EARLY POLEMICAL WRITINGS

KIERKEGAARD'S WRITINGS, I

EARLY POLEMICAL WRITINGS

by Søren Kierkegaard

Edited and Translated
with Introduction and Notes by

Julia Watkin

PRINCETON UNIVERSITY PRESS
PRINCETON, NEW JERSEY

Copyright © 1990 by Julia Watkin

Published by Princeton University Press
41 William Street, Princeton, New Jersey
In the United Kingdom: Princeton University Press, Oxford

Library of Congress Cataloging-in-Publication Data

Kierkegaard, Søren, 1813-1855.
[Endnu levendes papirer. English]
Early polemical writings / by Søren Kierkegaard ; edited and
translated with introduction and notes by Julia Watkin.
p.   cm. — (Kierkegaard's writings ; 1)
Translation of: Endnu levendes papirer.
Includes bibliographical references.
ISBN 0-691-07369-4 (alk. paper)
I. Watkin, Julia. II. Title. III. Series: Kierkegaard, Søren,
1813-1855. Works. English. 1978 ; 1.
PT8142.A6 1990
839.8′18609—dc20   89-28858

Preparation of this volume has been made possible in part by a grant from
the Division of Research Programs of the National Endowment
for the Humanities, an independent federal agency

Princeton University Press books are printed
on acid-free paper, and meet the guidelines for
permanence and durability of the Committee on
Production Guidelines for Book Longevity
of the Council on Library Resources

Designed by Frank Mahood

Printed in the United States of America by Princeton
University Press, Princeton, New Jersey

1 3 5 7 9 10 8 6 4 2

CONTENTS

III. *The Battle between the Old and the New Soap-Cellars*
103

HISTORICAL INTRODUCTION

When did Kierkegaard begin his authorship? In *On My Work as an Author* (1851) and *The Point of View for My Work as an Author* (1859), the authorship is clearly viewed as beginning with *Either/Or* in 1843,[1] but this omits not only *From the Papers of One Still Living* (1838) and *The Concept of Irony* (1841) but also several articles written in his student days. If one takes a closer look at the material, however, it is easy to see why Kierkegaard regarded *Either/Or* as his first work. The teasing newspaper articles are not consciously related to the basic aims of the authorship as expressed in *On My Work as an Author* and *Point of View*. *From the Papers* is a review originally intended for Johan Ludvig Heiberg's *Perseus*,[2] and *Irony* is Kierkegaard's master's dissertation.[3]

Although the authorship proper did not begin before *Either/Or*, some of its themes appeared in both published and unpublished material prior to 1843. In the period 1834–1838, Kierkegaard is clearly trying his hand at various styles of writing and is experimenting, if unconsciously, with various forms of expression ranging from newspaper article to drama.

As was usual with Kierkegaard later, his literary activity

[1] See *The Point of View*, *KW* XXII (*SV* XIII 494, 517).

[2] See *Kierkegaard: Letters and Documents*, Letter 9, *KW* XXV. Johan Ludvig Heiberg (1791-1860), poet and esthetician and introducer of Hegel's philosophy to Denmark, was a leading cultural figure, active as playwright, critic, translator, and director of the Royal Theater Copenhagen. His wife was the leading actress Johanne Luise Heiberg (née Pätges) (1812-1890). Among his literary productions was *Perseus, Journal for den speculative Idee* (1837-38). Heiberg appears to have been critical of Kierkegaard's style in *From the Papers of One Still Living*, but, in any case, *Perseus* had ceased publication in August 1838.

[3] The degree of Magister was the highest postgraduate degree in the faculty of philosophy and corresponded to the Doctor's degree in other faculties of Copenhagen University. In 1854, those with the M.A. degree were declared to be Doctors of Philosophy.

contained a response to what was going on in the world around him, but he was never involved in direct political engagement. At first glance, at least some of the material appears to be nothing more than light, dilettantish nonsense, contrasting strangely with the dedicated earnestness of people like Johannes Hage and Orla Lehmann.[4] Indeed, given the political conditions of Europe at the time, Kierkegaard's attitude would perhaps be noteworthy in its lack of political interest if we did not have an understanding of the situation in Denmark and the circumstances of his own life.

The French Revolution of July 27, 1830, had caused rebellion and disturbance throughout Europe. The urge to liberty seemed to express itself everywhere in revolt against oppressive government and control. The excitement of the various tumults even penetrated the Kierkegaard home in Copenhagen, for we learn from the diary of Søren's elder brother Peter Christian Kierkegaard (1805-1888) that during a stay in Paris, which happened to coincide with the 1830 July Revolution, he was forced to help with barricade building.[5] Further, in a letter dated September 14, 1830, from A. G. Rudelbach's

---

[4] Johannes Dam Hage (1800-1837), the Roskilde schoolmaster who became a pioneering figure in the movement toward a liberal constitution. Hage was well versed in the political and economic questions of the time and was considered to be a talented political writer. Added to other troubles, the law court ban depriving him of political expression and of his editorship of *Fædrelandet* became the final blow that caused him to commit suicide.

Peter Martin Orla Lehmann (1810-1870) began his career in the legal profession. Inspired by the July Revolution and gifted as a speaker, he soon became, like Hage, a pioneer figure in the Liberal movement and active in journalism. When, in 1835, *Selskabet for Trykkefrihedens rette Brug* was founded, he was a leading member, and it was Lehmann who in 1839 drew up and presented to Christian VIII the address asking for a free constitution. In 1842, Lehmann was imprisoned for three months for one of his political speeches and thereby won popularity for himself and the Liberal cause. Despite his successful legal and political career and his weathering of the vicissitudes of political life, he became disillusioned by the course of events after Frederik VII's death in 1863, and from 1864, with increasing bad health, was a broken man.

[5] See Carl Weltzer, *Peter og Søren Kierkegaard*, I-II (Copenhagen: 1936), I, p. 34.

sisters to Rudelbach, who was also abroad, we learn that another brother, Niels Andreas Kierkegaard, was in Germany (Hamburg), where there was also agitation.[6] J. L. Heiberg, writing to his exiled father on August 17, 1830, declared that "through the revolution, civilization has made an enormous step forward, not only in France but in the world as a whole."[7] The European situation in 1830 was not, however, reflected in Denmark in terms of a general political awakening or activity, partly because of the relationship between king and people and partly because of the restrictions on the freedom of the press.

Through a bloodless coup in 1784, Frederik VI (1768-1839) as rightful crown prince had taken over absolute monarchical power from his ailing father, Christian VII (1749-1808), and thus from the Guldberg government supporting the Queen Mother's party. Thanks to the availability of wise counselors during his regency, Frederik governed well at the beginning. His period of rule is marked by important reforms[8]—for example, the abolition of villeinage—but he patently lacked the diplomatic capacity to carry the country through a crisis with-

---

[6] Ibid., p. 33. Andreas Gottlob Rudelbach (1792-1862), pastor and theologian, was superintendent with pastoral office in Glaucha, Saxony, 1828-45. In 1848, he was appointed pastor in Slagelse, Sjælland, Denmark. He was author of various theological works.

Niels Andreas Kierkegaard (1809-1833) died in Paterson, New Jersey, after an illness.

[7] See *Breve fra og til Johan Ludvig Heiberg*, published anonymously through the agency of Johanne Luise Heiberg (Copenhagen: 1862), p. 132, letter to Peter Andreas Heiberg (1758-1841) in Paris. P. A. Heiberg, Danish author and translator, having made his presence felt in Denmark as a political satirist, was permanently exiled after various literary clashes with the government in the 1790s. He was condemned under legislation brought in after his offense, namely, the press law of September 27, 1799, and left Denmark on February 7, 1800. He was married to Thomasine Christine Buntzen (1773-1856), who later divorced him and in 1801 married the exiled Swedish baron, Karl Frederik Ehrensvärd Gyllembourg.

[8] On Frederik VI's life and reforms, see, for example, Axel Linvald, *Kronprins Frederik og Hans Regering 1797-1807* (Copenhagen: 1923); Marcus Rubin, *Frederik VI's Tid* (Copenhagen: 1895).

out competent advisers. The period brought terrible problems and losses. Besides the Copenhagen fires of 1794 and 1795 there was an unwilling involvement in the Napoleonic Wars with the loss of the fleet and the bombardment of Copenhagen by the English in 1807. To this can be added the ensuing national bankruptcy of 1813 and the loss of Norway in 1814. Any lack of capability in Frederik was matched, however, by characteristics that endeared him to his people; his frank, straightforward nature and his hard work and genuine personal concern for his subjects created a lasting bond of affection. It was no uncommon sight to see the royal family rowed round the canal in the palace gardens at Frederiksberg,[9] watched by the Sunday afternoon crowds who were also permitted to enjoy the gardens, and if a fire broke out in the city at night, the king could be seen personally directing the firefighting operations.

Because the beginning of Frederik's period as regent saw economic progress and a flowering of cultural life, there began to be an interest in politics and especially a sympathy for the ideas underlying the French Revolution. Although the execution of Louis XVI in 1793 dampened the popular enthusiasm, Frederik gradually became suspicious of anything that might directly or indirectly shake absolute monarchy, and he became especially concerned about the press and the free speech of such writers as Peter Andreas Heiberg and Malthe Conrad Bruun (1775-1826).[10] Both were exiled for life for infringing press restrictions, and the Ordinance of September 27, 1799, tightened the press laws to what was in fact a degree of censorship[11] and thus gave rise to a period of political passiv-

[9] The palace and gardens west of Copenhagen, in the present-day suburb of that name.

[10] Malthe Conrad Bruun was another polemical Liberal author. After his exile, he made a career for himself in Paris as journalist and geographer. He was given permission to return to Denmark, but he died before he could do so. P. A. Heiberg did not wish to return.

[11] Freedom of the press had been introduced by cabinet-minister Johan Frederik Struensee (1731-1772), with the ordinance of September 14, 1770. That the king had nothing to fear from his subjects is amply shown by their reaction to the performance of Daniel Auber's opera *Den stumme i Portici*

ity. More fortunate was Frederik's reaction later to the activity of Uwe Jens Lornsen (1793-1838), who, while in office as bailiff of Syld, published on November 5, 1830, a work, *Ueber das Verfassungswerk in Schleswig-Holstein*, asking for a free constitution for Schleswig-Holstein. Although Lornsen lost his position and was imprisoned for a year, the king also reacted more positively to the situation by introducing in 1831, and constituting in 1834, four Provincial Consultative Assemblies covering the entire country. Although membership of these assemblies was based on property ownership, it was a first step in the direction of greater political freedom, despite the fact that members were somewhat hindered in their advice-giving functions by lack of information from the higher powers.[12]

Hence, by 1830, although it was the "Golden Age" of culture,[13] the national political consciousness remained dulled, thanks to the king's "fatherly" control. By 1834, however, the press was beginning to find its voice and at least was reflecting some of the issues discussed in the Provincial Consultative Assemblies. Besides comments on the state of the national economy, there were complaints about the expenses of the royal court and the cost of the army. The king, who welcomed the idea of criticism from the assemblies about the conduct of state officials acting officially, was alarmed by the utterances of the press about other matters and reacted sharply with the proposed legislation of December 14, 1834, that would mean

---

(1828) at the Royal Theater Copenhagen. The opera, which, in Brussels on August 25, 1830, had inspired the Belgians to revolution, became in Copenhagen the occasion for expressions of loyal devotion to Frederik VI when he attended a performance on October 7 that year. See Teddy Petersen, *Kierkegaards polemiske debut* (Odense: Odense Universitetsforlag, 1977), pp. 20-21.

[12] A. Fabricius, *Illustreret Danmarkshistorie for Folket*, I-II (Copenhagen, Kristiania: 1914-15), II, pp. 556-60. There was especially a lack of information about the national economic situation.

[13] This period lasted approximately from 1800 to 1870 and includes figures such as the sculptor Bertel Thorvaldsen (1770-1844); the poet Adam Oehlenschläger (1779-1850); pastor, poet, historian, and hymnwriter Nikolai Frederick Severin Grundtvig (1783-1872); and Hans Christian Andersen (1805-1875).

full censorship without the possibility of appeal to the law courts. A petition against the legislation signed by over 570 respected people and delivered to the king on February 21, 1835, only provoked the famous reply of February 26, in which Frederik claimed that no one but himself [14] was able to judge what was best for the people. This reply in turn provoked the foundation of the highly successful *Selskabet for Trykkefrihedens rette Brug* [the Society for the Proper Use of Freedom of the Press] on March 6, 1835, a society that proved to be yet another step on the road to greater political freedom. Thus, by 1835, the year in which Johannes Andreas Ostermann[15] and Kierkegaard were to make the press the subject of their lectures to the Student Association, the press, here especially *Kjøbenhavnsposten* [The Copenhagen Post] and *Fædrelandet* [The Fatherland], despite all strictures, began to make itself felt politically.[16]

Kierkegaard, as he reminds us,[17] was born in the disastrous year of 1813, and in the period ending with 1838 he suffered severe losses at home. In 1819, his brother Søren Michael died as a result of a school playground accident, and 1822 saw the death of his sister, Maren Kirstine. In 1832, yet another sister, Nicoline Christine, died, and the following years took their toll: in 1833, Niels Andreas in America; in 1834, Kierkegaard's mother, Ane Sørensdatter Lund, and the last surviving sister, Petrea; in 1837, Kierkegaard's sister-in-law, Elise

[14] "*Ingen uden vi alene* [None but ourself alone]." See Christian Kirchhoff-Larsen, *Den Danske Presses Historie*, I-III (Copenhagen: 1942-62), III, pp. 80-89; Petersen, *Debut*, pp. 57-58. The proposed legislation became official as the rescript of December 16, 1834.

[15] Johannes Andreas Ostermann (1809-1888) graduated from the University of Copenhagen in 1839 and in 1840 was given a teaching post at the Metropolitan School, Copenhagen. He pursued a career as teacher and politician and became a member of Parliament under the new constitution in 1849.

[16] The esthetic period of *Kjøbenhavnsposten* prior to this change is well described through the figure of "the Translator" (Kierkegaard) in Henrik Hertz, *Stemninger og Tilstande* (Copenhagen: 1839), p. 219, quoted in Petersen, *Debut*, pp. 104-05.

[17] *JP* V 5725 (*Pap*. V A 3).

Marie; and finally, in 1838, his father, Michael Pedersen Kierkegaard, in his eighty-second year.[18] The many deaths in the family had been interpreted by Michael Kierkegaard as God's punishment for his cursing him when he was a child, the revelation and interpretation of which episode became the "earthquake" that shook Kierkegaard's life in the 1830s.[19] Kierkegaard, however, though deeply marked by the growing gloom of domestic events in the strongly pietistic home, did not succumb to it, since he was a livelier person than his more soberminded brother Peter. On October 30, 1830, he entered the university to read theology and embarked upon a decade of literary studies in a milieu that offered brighter perspectives than those of home.

It is in this period that we encounter a Kierkegaard chiefly interested in esthetics and then philosophy. He is well dressed; runs up bills for clothes, books, tobacco, etc.; incurs debts of honor, and gets behind with his subscription to the Student Association.[20] He is interested in theater and music,[21] but also

[18] Søren Michael died (at the age of 12) on September 14, 1819; Maren Kirstine died (24) on March 15, 1822; Nicoline Christine died (33) on September 10, 1832, after childbirth; Niels Andreas died (24) on September 21, 1833 (see note 6 above); Kierkegaard's mother died (67) on July 31, 1834, after a "nerve fever"; Petrea Severine died (33) on December 29, 1834, after childbirth; Elise Marie, Peter Christian's wife, died (31) on July 18, 1837, and Kierkegaard's father (81) on August 9, 1838.

[19] On "the great earthquake," see Grethe Kjær, *Søren Kierkegaards seks optegnelser om den Store Jordrystelse* (Copenhagen: 1983), where it is convincingly argued that in the period autumn–winter 1835-36 Kierkegaard thought that his father's guilt had to do with a sexual fall. Yet in the summer of 1837 "the great earthquake" occurred, the revelation that his father as a poor shepherd boy had cursed God. See also *JP* V 5427-32, 5874 (*Pap.* II A 802-07; VII¹ A 5). Kierkegaard later speaks of grief "from earliest childhood" (*JP* V 6025; *Pap.* VIII¹ A 205). With regard to his strict upbringing, it is interesting to note his description of the strictly brought-up child who comes to discover that the world offers other possibilities. See *The Book on Adler, KW* XXIV (*Pap.* VII² B 235, pp. 227-29).

[20] See *Pap.* I, p. xxvii; Walter Lowrie, *Kierkegaard* (Oxford: Oxford University Press, 1938), pp. 116-17; *Letters,* Letter 7, *KW* XXV.

[21] Kierkegaard was also one of the founders of the University Music Society (March 1836). See T. H. Croxall, *Kierkegaard Commentary* (London: Nis-

deeply concerned about the meaning of life and how one should live.[22] In May 1837, he meets Regine Olsen[23] for the first time and falls decisively in love. On September 1, 1837, he moves from home to Løvstræde 7 in Copenhagen. His father helps him pay off his debts, and he receives an annual allowance of five hundred rix-dollars.[24] In 1837-38, he teaches Latin at his old school, Borgerdydskolen.[25]

In the tension between his strict pietistic home with its secret guilt and the new possibilities presented through university life, Kierkegaard was to suffer much while seeming joyful. His final encouragement in the direction of an ethical-religious way of life was to come in this period, however, from three important events in 1838: the death of Poul Martin Møller, "the mighty trumpet" of Kierkegaard's awakening;[26] the experience of an "indescribable joy" on May 19;[27] and the death of his father on August 9. Thus Kierkegaard was to finish his theology degree and enter the Pastoral Seminary in 1840, the year of his engagement to Regine Olsen, but his view of life as it developed in the 1830s was to lead him existentially further.[28]

After a brief look at the historical background of the period— at the European scene, the Danish situation, and finally at

---

bet, 1956), p. 49; Sejer Kühle, *Søren Kierkegaards Barndom og Ungdom* (Copenhagen: 1950), p. 117.

[22] *JP* V 5100 (*Pap.* I A 75).

[23] Regine Olsen (1822-1904), daughter of Terkel Olsen (1784-1849) and Regine Frederikke Olsen (1778-1856).

[24] See *Pap.* II, p. xiv; *Glimpses and Impressions of Kierkegaard*, ed. and tr. T. H. Croxall (Digswell Place, Welwyn, Herts.: Nisbet, 1959), pp. 8, 10; Kjær, *Jordrystelse*, p. 64. Five hundred rix-dollars = c. $2,500 in 1973 money.

[25] It is possible that he took the post in order to help with the payment of his debts.

[26] *Pap.* V B 46. Poul Martin Møller (1794-March 13, 1838), writer and philosopher, professor of philosophy at the University of Christiania (Oslo), 1826-30, University of Copenhagen, 1830-38. He was Kierkegaard's favorite teacher, good friend, and a great influence on his life. See *JP* V 5302, 5961 (*Pap.* II A 209; VII¹ A 221); *JP* VI 6888, 6889 (*Pap.* XI¹ A 275, 276).

[27] See *JP* V 5324 (*Pap.* II A 228).

[28] See *JP* V 5368 (*Pap.* II A 347); cf. *JP* VI 6356 (*Pap.* X¹ A 138).

events in Kierkegaard's own life—it is now easier to understand the motivation behind the material coming under the
heading of "early polemical writings." One important feature
of the material is that the pieces are a response rather than an
initiative.

Among the revolutionary ideas coming from France in the
1830s was that of women's emancipation,[29] then a likely target
for the aspiring witty pen. In 1834, Heiberg had replaced Oehlenschläger as arbiter of literary style, especially among the
young;[30] so a successful article meant one acceptable to Heiberg. In Denmark, educated women from wealthier back-
grounds participated in cultural life, but usually as hostess in
the home in relation to a husband's position.[31] Otherwise they
ventured out in a man's world with caution.[32] Thus, although
F. C. Sibbern[33] and Heiberg thought women capable of grasping philosophical subjects, their view was not representative
of their time. To student Peter Engel Lind,[34] therefore, the
topic was eminently suitable for ironic, comic treatment, and

[29] The male dress and notorious free-living of author George Sand (Arma-
dine Lucile Aurore Dupin, Baronne Dudevant, 1804-1876) created a stir in
France as well as abroad; the Saint-Simonist movement pointed to an equality
between the sexes that must have seemed scandalous or ridiculous to the av-
erage bourgeois citizen. See Petersen, *Debut*, pp. 20-28.

[30] See Petersen, *Debut*, pp. 21-22; F. J. Billeskov Jansen et al., *Dansk Litteratur Historie*, I-VI (Copenhagen: 1976-77), II, pp. 429-30.

[31] A good example of this is Kamma (Karen Margrethe) Rahbek (née
Heger) (1775-1829), who in 1798 married Knud Lyne Rahbek (1760-1830),
writer and leading literary critic. For three generations the Rahbek home,
Bakkehuset, Valby in Frederiksberg, was the salon for the leading figures of
the day. Another lesser-known figure is Frederikke Brun, who gathered leading figures in her salon in Copenhagen. See Petersen, *Debut*, p. 24.

[32] See *"Fru Gyllembourgs litterære Testament"* to her son, in which she speaks
of the daring with which she ventured out as an author; *Breve fra og til Johan
Ludvig Heiberg*, pp. 220-22.

[33] Frederik Christian Sibbern (1785-1872), Danish philosopher and professor of philosophy at Copenhagen University from 1813, later Kierkegaard's
teacher and adviser. See Petersen, *Debut*, p. 21.

[34] Peter Engel Lind (1814-1903), a schoolmate of Kierkegaard's at Borgerdydskolen and at the university. He gained his theology degree in 1837, lectured at the university in 1840, was first a prison pastor in 1844 (Copenhagen,
later also Christianshavn), and then became pastor of the parish of Sæby and

his article was accepted by Heiberg for *Kjøbenhavns flyvende Post* [Copenhagen's Flying Post].[35] It is not clear whether Lind directly provoked Kierkegaard's piece on women,[36] but on December 17, 1834, Kierkegaard pseudonymously made his literary debut with an article that was a "follow-up" to Lind's. Both contributions are typical of the time in being male-oriented and devoid of serious interest in the subject of women's position in society, but Kierkegaard here clearly demonstrates a wit and humor far superior to Lind's and not surprisingly gained a place in print and the attention of the circle surrounding Heiberg, whom he daringly teases in his article.[37]

Hallenslev (1855). Finally he was bishop of Aalborg (after Kierkegaard's brother), 1875-88.

[35] *Kjøbenhavns flyvende Post*, a Danish paper in the period 1827-37, edited by Johan Ludvig Heiberg. Initially it was almost entirely devoted to the world of the theater and literature, and although nearly all the rising young authors had their contributions printed in it, it contained chiefly Heiberg's own material on esthetics. It came out twice weekly, 1827-28, then, after a year's break, three times a week in 1830. After another break, 1831-33, it appeared at irregular intervals as an "intermittent paper" (*Interimsblad*), 135 numbers from 1834 to 1837.

With the French July Revolution of 1830, the paper began to take on a more political tone. By 1834, it was clearly a conservative organ. By the last number, the political material was dominant, and Heiberg had almost completely disappeared from its columns.

It is not surprising that Heiberg welcomed Lind's article, since despite his many new viewpoints Heiberg was conservative in outlook. See Petersen, *Debut*, pp. 25-26. For Lind's article, see Supplement, pp. 131-33.

[36] See Henning Fenger, *"Kierkegaard, P. E. Lind og 'Johan Gordan',"* *Kierkegaardiana*, VII, 1968, pp. 7-18; Petersen, *Debut*, p. 22.

[37] "Another Defense of Woman's Great Abilities," pp. 3-5. Nothing callous should be seen in the fact that Kierkegaard's article appears only a few months after his mother's death. His mother did not belong to the cultured elite and her entire interest was centered on her family and domesticity. See Henriette Lund, *Erindringer fra Hjemmet* (Copenhagen, Kristiania: 1909), pp. 19-20. In *Af mit Levnet*, I-III (Copenhagen: 1882-83), I, pp. 78-79, the author, Hans Lassen Martensen, tells us the following (ed. tr.): "My mother has told me that when I was abroad he [Kierkegaard] often called to ask if there was news from me. She also told me something I do not want to omit here, that sometimes he stayed, and that she took great pleasure in his conversation. Once he called in great distress and told her that his mother was dead. My

If it is correct that the Kierkegaard family skeleton began to make itself felt in the autumn and winter of 1835-36, then perhaps Kierkegaard was turning for consolation to his "eminent mental faculties"[38] when he gave a paper in the Student Association[39] on November 28, 1835. Responding to a paper given by Johannes Ostermann,[40] he again exercised his literary wings, this time in the discussion of a topical issue. Yet even though he now addressed himself to the subject of the press and the arena of politics, there was, in this period, no dominating view of life.[41]

The outlook of the Student Association at this time was politically moderate and perhaps best reflected in Johannes Ostermann's statement on its behalf (in June 1837) that the Student Association ought not to be of any political significance and therefore should not exert its influence politically one way or the other.[42] This moderate outlook appeared already in his serious and sober paper to the association in 1835, where, as a temperate Liberal, he criticized the "rocket literature"[43] but not the Liberal papers *Kjøbenhavnsposten* or *Fædrelandet*. Although he was against sudden revolution, Ostermann felt sympathy for several of the new tendencies of the time and in his lecture expressed the view that, to a great extent, the press was responsible for the latest political initiatives.

In his response to Ostermann, Kierkegaard produced a pa-

---

mother has repeatedly assured me that she—and she had considerable experience—had never in her life seen a person in such great distress as S. Kierkegaard was over his mother's death, from which she concluded that he must have an unusually profound temperament. She was correct in thinking so."

[38] See *JP* V 5431 (*Pap.* II A 806).

[39] The Student Association was founded in 1820. See Hans Carl August Lund, *Studenterforeningens Historie 1820-70*, I-II (Copenhagen: 1896-98). See *JP* VI 6310, p. 94; IV 4201; VI 6625 (*Pap.* X¹ A 42, p. 33; X⁴ A 51; X³ A 112).

[40] The Student Association's *Rapportbog for Inspectionshavende*, October 1833-April 1837, tells us that philology student J. A. Ostermann gave a paper on Saturday, November 14, 1835.

[41] On Kierkegaard's view later, see, for example, *JP* IV 4170; III 2952; IV 4238 (*Pap.* X² A 351, 390; XI² A 108).

[42] See H.C.A. Lund, *Historie*, I, p. 379; Petersen, *Debut*, pp. 55-59.

[43] See Supplement, pp. 189-99.

per that dissects and refutes Ostermann's. Through an analysis of *Kjøbenhavnsposten* for 1829-1834, he sought to show that
the political initiative came essentially from Frederik VI.[44] For
the first time Kierkegaard publicly demonstrated his capacity
for polemic against a direct target, and clearly one of his goals
here is the exercise and demonstration of this capacity. A Kierkegaardian characteristic that also appears in the articles in
Kjøbenhavns flyvende Post is his gift for discovering and hang-
ing on to weaknesses in his opponent's position—weaknesses
that, however small, he exposes from every possible angle,
even if he risks somewhat obscuring the main issue. Yet although Kierkegaard's lecture may seem a rather one-sided defense of the establishment, a defense in which he airs a polemical temperament, one can detect the beginnings of an
enormous capacity to look at the other side of a question and
bring its various possibilities to light in their smallest details.
At the same time, his defense of the establishment is not a
blind one. If he underestimates the power of the press in the
realm of politics, he wishes to give Frederik VI his due, and
his paper may even be viewed as an indirect, although probably unconscious, attempt to muzzle the press as an unortho-
dox and unauthorized source of political power. By arguing
for Frederik's initiative and refusing to take into proper account the influence and effect of the press on the king, he directs attention away from the press as a possible political
weapon through which "premise-authors"[45] can provoke
forces in society inimical to true community life.

If Kierkegaard's view of the press[46] here can perhaps be criticized for being too negative regarding politics, he at least sees
what probably many of his contemporaries failed to see at this
point: that the press is a double-edged weapon and a mixed

---

[44] See Addendum, pp. 35-52 (*Pap.* I B 2). In his paper, Kierkegaard advo-
cates a moderate conservatism and opposes what he regards as the precipitous
growth of a liberalism lacking firm roots. See Petersen, *Debut*, p. 157.

[45] Kierkegaard's term later for those writing without a genuine life-view or
perspective on life. See *Adler, KW* XXIV (*Pap.* VII² B 235, pp. 5-29).

[46] On Kierkegaard's ultranegative view of the press later, see, for example,
JP II 2148, 2158, 2173-4 (*Pap.* VIII¹ A 137; IX A 468; XI¹ A 232, 342).

blessing. Where Ostermann and others emphasize its political power primarily in terms of its positive benefit, Kierkegaard's lecture can be seen as an existential tactic aimed to hinder a development of the negative. If this is so, then another Kierkegaardian feature comes to light here: his ability to be very seriously engaged in discussion of an issue under the guise of not seeming to be so.

The year 1836 saw an upswing in the mood of the Kierkegaard home with the marriage of Peter Christian to Elise Marie Boisen on October 21. For his younger brother Søren, 1836 was a year in which he enjoyed student life to the full, and in three articles for Heiberg's *Kjøbenhavns flyvende Post* he managed to take on two leading lights of the Liberal opposition: Orla Lehmann and Johannes Hage.[47]

In the same year as the two papers in the Student Association, Jens Finsteen Giødwad[48] and Orla Lehmann had come to an agreement with the editor of *Kjøbenhavnsposten*, Andreas Peter Liunge,[49] under which they would edit the paper's political matter. With this they created a Liberal link between the Student Association, where Orla Lehmann had already made

---

[47] See Petersen, *Debut*, pp. 103-12.

[48] Jens Finsteen Gi(j)ødwad (1811-1891), political journalist on *Kjøbenhavnsposten* 1834-37, editor 1837-39, and an editor with Orla Lehmann and others of *Fædrelandet* when it became a daily in 1840. Giødwad was charged several times for infringing the press laws, and although he was acquitted, in 1838 he had to pay some of the costs of the court case. See Supplement, p. 215 (*Pap.* II A 728). Despite Giødwad's Liberal outlook, he was a friend and great admirer of Kierkegaard. He acted as intermediary between Kierkegaard and the printer and bookseller of the pseudonymous works. See Petersen, *Debut*, pp. 105-06.

[49] *Kjøbenhavnsposten*, a daily paper begun in 1827 by Andreas Peter Liunge (1798-1879) together with Ove Thomsen (1801-1862), who remained with it only for that year. Aiming to depict current Copenhagen news and events abroad, the paper at the beginning was issued twice weekly and, literary in character, served as an organ for the opponents of J. L. Heiberg. According to an agreement made with Liunge by Orla Lehmann and Jens Finsteen Giødwad in 1835 for the regular publication of political articles, *Kjøbenhavnsposten* changed in character and became the first Liberal newspaper. In 1837, when Liunge retired to the role of publisher only, Giødwad became editor (with Orla Lehmann as leading journalist) until 1839, in which year Johan Peter Grüne (1805-1878) took over the editorship. Liunge gave up the post of publisher in 1845, and the paper finally closed in 1859.

his oratorical talent felt,[50] and a wider public. Similarly, C.G.N. David, professor of economics, with his paper *Fædre-landet*,[51] in which Johannes Hage was the driving force, also made a link between Liberalism in the university and the general public. Thus when Kierkegaard again demonstrated his talents concerning press and politics, it was not only before a university audience, it was also before the general public and, of course, Heiberg.

In part V of his long article on the freedom of the press in *Kjøbenhavnsposten*, Orla Lehmann speaks of the political stagnation of the country in the period ending at the beginning of the thirties.[52] One remedy for such a state of affairs is the press, he states, and even if it "makes mistakes," this is certainly no reason for suppressing it. The previous "sentimental-idyllic" mood of the people is to be replaced by the dawn of political awareness, the "dawn of the life and freedom of the people."

For a Kierkegaard interested in flexing his pen, the chance presented by Lehmann was not to be missed. Lehmann's oratory not surprisingly appears in his style of writing, and so there are plenty of phrases for Kierkegaard to find fault with. Expressions such as "dawn of the life and freedom of the people" and "sentimental-idyllic" are taken up and flung back in a witty, comic irony as Kierkegaard goes to the attack—and deprives the oratory of power by drawing attention to such expressions. Of particular importance is the fact that Orla

---

[50] See H.C.A. Lund, *Historie*, I, pp. 286, 293-322.

[51] *Fædrelandet*, a weekly paper begun in September 1834 by national economy professor Christian Georg Nathan David (1793-1874) at the instance of his colleague on the paper, Johannes Hage. Its aim was to create interest in public affairs, in a moderately Liberal direction, but by December, David found himself in conflict with the press laws. During the case proceedings (he was acquitted but lost his professorship), David handed the editorship over to Hage in 1835. Hage's own conflict with press law led to sentence and loss of the editorship in 1837. This did not prevent the paper from becoming the chief organ of national Liberalism, inasmuch as after Hage's death (David was again editor from 1837 to 1840) Giødwad and Lehmann joined the staff in 1839 and made *Fædrelandet* into a daily paper that was to survive until 1882.

[52] See Supplement, pp. 134-41.

Lehmann has suggested a previous state of decay in which the people "estheticized" and "played."[53] Undoubtedly this in particular has provoked Kierkegaard's reply, given his admiration of Danish romanticism, especially that of Oehlenschläger, Henrich Steffens, and J. P. Mynster.[54]

A couple of weeks later, the polemic enters a new phase. Johannes Hage in *Fædrelandet* comes to Lehmann's defense. In a section of his article, he characterizes Kierkegaard's attack as lacking factual information and having a polemic built upon a ridicule of specific words and phrases. The editor of *Kjøbenhavns flyvende Post*, Hage says, is striving, through Kierkegaard, "to bring down his opponent with mockery and witticisms" instead of collecting data and embarking on "discussions about reality."[55]

If Hage's response seems harsh, it must be remembered that he possessed a thorough grasp of his country's affairs and that there was already friction between the Liberal press and Heiberg's organ on the subject of economics. Heiberg's *Kjøbenhavns flyvende Post* indicated a surplus in the national budget, but the Liberals were certain there was a deficit.[56] That Kierkegaard was uninterested in the niceties of the current economic situation can be seen from his own copy[57] of *Fædrelandet* for March 4, 1836. Whereas the paper is heavily marked in the section dealing with Kierkegaard's article, the large piece dealing with the economic situation is totally untouched. Kierkegaard did not enter into the economic debate, and his article seemed to suggest that the author was out to get a foot on the ladder of literary success. It looked as if Kier-

---

[53] See Supplement, p. 135.

[54] Henrich Steffens (1773-1845) was the Norwegian-born Danish-German philosopher who introduced romanticism into Denmark. See Jørgen Bukdahl, *Søren Kierkegaard og den menige mand* (Copenhagen: 1961), pp. 12-14. Jakob Peter Mynster (1775-1854) was bishop of Sjælland and primate of the Danish Church from 1834 until his death. Mynster was the Kierkegaard family's pastor. See Petersen, *Debut*, p. 109.

[55] See Supplement, p. 142.

[56] See Hage's article *"Om Flyvepostens Polemik"* in *Fædrelandet*, 77, March 4, 1836, col. 634-42; Petersen, *Debut*, p. 109.

[57] Now in the Royal Library, Copenhagen.

kegaard wanted to glorify his "own little self," as Hage put
it.[58]

While it is correct that Kierkegaard was still at the stage of
showing himself and others what he could do, and it is true
that he avoided entering into serious political debate, it would
be wrong to regard him as simply indulging a vain self-
esteem. In Lehmann's disapproval of an esthetics without politics, his somewhat flowery oratorical style with its dash of
rhetoric should especially be noted. It may be that Kierkegaard here instinctively reacted to the use of language as a tool
to persuade the masses. As we have already observed, by at-
tacking the expressions he deprived them of power. Moreover, a tacit refusal to be drawn into serious political debate
may indicate a nonserious, self-preoccupied mind, but it may
also be the sign of a profounder understanding of politics and
the true good of the nation. Kierkegaard at this point was possibly just exercising his pen in the championship of estheticism, but perhaps in his polemic lie the seeds of something
deeper: a healthy contempt for political oratory and a suspi-
cion of attempts to correct externals, as if such attempts could
heal the natural human condition grounded in self-preserva-
tion and self-seeking. If at this point Kierkegaard still has not
existentially grasped the idea for which he can live and die,[59]
it is not impossible that he already realizes that national and
political problems are intimately bound up with personal
ones.[60]

In the second article "On the Polemic of *Fædrelandet*," Kierkegaard replies to Hage's counterattack in the same manner as
before, although at an exaggerated length, his article running
into two issues of Heiberg's *Kjøbenhavns flyvende Post*. Again
he fastens on the expressions and turns of phrase used by his
opponent, and he has by no means forgotten Lehmann's
expression "sentimental-idyllic." He refuses to accept the sug-

---

[58] See Supplement, p. 144.

[59] See note 41 above.

[60] Note that in the articles against Lehmann and Hage, Kierkegaard signs
himself as "B," the pseudonym later associated with the ethical Judge William
of *Either/Or*.

gestion that there was a period of "esthetic decay" at the beginning of the century. By the end of his reply to Hage, Kierkegaard has extended his polemic to include not only the
entire staff of *Fædrelandet* but the entire Liberal movement,
which he describes as being "a kind of motley militia."[61] Up to
now, the polemical battle has been conducted (officially) anonymously and pseudonymously, as were most newspaper bat-
tles, but this final prick has the result that Orla Lehmann as a
leading Liberal replies to Kierkegaard in his own name. In
Kjøbenhavnsposten, 96,[62] he summarizes the course of the polemic and correctly points out that while the Liberals have been
concerned with the country's political and economic conditions, Kierkegaard has concentrated his attention on the esthetic and on the polemic. While admitting and even admiring
Kierkegaard's literary talent, he regards his attack as one
founded on false premises and cannot see the point of it. Noteworthy in Lehmann's "reply" is his conciliatory tone. He
wishes to straighten out the facts yet wants to terminate the
polemical combat. Gadfly to the end, Kierkegaard replies to
Lehmann's reply, also in his own name, in the same manner as
previously. In this way, refusing any conciliation and insisting
on the last word, Kierkegaard successfully maintains the upper hand. He has demonstrated his literary and polemical ability to the university and to Heiberg,[63] has gained a deserved
respect, and is now ready for the next literary encounter.[64]

---

[61] See p. 22.

[62] See Supplement, pp. 152-59.

[63] Some thought that the article in *Kjøbenhavns flyvende Post* was written by
Heiberg. See Supplement, pp. 149, 214 (*Pap.* I B 7).

[64] That Kierkegaard did not reply to the witty attack by the "Humoristic"
papers (Supplement, pp. 160-88) seems to have been because Heiberg did not
think much of the quality and felt that it would be undignified to reply. Kierkegaard also gives as a reason the length of time since his articles had been
printed and that there was a poor opinion of the "Humoristic" papers in the
Student Association (Supplement, pp. 211-12; cf. pp. 212-14 [*Pap.* I B 6]).
Petersen (*Debut*, pp. 146-51) thinks that the "Humoristic" author's style and
below-the-belt attacks acted as a deterrent. Kierkegaard may have felt it was
better to stop with Heiberg's approval and the successful encounter with two
leading names.

If the summer of 1837 was the period of "the great earth-quake," the year 1838 was not without severe blows for Kier-kegaard, bringing as it did the deaths of his father and Poul Martin Møller. Yet, despite this, by 1838 Kierkegaard seemed to be emerging from sorrow rather than succumbing to it. He moved back to the family home, probably in April,[65] and was reconciled with his father. In the journal entry of May 19, 1838, he reports the experience of "an indescribable joy." It is against this background that we must look at two Kierkegaard productions of 1838: *From the Papers of One Still Living* and *The Battle between the Old and the New Soap-Cellars.*[66]

On November 22, 1837, Hans Christian Andersen's third novel,[67] *Kun en Spillemand* [Only a Fiddler], was published. At this point Andersen was thirty-three years old[68] and already an established name as poet, novelist, and writer of fairy sto-ries. Kierkegaard, on the other hand, was still not really known outside the academic circle. When Kierkegaard says he did not know Andersen personally,[69] this is probably correct.

[65] Kierkegaard may have moved in April 1838. There was an official "mov-ing day" in Copenhagen at that time. One could change one's place of resi-dence twice a year, in April (on a date falling between the fifteenth and the twenty-ninth) or in October.

[66] *From the Papers* was composed in the period between late April or early May and mid-August 1838 and was published on September 7, 1838. See Alastair McKinnon and Niels Jørgen Cappelørn, "The Period of Composi-tion of Kierkegaard's Published Works," *Kierkegaardiana*, IX, 1974, pp. 132-46. The draft of Kierkegaard's unpublished play (pp. 103-24 [*Pap*. II B 1-21]) appears to have been written in the spring or summer of 1838, although there is some debate about the dating. It is notable that Kierkegaard considered calling his play: "*The All-embracing Debate on Everything against Everything or The Crazier the Better. From the Papers of One Still Living / against his will pub-lished / by / S. Kierkegaard*" (p. 105 [*Pap*. II B 3]). See Niels Thulstrup, *Kierkegaard's Relation to Hegel*, tr. George Stengren (Princeton: Princeton University Press, 1980), pp. 166-200; Henning Fenger, *Kierkegaard-Myter og Kierkegaard-Kilder* (Odense Universitetsforlag, 1976), pp. 113-16; *Kierkegaard, The Myths and Their Origins*, tr. George C. Schoolfield (New Haven: Yale University Press, 1980), pp. 138-42.

[67] The two previous ones were *Improvisatoren* (1835) and *O. T.* (1836).

[68] Andersen lived to be seventy.

[69] See p. 83. Although Kierkegaard and Andersen appear as "the Transla-

Although Andersen, too, was a member of the Student Association and they possibly met occasionally also in the Music Society, it would seem that they were more acquaintances than friends. This is hardly surprising, given the difference in their temperaments. Andersen was a spontaneous person, oversensitive in his emotional reactions. He was an admirer of H. C. Ørsted's romantic philosophy of nature[70] and possessed, throughout his life, an unreflective, childlike confidence in God. Such a person was poles apart from the reflective personality of Kierkegaard, whose view of faith was to develop into the definition: "immediacy after reflection."[71]

Andersen tells us that after *Kun en Spillemand* appeared, Kierkegaard met him in the street and told him he would write a positive review of the work. He expressed the opinion that Andersen was generally misunderstood by the critics.[72] Later, however, Kierkegaard appears to have let Andersen know that he had changed his mind, for, on August 30, 1838, Andersen noted in his calendar that he felt an agony of mind over "Kierkegaard's still unpublished review."[73] As soon as

---

tor" and "Amadis" in Hertz, *Stemninger og Tilstande* (cf. *JP* V 5399 [*Pap*. II A 508]), no historical reality is indicated.

[70] Hans Christian Ørsted (1771-1851), Danish scientist and professor of physics at Copenhagen University, is known primarily for his discovery of electromagnetism (1820). He was also keenly interested in philosophy and literature and wrote on natural philosophy in *Aanden i Naturen*, I-II (Copenhagen: 1850; *ASKB* 945 [I]).

[71] See *JP* V 6135 (*Pap*. VIII¹ A 650); Christian Svanholm, *H. C. Andersens Ungdoms-Tro* (Trondheim: 1952); H. S. Holbeck, *H. C. Andersens Religion* (Copenhagen: 1947).

[72] See Hans Christian Andersen's autobiography, *Mit Livs Eventyr* (Copenhagen: 1855), p. 198. At the time Kierkegaard apparently was acquainted with at least some of Andersen's poetry, with the novels *Improvisatoren* and *O. T.*, several fairy stories, and probably with *Agnete og Havmanden*. See p. 78; *JP* V 5077, 5211, 5668 (*Pap*. I C 46; II A 42; IV A 113). See also Elias Bredsdorff, *"H. C. Andersen og Søren Kierkegaard"* in *Anderseniana*, ed. Niels Oxenvad (Odense: H. C. Andersens Hus), *3. række*, III, 4, 1981, pp. 230-32.

[73] Quoted in Bredsdorff, *"Andersen og Kierkegaard,"* pp. 229-30. That Kierkegaard in 1838 may also have toyed with the idea of a newspaper article or articles about Andersen is indicated by two journal entries. See Supplement, pp. 216, 217 (*Pap*. II A 768, 781).

From the Papers was published, Andersen received a copy. On September 6, he noted that it arrived just after an "outrageous letter" from his friend and benefactor Commander Wulff (who had erroneously accused him of slander and forbidden him his house).[74] The Wulff episode, lasting as it did for three weeks, overshadowed everything else, and it seems clear that Kierkegaard's review did not trouble Andersen too greatly. On December 9, 1838, the poet B. S. Ingemann (1786-1862) wrote a consoling letter to Andersen in which he criticized Kierkegaard for a one-sided emphasis on the book's demerits yet pointed out that the review contains no malicious desire to wound. He noted that the ending of the work, though strange, suggested a friendly attitude on the part of the reviewer.

Andersen himself, in a letter to a Henriette Hanck on February 1, 1839, speaks only of the "whimsicality" of one public voice condemning the book at home whereas abroad everyone likes it.[75] In his memoirs, he recalls that Kierkegaard's review was "somewhat difficult to read because of the Hegelian heaviness of expression." He further relates that for this reason it was said of the review that only Kierkegaard and Andersen had read it.[76] Finally, he reports that later he came to understand Kierkegaard better and that the latter came to show him friendliness and regard.[77] Andersen, however, could not resist revenging himself on Kierkegaard through the figure of the hairdresser in *En Comedie i det Grønne* (1840),[78] and as we can

---

[74] See Bredsdorff, "*Andersen og Kierkegaard*," pp. 235-36.

[75] Ibid., pp. 236-37; see *Mit Livs Eventyr*, pp. 198-99.

[76] See *Mit Livs Eventyr*, p. 198. At the time, Andersen understood from the review that he was not a poet but a poetic figure out of group and that a future poet must put him back in his proper place or else use him as a character in a piece of poetry in which what Andersen lacked would be created for him. See pp. 75-76, 83-84 fn.

[77] *Mit Livs Eventyr*, p. 198. See *Letters*, Letter 206, *KW* XXV. Kierkegaard gave Andersen a copy of *Either/Or* in 1849, but Andersen had already sent Kierkegaard a copy of his *Nye Eventyr* (1848) with a friendly dedication. See also Bredsdorff, "*Andersen og Kierkegaard*," pp. 244-45, 254; *JP* VI 6413 (*Pap.* X[1] A 402).

[78] See Supplement, pp. 202-04. Kierkegaard bought the play (which was

see from the unpublished reply,[79] Kierkegaard was annoyed with Andersen for his late retaliation and for parodying him as a Hegelian.

Kierkegaard's change of heart regarding Andersen's novel may well have been caused by a change in Kierkegaard's basic attitude to life. If in this period he has undergone a conversion experience and has won through to an ethical-religious life-view, it is understandable that his original good opinion of Andersen's work was affected and that friendly praise of Andersen at the beginning of *From the Papers*[80] is lost in the following heavy concentration on the defects of Andersen and *Kun en Spillemand.* Just as Pastor Adolph Adler was to become the occasion for Kierkegaard's analysis of religious revelation,[81] so, here, Andersen became the occasion for Kierkegaard's discussion of the individual and the successful novel. Whereas with the Adler book Kierkegaard refrained from publication because of its personal involvement with Adler, in *From the Papers* he had to rescue the personal situation by writing the friendly conclusion in which he hoped Andersen would hold up what he had written with sympathetic ink to "that light which alone makes the writing readable and the meaning clear."[82]

As we have seen above, the reception of *From the Papers* was extremely quiet. Few cared to battle their way through Kierkegaard's difficult prose. For this reason, and because it was only a review[83] of a book, a second edition did not appear until thirty-four years later, in 1872. The third edition (1906) is

---

first performed on May 13, 1840, and printed in *Det Kongelige Theaters Repertoire*) on October 27, 1840 (*ASKB U* 14).

[79] See Supplement, pp. 218-22 (*Pap.* III B 1). Kierkegaard's "reply" remained unpublished because Andersen went on a long trip abroad.

[80] Kierkegaard does not begin the actual review of Andersen's work until after the first eight or nine pages. See p. 69.

[81] *Adler, KW* XXIV (*Pap.* VII² B 235); Søren Kierkegaard, *Nutidens religieuse Forvirring* (Copenhagen: 1984).

[82] See p. 102; Bredsdorff, *"Andersen og Kierkegaard,"* p. 235.

[83] See Kühle, *Kierkegaards Barndom og Ungdom,* pp. 123-25. Naturally there are no reviews of this review.

identical with *SV* XIII 42-92.[84] It is possible that *From the Papers* was first published in the usual edition of 525 copies, but because of lack of documentation we have no precise details. We do know, however, that 121 copies were sold in the period from June 1839 to March 1850,[85] and of course there were a number of gift copies.[86] For the second edition (together with the second editions of *Repetition* and *Prefaces*), C. A. Reitzel's[87] made a payment of sixty rix-dollars to Peter Christian Kierkegaard, who represented the heirs to Kierkegaard's estate.[88]

In *From the Papers*, Kierkegaard's view of the individual emerges especially in his thought that authentic existence lies in more than fragmentary experience or the holding of abstract propositions. There has to be a "transubstantiation of experience . . . an unshakable certainty in oneself won from all experience." If a person consistently refuses to let his life be dissipated in the multiplicity of experiences and refers each experience back to himself, to his view of existence, then life can be "understood backward," experience be interpreted in the light of the "idea" or life-view. Not any idea can be a life-view, of course, least of all a fixed idea. It has to be one that authentically develops the person as an individual. It may be a purely humanistic life-view—Stoicism, for example—or it may have a heavenward direction in a religious outlook that provides a center for both heavenly and earthly existence and wins the Christian conviction that nothing can separate the individual from the love of God.[89] In either case, Kierkegaard

---

[84] In some sets of the first edition of the *SV*, the pagination from the third edition has been retained.

[85] See Frithiof Brandt and Else Rammel, *Kierkegaard og Pengene* (Copenhagen: 1935), pp. 17, 20.

[86] For example, to Frederik Fabricius (1789-1873), secretary of the Royal Library and co-founder of the Student Association. See *Letters*, Letter 12, *KW* XXV.

[87] The prominent bookshop and printing house founded by Carl Andreas Reitzel (1789-1853).

[88] See Brandt and Rammel, *Kierkegaard og Pengene*, pp. 22-25.

[89] See pp. 76-78. Cf., for example, Judge William's outlook in *Either/Or*, II, pp. 166-68, 229-30, 324, *KW* IV (*SV* II 151-52, 205-07, 291). The Judge, too, sees the need for an authentic consolidation of the personality.

views the authentic individual as one who does not depend on external events in order to survive as a person and who does not go under at the first breath of adversity.

Both from a humanistic standpoint and from a religious one, Kierkegaard is thus critical of Andersen in his relation to *Kun en Spillemand* as author and hence of the finished work. The authentic novel must express an authentic view of life and not be a projection of personal problems and a revelation of other deficiencies. To the central proposition of Andersen's novel, that "genius is an egg that needs warmth for the fertilization of good fortune," Kierkegaard reacts violently. He is clear that because Andersen lacks a total view of life he lacks insight when he constructs a passive genius who succumbs to the blows of fate. Kierkegaard contends that a genius is a person having the consolidated and consolidating power of a genius's personality, in which case unfavorable circumstances will encourage rather than discourage the person. Andersen's hero, in whom he so blindly believes, is thus not a genius but a weakling who passively succumbs to fate and evil circumstances. He becomes a "poor wretch" because he was one.[90] On top of this, Kierkegaard is critical of Andersen's solution of his hero's problems by finally turning him into a pietist. Since Andersen cannot look "into the history of hearts," he fails to explain how the character he describes could possibly undergo such a conversion.[91]

In his analysis of Andersen's novel, Kierkegaard begins with the contemporary tendency to turn in distrust from the previous historical development to political initiative.[92] In so doing, he again avoids any direct engagement with the political world and enters into a discussion of the work of novelists

---

[90] See pp. 74-100. Andersen himself disproved this view of genius, since he did not succumb to adversity. See Bredsdorff, *Andersen og Kierkegaard*, pp. 234-35.

[91] See p. 100-01.

[92] See Richard M. Summers, "A Study of Kierkegaard's Philosophical Development up to *Om Begrebet Ironi*" (diss., London University, 1980), p. 170. Summers points out that the trends that Kierkegaard attacks here were represented particularly by the *junge Deutschland* [Young Germany] school.

with something to say about life. From the work of Steen Steensen Blicher and Thomasine Gyllembourg,[93] the younger generation can learn something because their view of life emerges in their stories. Finally coming to Andersen, Kierkegaard praises his lyrical productions but complains of his lack of the epical. Andersen has succumbed to the urge to turn out novels instead of developing himself and hides "an inner emptiness under motley pictures." He cannot avoid reproducing his own joyless battle with life, his dissatisfaction with the world, because he cannot reflectively distance himself from his own situation and rise above it in a higher view. He lacks the proper vantage point. He fails to win himself a competent personality, which, Kierkegaard says, is a dead and transfigured one, not one consisting of raw personal encounters with the world.[94] Lack of a life-view means a misrelation to his person and to the fund of knowledge necessary for a novelist. According to Kierkegaard, situations and comments repeatedly occur in *Kun en Spillemand* that are poetic but not at all in keeping with the story. Andersen expresses himself in various faults: for example, in an inability to think himself into the outlook of a child, in unhelpful comparisons, incidental knowledge and associations of ideas, and an inappropriate expression of livid indignation.[95] Finally, Kierkegaard ends his review by distinguishing between a reading and a criticizing public. As reader and not critic, he can remember with pleasure poetic moods evoked by the book and feel thankful to Andersen, who, despite his literary faults, has still (in Kierkegaard's view) not succumbed to involvement with politics.[96]

---

[93] See pp. 64-69. As Summers points out (see Summers, "Kierkegaard's Development," p. 176), by praising the work of Heiberg's mother, who wrote from Christian convictions, Kierkegaard could identify with the Heibergian esthetic ideals without committing himself to Heiberg's philosophy.

[94] See pp. 70-82.

[95] See pp. 83-95.

[96] See pp. 101-02. Andersen was not, however, entirely free from sympathy with political causes, for example, the Polish rebellion. See *Skyggebilleder* (1831); Petersen, *Debut*, p. 155.

The idea that was indirectly indicated by the newspaper articles earlier now begins to take definite form in *From the Papers*. The concentration on political externals arising from dissatisfaction with the world is here viewed as an evasion of actuality. People cannot divorce themselves from their historical heritage, and the world does not become automatically wiser. The individual must first take on the task of becoming an authentic self, the fundamental prerequisite for genuine social and cultural existence. The task may be undertaken from a humanistic standpoint, an idealist philosophy, but this falls short insofar as it keeps itself from contact with the deeper experience belonging to the religious, the heavenward direction provided by Christianity.[97]

That Kierkegaard should be regarded as here espousing Hegelianism in any form is thus a misunderstanding of his aim and intention.[98] Granted, he intended his review for Heiberg's *Perseus*, but this in itself is no proof of Hegelianism. It would be entirely like Kierkegaard to write an article for a speculative journal, and in that article show a thorough grasp of Hegelian principles but deliberately point away from Hegelianism.[99] Indeed, Kierkegaard's style here is so heavy, with its lengthy syntax and wordy, obscure language, that it may well be a deliberate exaggeration.[100] Finally, for Kierkegaard, as for generations of students, there is the factor of reaction to mental fatigue in studying a subject. Many students have parodied a style or a philosophy, not because they were for or against it

[97] See pp. 63-81.

[98] See p. xxvii and the references to Thulstrup and Fenger in note 66 above. See also Summers, "Kierkegaard's Development," pp. 169, 174-81.

[99] This is not to deny any Hegelian influence on Kierkegaard. See, for example, *JP* IV 4281 (*Pap.* X³ A 477), where Kierkegaard reproaches himself as a "Hegelian fool" in this period.

[100] It should be noted, however, that Hans Peter Holst (1811-1893), the Danish poet and a school companion of Kierkegaard's, stated in a letter to H. P. Barfod that Kierkegaard at that time wrote in a "Latin-Danish" full of participles and involved sentences. Holst claims to have helped Kierkegaard by rewriting Kierkegaard's Andersen review for him. See *Af Søren Kierkegaards efterladte Papirer, 1833-55*, I-VIII, ed. Hans Peter Barfod and Hermann Gottsched (Copenhagen: 1869-81), I, pp. l-li.

but out of a healthy, humorous reaction to the effort of serious concentration on serious subjects.

Whether Kierkegaard's play, *The Battle between the Old and the New Soap-Cellars*, was written before or after *From the Papers*, or even at the same time, it is obviously intended for performance in the academic world (for the Student Association?), where the students and professors would recognize the characters and elements of satire obscure to us today. The main themes of the play as we have it treat of philosophy and politics, with a few allusions to religion, while the whole is a satire on superficial Hegelianism or at least on the jargon bandied about in the academic sphere.

The action of the play[101] takes place in the world of actuality (Act I) and thereafter in the realm of ideality. The chief character, Willibald (a Faustian doubter), returns home from a party with serious identity problems. He is sick, possibly because of all the literature he has swallowed. In his flight from the world of actuality and himself (Echo), he encounters some born-again Christians (Grundtvigians)[102] but succeeds in avoiding religion. He arrives safely in the world of philosophical ideality. The realm of philosophical ideality (Act II) is not, however, free of a political element, and doubt has its home there in the philosophical debate. Holla Hurrison, bearing a striking resemblance to Orla Lehmann, does not want to be plagued with "the old story about the past" but wishes to "intervene in things." Hegelian philosophers von Jumping-Jack and Phrase discuss the problem of whether the results of scholarship can be made understandable to people. Von Jumping-Jack is skeptical and sometimes doubts whether he has doubted enough. He has, however, learned from Descartes, the father of modern philosophy, that "everything must be disputed."[103] After Ole Wadt's support of Phrase's compro-

---

[101] See pp. 105-24.

[102] See p. 112; cf. *JP* V 5156 (*Pap.* I A 220).

[103] See p. 114. Here Kierkegaard attacks the thoughtless repetition and misinterpretation of Cartesian propositions leading to a philosophy based on illusion. Later, in *Johannes Climacus*, pp. 113-72, *KW* VII (*Pap.* IV B 1), he takes

mise, that one should at least write for "the educated middle class," Hurrison rejects philosophy. It is not philosophy that counts but the practical questions of life. At this, von Jumping-Jack chimes in with his question as to what life is. He wants to know how he can acquire a firm foothold, a fast Archimedean point in the sphere of reasoning.

Willibald now arrives, wanting to be cured of his relativity, his doubt. All he receives is a long lecture on philosophy from von Jumping-Jack (encouraged by Phrase), who tells him that modern philosophy suffers greatly from the same disease. Despite efforts by the president of the prytaneum to stop him, von Jumping-Jack in his historical exposition manages to reach Hegel and hence the end of world history; the only alternative is Straussian mythology. Phrase, his disciple, jibs at this, since he has "gone beyond Hegel"—even if he does not know where. Willibald, the existential doubter, is naturally not helped by the philosophical doubters and raises a serious question for public discussion. In the meantime, however, he is sent to the unfinished World-Historical College, where he is won over to the current philosophical views and comes to regret his question, namely, why the prytaneum's sun stands still in an eternal timelessness. Hurrison's reply at the annual general meeting is that it is the dawn of enlightenment as it throws off the final endeavors of darkness and introduces the existential golden age. Von Jumping-Jack maintains it is the light of philosophy as the evening of life. Hegel has drawn the previous rational systems together, and the world-historical culmination has begun. Hurrison, fighting for freedom, demands that the question be decided by balloting, a political solution that von Jumping-Jack views as giving rise to the "spurious infinity." Willibald manages to calm the resulting commotion by assuring them all that the physical sun does, of course, change its position, and all he wished to express was

---

up the proposition that modern philosophy began with doubt and discusses how the individual should relate to that proposition. See also Summers, "Kierkegaard's Development," pp. 178, 182.

the "poetic, philosophical, cosmopolitan eternity" that has in a spiritual sense already entered the prytaneum.

For Willibald, it is the dawn of truth, and Act III finds him strolling about in a state of bliss, proclaiming his enthusiasm for the absolute spirit. When a fly goes past reciting Hegelian propositions, Willibald sees the complete harmony of a completed world history that includes the natural order. Encouraged to bring about a reconciliation between prytaneum members after the recent disagreement, he proposes a new time-reckoning and a new name for the learned association to indicate that peace is restored: "The New-and-the-Old-Prytaneum." Von Jumping-Jack realizes that the entire incident sheds light on the myth of the battle between the old and the new soap-cellars, and that the mythical contains an anticipation of history. Here Ole Wadt suggests the erection of a monument to commemorate their unforgettable day, and the play ends with the erection of the monument amid enthusiastic toasts.

The serious theme underlying Kierkegaard's satire is the problem of human existence and the need for an authentic philosophy of life by which to live. Like *From the Papers*, it is concerned with the result of trying to begin again from the beginning and from nothing,[104] but here it approaches the problem of the idea for which one can live and die from a purely humanistic basis. Where *From the Papers* points to the religious, the soap-cellar drama portrays the failure of politics and philosophy divorced from real life and genuine personal existence. Willibald doubts himself and the actual world because he has not found an authentic life-view. The philosophers in their doubt ask what existence is really about and how one can find firm ground in the realm of thought. Thus both Willibald and the members of the prytaneum are faced with the problem of finding an authentic self by means of an authentic life-view. Willibald needs a life-view by which to exist; the philosophers according to their pretensions should be able to give him one. Unfortunately, the philosophical doubters in

---

[104] See pp. 61-62.

their ivory tower of superficial knowledge are themselves sick and cannot heal the sickness of anguished existential doubt. They therefore try to solve their problems by beginning again in the same old way under a new name. The politicians also wish to begin again, turning away from the past and rejecting philosophy in favor of the everyday world where they hope a vote will settle issues. However, in talking about the practical questions of life, they do not know what life is, and so they, too, cannot help Willibald. The politicians hope for the coming of the golden age, the philosophers look back into history. Both are unrealistic, and Willibald's disturbing question to the annual general meeting draws attention to the fact that they are all living in an illusory, idealistic eternity, in a state of abstract still life. The philosophically converted Willibald solves the problem of his unfortunate question by reassuring them that life is really going on and by pretending his question was another. He has finally let himself be brainwashed by the philosophical jargon that does not doubt radically enough to doubt its own jargon. That he has avoided considering a religious solution to the problem of existence is not surprising. Its representatives were egocentrically wrapped up in themselves, busy discussing their sins. There is, however, a hint of authentic religiosity at the edge of this crazy world. At the beginning of his drama Kierkegaard has Luther sitting in a tree cutting switches for people who "ask useless questions," while at the end the sinner Zacchaeus looks down on Christ from his sycamore tree.[105]

Many comic elements in Kierkegaard's play are hidden from us because we have insufficient knowledge of the contemporary situation. Neither can Kierkegaard's talent as a playwright be judged from the rough draft he has left us. Nevertheless, with its surrealist elements it may on the one hand strike us as rather modern, while with its "otherworldly" motif it is not untypical of the period.[106] The pas-

---

[105] See p. 105.
[106] See, for example, the fantastic elements in Andersen's first book, *Fodreise fra Holmens Canal til Østpynten af Amager* (1829).

sages taken from philosophical lectures and appearing in the lines of von Jumping-Jack and Phrase[107] would undoubtedly have provoked gusts of laughter, as would Sibbern's definition of life,[108] the characterization of Lehmann, the political allusions, and the sprinkling of Grundtvig's favorite expressions. Underlying the humor of the satire, however, remains Kierkegaard's polemic against false, illusory existence. The Archimedean point gradually emerging from his early polemical writings is thus his understanding of the self—the competent "dead and transfigured personality"[109]—in its relation to a right idea of existence, a theme Kierkegaard is to begin to explore in his discussion of Socrates' relation to the state[110] and his contemporaries in *Irony* (1841).

[107] The substance of such lectures is well indicated by Kierkegaard's notes on Martensen's lectures. See *Pap.* II C 25 (XII, pp. 280-331). See also *Pap.* II C 26-28 (XIII, pp. 3-116).

[108] See p. 115 and note 52.

[109] See p. 82.

[110] Note Kierkegaard's comic definitions of the state here, p. 122. See also *The Concept of Irony, with Continual Reference to Socrates*, pp. 178-83, *KW* II (*SV* XIII 260-65).

I

Articles from Student Days,
1834-1836

ANOTHER DEFENSE OF WOMAN'S GREAT ABILITIES[1]

So much has been said against the ladies' seeking to educate themselves in a theoretical as well as in a practical direction. Yes, even through no. 33 of this paper[2] an irony over this is presented to the public, chiefly regarding the academic education offered them at the present time through lectures.[3] But how unreasonable! History throughout the ages shows that woman's great abilities have at least in part been recognized. Hardly was man created before we find Eve already as audience at the snake's philosophical lectures,[4] and we see that she mastered them with such ease that at once she could utilize the results of the same in her domestic practice. This talent for speculation and the allied craving for deeper knowledge already manifest here, the East tried to satisfy; therefore women were confined in seraglios. And whenever an occasional traveler ventured into these sanctuaries, he was certainly driven solely by a thirst for knowledge. Therefore they went veiled in order not to be disturbed in their trains of thought. Yet not all were thus torn from life in order to brood on more abstract subjects. A great majority sought rather to assert their competence in life. As a speaker, woman has so great a talent that she has made history with her own special line: the so-called bed-hangings sermons, curtain lectures,[5] etc., and Xanthippe[6] is still remembered as a pattern of feminine eloquence and as founder of a school that has lasted to this very day, whereas Socrates' school has long since disappeared. Although Christianity was certainly hard on women by forbidding them to speak at meetings,[7] it still allowed them an arena for their eloquence inside the home. And when the rabbis forbade them to put in their word, it was solely because they were afraid that the women would outshine them or expose their folly. In the Middle Ages, the countless witch trials sufficiently showed the deep insight woman had into the secrets of nature.

Yet many centuries elapsed before woman's great abilities

were *properly* recognized. This was reserved for France, and here we shall refer solely to two phenomena: that reason in the French Revolution was represented by a female[8] and that the Saint-Simonists[9] placed them on a totally equal footing with the men. If to this we now add the fact that no one has ever yet succeeded in getting the better of a lady in an argument, that woman's dialectic capacity has reduced many an opponent to silence, then one certainly comprehends her superiority in intellectual matters, a superiority that extends to all branches of the mental faculties. And it is probably also because of this that anterooms swarm with ladies who nevertheless are married, for their discernment, inventiveness, etc. far surpass the men's.

Neither do the ladies of our time let us lack examples of woman's great abilities. We owe to ladies several theatrical works, one of which, enriching casuistry with new instances of collision, is making a stir.[10] In the last few years, a lady[11] is the only one who has proved the immortality of the soul—a book that together with Christiane Rosen's cookbook[12] has served to keep life in many. With hurried step the ladies hasten forward to their exalted goal: in esthetics, reviews are supplied by ladies; in medicine, the Department of Health gives them its blessing to let people jump from the pitch cap.[13] In art, they concern themselves with the most elevated subjects: they conjure up supernatural beings on canvas[14] and work together with the men for the spread of art. When it comes to manufacturing, they are the first to invent the making of gloves from stockings. Regarding history, they keep abreast of events, and many a paper, many a journal that man considers insignificant does not escape their keen eye—in fashion magazines they study the spirit of the age. Thanks, therefore, to you, great men, who help them up to the peaks of knowledge but nevertheless do not forget the other sex. Therefore it is so lovely to see that the man who *especially* wishes to have an effect upon the *ladies* does not, however, forget *the men* and finally extends his philanthropic enthusiasm to *all*.[15] With pleasure I look forward to the time when the ladies will know how to make clear to themselves what love really is, will have

XIII
7

a clear conception of the nature of warmth, will far surpass the men in accuracy in the study of history, since they will even know what Hagbart and Signe[16] ate for dinner and whether they ate anything at all, will probe deeply into the secrets of the Trinity (although this doctrine will be especially difficult for them, because hitherto they have had a bad time grasping that two can agree). So return, time of chivalry of the Middle Ages, in another sphere! Just as of old the ladies were ac- knowledged as umpires, so now shall dissertations, plays, philosophical works, be submitted to your judgment. Just as each knight bore his lady's colors, so shall there no longer be reference to Kantians, Hegelians, etc. No! From now on, the designation *the blue*, *the red*, etc. shall appear instead. From Eve's hand we shall receive the apple of knowledge. So ele- vate yourselves, then, above the earth! Already you are chang- ing at the top into winged birds.[17] Only fill your great sleeves with air and disappear before our eyes, before the eyes of the great multitude who will be present at the ladies' ascension. So fly, then, from this ungrateful earth, raise yourselves on the wings of philosophy and look down with contempt on those whose cowardly, servile minds would, with the Jews of old,[18] prefer to remain behind by the fleshpots. And then, when the men in this cold winter have repented their sin, then will spring smile at your return, then shall woman again stretch forth her hand to man—a snowdrop and a winter fool.[19]

XIII
8

A.[20]

THE MORNING OBSERVATIONS IN
KJØBENHAVNSPOSTEN NO. 43[21]

Home went the valiant Peter
The kettle on his back,
They blew upon the trumpets, etc.[22]

It is not the first time that *Kjøbenhavnsposten* [The Copenhagen Post], probably because it is on friendly terms with the tower watchman* of political life, has informed us that it is not yet day and dawn is still continuing. We have to some extent been confirmed in this observation through continually hearing the political cockcrow of *Kjøbenhavnsposten*. In vain one has tried
to get *Kjøbenhavnsposten* to discard the now surely somewhat worn negligee in which it has hitherto appeared and step forward so one can see with whom one has to do. It is probably this dawn also that has given *Kjøbenhavnsposten* the chance to produce a great many jokes and journalistic juggling tricks. After "the complaints have almost entirely ceased" (p. 169, col. 1, line 4 down),[26] by conveying to itself some of the praise generally awarded to *Fædrelandet* [The Fatherland] and shoving some of the blame from itself onto *Fædrelandet*, *Kjøbenhavnsposten* tries to bring it about that it can either heroically blow up itself and *Fædrelandet* or conquer completely. But we have a great deal to object against this observation, for the complaints about acrimony have been aimed almost solely at *Kjøbenhavnsposten*, and we therefore wish to exonerate *Fædrelandet* from any share in the supposed defense of *Kjø-*

---

* Incidentally, it seems that the observer to whom *Kjøbenhavnsposten* has appealed is not entirely reliable, for otherwise one would probably not find such confusion in his assertions: "It is dawn" (p. 169, col. 2, line 9 up); "The rays of truth dispel their vague phantoms" (p. 170, col. 2, line 6 down).[23]— "Life is in its early childhood" (p. 169, col. 2, line 13 up);[24] "the universal faintheartedness matched hardly at all the universal reforming spirit one otherwise regards as the salient feature of our time" (p. 170, col. 1, line 4 down).[25]

benhavnsposten, just as we also exonerate *Kjøbenhavnsposten* from its broker's business regarding *Fædrelandet*.

It thus remains to consider how *Kjøbenhavnsposten* has put its own house in order. After it has tried in its own way to show that the aforementioned complaint is on the whole unreasonable, it undertakes to come to terms with its creditors, solemnly confessing "that the press, however, is not completely guiltless" and "that it has also made itself guilty of some abuse or other."[27] —A very naive expression, indeed, which at best can be explained by the pleasant mood in which *Kjøbenhavnsposten* has perhaps been put by reading that piece which arrived rather *post festum* [after the party] in *Politivennen* [The Policeman's Friend]: "Even *Kjøbenhavnsposten* can make mistakes."[28] But if we wish to speak as human beings and not completely cut out all intellectual communication, then it surely should be *in confesso* [generally admitted] that when one says of *Kjøbenhavnsposten* that it is acrimonious and makes mistakes, one means that it is more acrimonious and makes more mistakes than one could wish. This newspaper, however, regarded as a human undertaking, must still be seen in relation to what has been accepted since the creation of man, and one must be very easy to satisfy if one will let oneself be fobbed off at all with the admission by *Kjøbenhavnsposten* that it is a human product.

After these preliminary observations, we shall now go on to the historical development of the individual complaints, a development, however, that by making these complaints into a "natural, easily explained, almost necessary item,"[29] and yet again, into an "inexplicable and impossible"[30] one, contains nothing particularly attractive for the observer. It is well known from the art of painting that a black ground contributes a great deal to making the colors stand out, and it is therefore an easy matter, by describing a previous state as sentimental-idyllic[31] or patriarchal-idyllic, to make the present surpass it in vigor. Yet this is always strange, because it is precisely "childhood" in which we are living when it is the sentimental, as the nebulous, dawning vigor that has not yet attained clarity, and the idyllic that are usually predominant.

Now it is certainly true that *Kjøbenhavnsposten* has long since lost its esthetic, and then its political, chastity, and to that extent it can well smile at a supposed state of innocence. There is also a palpable discrepancy between that time's so-called barrel-organ music[32] and the melodramas of *Kjøbenhavnsposten* to the accompaniment of the revolutionary clarinet.[33] There is certainly a great difference between that time's unpretentious simplicity and the swagger-booted, high-tragic posture of *Kjøbenhavnsposten*, which is indeed strangely suited to its morning observations and reminds one of Don Quixote,[34] who springs up in a dream and, with nothing on but his shirt, conducts himself as a hero—a posture that becomes still more elevated in that the hero has equipped himself with an "umbrella."*[35] (It must then presumably be a family umbrella, since all members of the staff of *Kjøbenhavnsposten* and consequently the compositor also** have to go under it.)
There is, sure enough, a great difference between the aforementioned time described by *Kjøbenhavnsposten* and the time that begins its era from the well-known metamorphosis of *Kjøbenhavnsposten*.[37]

But when was that time then? one may well ask, and we shall now try to discover the answer to this from the historical observations of *Kjøbenhavnsposten*, which, of course, distinguish themselves sometimes by grandiose abstract groupings, sometimes by totally individual concrete trifles, almost like someone who with seven-league boots strides over a whole kingdom and then trips over a little stone, which he then picks up, firmly convinced that he now knows that land's geography perfectly. So when was that time? It begins with 1799.[38] And when does it cease? Yes, that is just the problem. It begins to go out of fashion, for the entire people's way of life "has

XIII
12

XIII
11

XIII
12

---

* Page 171, col. 2, line 4 up.
** That the compositor is actually a member of the staff of *Kjøbenhavnsposten* it seems to have recognized itself, since it does not, like other papers, make a distinction between the authors' errors and the compositor's (printing errors) but elevates the whole to a higher unity under the designation "corrections,"[36] from which it then becomes a consequence that the authors can use the compositor as a shield.

taken a far more dignified, more serious, and more positive direction,"³⁹ and it must presumably be as good as totally gone out of fashion, since those complaints "have almost totally ceased."⁴⁰ And it was, of course, that much-mentioned state of mind that provoked and made those complaints "natural, easily explained, yes, almost necessary,"⁴¹ and consequently that state of mind as their cause has surely disappeared some time ago. Yet it was precisely these complaints that "are in fashion at the moment—or at least were so a short time ago."⁴² How was that time constituted, then, that sentimental-idyllic time—let this be said *in parenthesi*—characterized by perhaps the greatest literary activity Denmark has ever seen—how was it constituted? One was "content with everything; everyone took care of his own business and let the government take care of the rest."⁴³ But besides that, one was "really afraid and sang out of terror, just like children in order to banish or at least drown their anxiety."⁴⁴ "The state of the country was less satisfactory.⁴⁵ The people were weighed down by sorrow and grief in those cheerless times,"⁴⁶ and yet "one was happy and delighted, went on picnics, and rejoiced over every forget-me-not one found in Danavang."⁴⁷ But even if it was a fact that in the time of sorrow one looked back to the vanished days of prosperity, was there, then, anything wrong in it? There must indeed have been a consciousness of something wrong and miserable at that time, since this was what caused people to look back. And is not, then, the consciousness of what one has once been, precisely that which strengthens one most for a new and powerful activity? I certainly know that it goes with states as it does with individual people, and that an individual who has never been any good at anything is always in a terrible hurry to rush into the future and never dares to look back for fear that the abomination of desolation lying behind him will turn him to stone, just like Lot's wife of old.⁴⁸ Yet for the one who has had better times, such retrospection is certainly to a great extent beneficial. Now, regarding the estheticism of that time, *Kjøbenhavnsposten* surely cannot be thinking of that brilliant esthetic period from 1803⁴⁹ and thereafter, but rather, yes, that must be it, of that esthetic

XIII
13

shortcoming[50] *Kjøbenhavnsposten* exhibited for a number of years as a warning to all other esthetic artisans, a period to which it now perhaps thinks back with "contrition."[51]

But it was acrimony we were talking about.[52] *Kjøbenhavnsposten* thinks that it is wronged by these complaints about acrimony. "And what is it, then, that is most often complained about? Some trifling expression in an article with which one is otherwise very satisfied."[53] Certainly *Kjøbenhavnsposten* thinks "that to many it seems unesthetic and tone-deaf to speak of making the national finances public and of the abolition of villeinage"[54] (which indeed is not a trifling acrimony in "an article with which one is otherwise very satisfied"). But we will not be particular about that. There is certainly a noble heat in battle that can easily induce a writer to use a somewhat acrimonious expression. But one readily forgives him that. One tolerates a large dog barking, even in the wrong place, but these little dogs that always yap, and in the moment of danger creep into hiding ("into a gateway in a thunderstorm"[55]), are intolerable. The energetic reforming spirit going through *Kjøbenhavnsposten* has now been spoken about for a long time, but I must admit I have never yet been able to find it, and should *Kjøbenhavnsposten* continue with "Mette"[56] to maintain "there stands a hero, traitor," then I say as before, "Madam, there stands a tailor." Where, then, is that energetic, that serious, reforming spirit? Is it identical with those anonymous reformers (I can hardly say these words in one breath[57]) who have their prototype in that anonymous or rather pseudonymous reformer, the snake of Eden?[58] And shall I class with them all the world's reformers straight from Moses,[59] who, although he used Aaron's mouth, nevertheless did not stay in the background in order to let him fall victim to Pharaoh's wrath but faithfully met all dangers and difficulties— through Luther to an O'Connell[60]—those anonymous reformers who work under the auspices of Liunge?[61] And it is Liunge, the editor responsible under press law, who is fattened up and well fed like a sacrificial lamb, in order one day to fall under censorship's razor, this Liunge who, however, in a certain respect is too good to be editor of *Kjøbenhavnsposten*, since its staff might prefer to have a perfect nothing instead. Neither do I doubt, therefore, that one day in the future, just as in England one sells one's corpse to the dissecting room, in the same way here one will sell one's body to be used as editor of *Kjøbenhavnsposten*. Yes, certainly *Kjøbenhavnsposten* is reforming, but on closer examination it is rather a parody of the reforming endeavor, and I do not doubt that when the sun first really rises one will find the staff of *Kjøbenhavnsposten* standing just like the guests in Auerbach's cellar (see Goethe's *Faust*), the one holding the other by the nose, ready to cut.[62]

My discussion of the present no. 43 of *Kjøbenhavnsposten* is finished; yet I cannot leave it without the opinion forcing itself on me that the whole thing, after careful selection and classification of the heterogenous elements, can be conceived in the form of a great performance in three acts. Act one: mimicplastic[63] display of energy. *Kjøbenhavnsposten* is seen using a more forceful style.[64] Act two: A great deal of *non plus ultra* [second-to-none] dialectical rope dancing, both with and without balancing pole, interspersed with recital pieces. Of the dialectical rope dance we have seen enough examples in the foregoing, and that *Kjøbenhavnsposten* has used *Fædrelandet* as a balancing pole we have also seen. As to the recital pieces, however, these consist of a number of short story anecdotes, scenes from real life at the beginning of the nineteenth century: "The Privateering Time," "The Jolly Time,"[65] "The Cheerless Times,"[66] scene from "Thunderstorm in a Gateway,"[67] etc. Act three: Great fantasia for the journalistic Jew's harp on the given theme: a "glance into the future that one day will harvest what *Kjøbenhavnsposten* sows."[68] Only one thing is lacking: that the proceeds from the individual copies of this number go to, for example, schoolmaster Brodersen.[69]

B.[70]

XIII
15

Stay my fine Count, for I want you to learn
That I, though poor, my honor esteem;
Not your piping will I obey,
No, you shall dance to the tune that I play. [72]

I.

After being silent for a long time in the field of polemics, *Fædrelandet* [The Fatherland] has again become vocal in a piece that admittedly seems to us to be rather stammering. This strange article is to be found in *Fædrelandet*, no. 77, under the title "On the Polemic of the *Flyvende Post* [Flying Post]." Considered in its entirety, it can at most be regarded as a plan for a complete polemic, albeit that the ending[73] (p. 647) seems to cut away every hope of this. The piece begins[74] in a subdued, quiet, and instructive tone, furnished with little witticisms so useful for that purpose. But the tone gradually rises until it (circa p. 642) reaches the highest pathos of moralizing's most shrill and heartrending falsetto, after which, as if exhausted by this great violent effort, it noticeably decreases and with conciliatory warmth has mercy upon the author of the pieces "on the so-called Liberal journalists,"[75] and the whole thing ends with a kind of *Post Scriptum* saying that for the future it [*Fædrelandet*] does not intend to reply. We are not concerned with the beginning and ending of the present article. On the contrary, our place is in the middle, and because we are here involved in a terrible hullabaloo, since nearly all winds—morality's northeast and intelligence's southwest, grammar's[76] east and compassion's south—blow all at once, we must ask pardon of the readers for speaking a little loudly in order not to be drowned by this journalistic Niagara Falls.

It has surely surprised more than the author of these lines that *Kjøbenhavnsposten* [The Copenhagen Post], while it continually replies to every attack by *Dagen* [The Day], Berling's paper,[77] and *Politivennen* [The Policeman's Friend], has never engaged with the *Flyvende Post*[78] but has either rejected its attacks as "low and ignorant"[79] or not noticed them at all. It has surely surprised many that when the reply finally arrives it comes only after a long time has passed and, moreover, rather out of breath. But many have surely been surprised to see that an article aimed exclusively at *Kjøbenhavnsposten* and trying specifically to isolate *Fædrelandet* from this paper finds its reply in *Fædrelandet*. Yet this surprise will probably soon cease if one remembers that, according to a well-known Jewish law,[80] when the husband is dead the closest relative must marry the widow.* Preeminently worth noticing is also the circumstance that this reply is found in a piece by *Fædrelandet* that says at the very beginning[83] "that for a long time we have not replied to the attacks the *Flyvende Post* has repeatedly made on *this paper*" (i.e., *Fædrelandet*) etc., and again, "We shall here contribute an article about *our* opponent's polemic." It is indeed very evident here from both quotations that there is solely mention of an opponent of *Fædrelandet* and not of an openly declared opponent simply and solely of *Kjøbenhavnsposten*. Admittedly, *Fædrelandet* itself mentions (p. 643) that our piece in no. 76 of the *Flyvende Post* "is aimed against no. 43 of *Kjøbenhavnsposten*,"[84] but this remark looks very strange in the context of all the rest because the other pieces in the *Flyvende Post* are either directed against *Fædrelandet* alone or *Fædrelandet* has at least a share of the business, whereas the piece in no. 76 is directed solely against *Kjøbenhavnsposten*. Consequently, it is the circumstance that *Fædrelandet* has undertaken the defense against our attacks on *Kjøbenhavnsposten* that compels us, who were not originally its opponents, to fight against it for the moment.

We shall now go on to consider the lion's share allowed us

XIII
18

---

* That *Kjøbenhavnsposten* actually is a widow is to be seen from her need of a guardian.[81] But we shall by no means therefore prevent her from running a small retail business on her late husband's mercantile license, and do not doubt that through "great industry and love of truth"[82] she will guarantee her customers the fairest treatment.

XIII
17

by *Fædrelandet* in its criticism of the *Flyvende Post*. After having tried to find out the nature of the factual information the *Flyvende Post* "*only rarely* communicates,"[85] it goes on to acquaint its readers with some "other weapons the *Flyvende Post* *not infrequently** uses." It begins, of course, with the usual invectives against the author's lack of a love of truth, an accusation that is indeed very hard when one's love of truth is being compared with *Kjøbenhavnsposten*'s well-known love of truth. Yet all the moralizing with which this piece is saturated to so great an extent we reserve for special treatment—even though we were almost tempted to ignore it, scorning every such attack, especially one so unmotivated as is here the case. But because we regard it as a remarkable feature in the polemic of the Liberal papers, we shall, as aforesaid, come back to it later. The author, in mentioning no. 43 of *Kjøbenhavnsposten*, immediately barricades himself in with the comment "this on the whole well-written article,"[87] a comment that we would indeed have preferred saved until the end of the production of evidence, where it would have looked rather curious. For this much is certain, that if nothing else than what is quoted by *Fædrelandet* is put forward in favor of that article's being well written, certainly not many will be tempted to vote for the description conceded this piece by *Fædrelandet*: well-written. The concise summary of the contents of that article in no. 43 of *Kjøbenhavnsposten* will, since it must essentially be included in the following more detailed comment, find its elucidation there.

On the other hand, a couple of remarks about the piece in *Kjøbenhavnsposten* will best find their place here. For some time complaints in general have been made against *Kjøbenhavnsposten*, to which the reply was that they were general complaints which, as such, prove nothing. In the aforementioned no. 76 of the *Flyvende Post*, we therefore tried to point

XIII
19

XIII
18

* Now, among other things it is remarkable that factual information that the *Flyvende Post* "*only rarely supplies*" is to be found in almost all of the pieces dealt with by *Fædrelandet* in this article, whereas only one piece or at the most two pieces are cited as examples of the weapons the *Flyvende Post* "*not rarely uses*."[86]

out a number of errors that were found in precisely that no.
43 of *Kjøbenhavnsposten*. In that regard, we drew attention to
a striking confusion in that piece, and it is something that we
want to point out again now, because *Fædrelandet* does not
mention it at all in its defense. There is a certain gadding about
in ideas, a certain, if I may say so, intellectual vagrancy, and it
is for this reason, among others, that *Kjøbenhavnsposten*, not
for the first but rather for the sixth time, has now been prosecuted. An odd criterion must surely be used for such a piece
to be considered "well written," in which, without seeking or
hunting, one can produce such a soiree of contradictions that
look in amazement at one another without comprehending
how they have come together, an exhibition of contradictions
that is still conveniently on view in *Kjøbenhavns flyvende Post*,
no. 76. It is this paddling backward and forward, it is this confused conception of the past, that has provoked our attack. Yet
we thereby approach naturally the actual assessment of the
squint-eyed conception of the past in *Kjøbenhavnsposten*,
whereas just above we referred more to the total lack of all
logical, even merely moonlight, illumination,[88] something we
have already sufficiently stressed in no. 76. Although these
observations in a certain sense now converge, because the unclearly expressed is also the unclearly thought,[89] we shall, following on the whole the course indicated to us by
Fædrelandet's defense, leave this observation on one side until
further notice and first of all dwell on the point first mentioned by *Fædrelandet*. The wording goes as follows:[90] first,
"the author in *Kjøbenhavnsposten*, whom we shall denote with   XIII
a K.,[91] is accused of conveying to himself some of the praise   20
generally bestowed upon *Fædrelandet* and of shoving a good
deal of the blame from himself onto *Fædrelandet*. In K.'s article
we cannot find the least thing to justify this accusation. Is it
perhaps the fact that K. mentions the press in general, not
Kjøbenhavnsposten in particular, that has provoked this accusation? Or is it because K., against unjust critics, recommends
what we once said—not anxiously to pay attention to gossip?[92] But in both cases the groundlessness of the accusation is
glaring." We reply: It is not for either this reason or that but

because, as we have already said in no. 76 of the *Flyvende Post*,[93] "The complaints about acrimony have been aimed almost solely at *Kjøbenhavnsposten*." As long as this is not denied, we think we are right in our assertion. As long as *Kjøbenhavnsposten*, in a piece in which it tries to defend the press, keeps to the complaints about the press in general, which, of course, it has done in part in a previous number[94] of the series to which no. 43 belongs, as long as it does that, we shall not make accusations of that kind, but of course we shall when in a piece of a general nature it [*Kjøbenhavnsposten*] enlarges the accusation made especially against itself into a complaint against the press in general. If an individual official in the police force, in a defense against attacks directed against the whole force, also were to mention as accusations against the police in general, for example, complaints about his own vehemence and impetuosity, with the result that one must presume that the whole police force had the same fault as this particular individual official, we believe rightly that we ought to protest and if possible prevent such a *commune naufragium* [common shipwreck]. Whether the complaints about acrimony have been directed almost solely against *Kjøbenhavnsposten*, everyone who has lately lived in Copenhagen can decide for himself.

We now go on to the next point mentioned by *Fædrelandet*, a point that in a way we have already touched upon before when we spoke about the confusion found in that piece by *Kjøbenhavnsposten*. The author seeks to reject our censure[95] with the comment "that *Kjøbenhavnsposten* has not blamed the past in general; it has presented only its lack of interest in common affairs and presented it as something that must of necessity follow from the course of events." If the case actually had been put thus, as is here described and as it is also put a few lines above in the short summary given by *Fædrelandet* about the content of the said piece, we would not have tackled it in this way. On the contrary, we so completely agree with *Fædrelandet* in what it says, "that this dwelling on the past must not weaken the vigor with which we are going to meet the future"[96]—we agree so completely with it, we say, that we

XIII
21

can only think that *Fædrelandet* has added this ending in order to urge the same proposition we have maintained in the *Flyvende Post*.* Even if, for the time being, we admit that *Kjøbenhavnsposten* has not spoken about the past in general, we must still point out that on the whole it has vented an opinion in a manner that essentially diverges from the summary in *Fædrelandet*, for if this latter is to be reliable it must also be demanded that on the whole it reproduce the tone. There is a great difference between someone's saying, for example (as would be said in a summary in the style of *Fædrelandet*), "He reprimanded them for their errors and exhorted them to improve," and someone's flaring up and demolishing something in the most violent terms. Thus, in the present case, *Fædrelandet* speaks about "a nostalgic dwelling on past events," about "misplaced patriotism,"[98] while *Kjøbenhavnsposten* relates[99] that "one played with old Denmark and the Dannebrog,"[100] flirted with "Sjælland's beech groves and Kodan's[101] billows," and "among all these baubles forgot or lacked courage to get down briskly to what it was really all about." It speaks about "a patriotic jingle of Danishness,"[102] besides all the other nonsense and self-contradiction that we have adequately pointed out in no. 76 of this paper.[103] Even if we therefore admit that *Kjøbenhavnsposten* has not spoken about the past in general, the way in which it has mentioned the past, albeit in a special respect, must yet entitle us to a censure in which we, granting that retrospection, mention it in a worthier manner. In particular, the author in *Fædrelandet* must be willing to grant us that, since he, in bypassing those at least indelicate witticisms and saying in other respects the same as we have already said once, is so far from writing against our piece that in a way by his authority he seems to give it more influence.

We shall now consider a little more closely whether we really can grant *Fædrelandet* that *Kjøbenhavnsposten* has not

XIII
22

* See no. 76: "And is not then the consciousness of what one has once been precisely that which strengthens one most for a *new and powerful activity*,"[97] in which, of course, precisely the labors conditioned by that retrospection are emphasized.

XIII
21

spoken about the past in general, but only in a special respect. We shall in this respect remind readers that *Kjøbenhavnsposten* characterizes that vanished time as "sentimental-idyllic,"[104] as "years of enfeeblement." But if this is the case, then we must categorically declare that time destitute of the power and ability that we must concede to it in many other respects. For an age can perhaps lack receptivity to a certain type of impression, but it cannot, if it is otherwise competent (which I with so much the more right can claim, since I have stated facts, and neither *Kjøbenhavnsposten* according to the explanation by *Fædrelandet* nor *Fædrelandet* has denied it), be sentimental-idyllic or enfeebled in one direction, respecting which I shall merely request *Fædrelandet* as well as *Kjøbenhavnsposten* to try an experiment with just one person. I shall merely permit myself an attempt at an explanation regarding this matter.

With an ordinarily competent person, at times when many sorrows and troubles burst in on him, it is not unusual that it is precisely intellectual competence that reacts most powerfully; gaining the upper hand in the temperament, it lets the sorrow be forgotten or gives him strength enough to bear it. One can, then, by no means accuse that person of being sentimental-idyllic or enfeebled regarding the aspect of his temperament that responded to those sad and melancholy impressions. Similarly, I would also say that it was precisely the competence of the state that made it able to bear the many pressures it suffered politically, so that precisely its power was the condition that made it able to bear adversity. If that age actually had been weak, then it would have succumbed to all those tremendous sufferings, its life would have been a shadow life, but this is so far from being the case that, on the contrary, we must admire its rich poetic abundance. It is therefore an injustice, as well as a psychological inconsistency, to accuse that time of having been sentimental-idyllic, for, since every age has its own fundamental stamp, its character, from which all its expressions of life must take their color, so also here the political life must stand in a necessary relationship to the vigor that *Kjøbenhavnsposten* itself concedes to that age on the whole.[105] It would be unfair to accuse the knight

who, after having lost what was to him the dearest thing here
on earth, went out in search of adventure and yet often remembered his loss with sadness—it would be unfair and un-
psychological to accuse him of being sentimental-idyllic. If
our own age had any power in the direction that it has made
its life's task and if one must not rather regret seeing so many
drunk with the penny ale offered this age by the journals, if
what they contributed up to that point was not rather to be
regarded as a little early parsley for the strong soup of which
there is still only talk—it would be unfair to accuse it [the age]
of being sentimental-idyllic because of its lack of interest in
esthetics and in the higher purposes of life. One age cannot do
everything, and if our age can take it as far in political intelligence as that time [did] in esthetics, then it can lie down in the
grave in peace, even if an avenging nemesis lets follow a generation that conjures up [our age], in order, in fancied competence, to triumph at its expense.

In addition to this, *Fædrelandet* mentions[106] a couple of comments by the *Flyvende Post* "about little dogs that always yap
and, in the moment of danger, creep into hiding." *Fædrelandet*
will "disregard" them. We shall do so, too, and, referring to
the whole context in which these words appear, shall add, in
order to complete the quotation by *Fædrelandet* from our piece
with our quotation from *Kjøbenhavnsposten*, "into a gateway
in a thunderstorm."[107]

II.

On the other hand, we want to say something about the so-
called "shameless stab"[108] at Liunge and the defense of him by
Fædrelandet. *Fædrelandet* can keep the whole long passage, because it is nothing more than a long-winded commentary on
the words that are to be found in our piece: "Liunge—who,
however, in a certain respect is too good to be editor of *Kjøbenhavnsposten*."[109] We have certainly never denied Liunge "zeal
in gathering materials and industry in working them up."[110]
Yes, concerning the first quality, we readily believe him [to
be] in possession of a true Dionysius-ear.[111] We shall also

XIII
24

credit him with "deep respect for truth,"[112] something we shall say a couple of words about in our examination of the moralizing in general by *Fædrelandet,* both when it ascribes to friends superior moral qualities and when it denies them to opponents. But to get back to the defense by *Fædrelandet,* we must point out that in the whole of the context in which we have spoken about Liunge and his relationship to *Kjøbenhavnsposten* as editor, we have spoken about the reforming endeavor that goes through a number of articles and that precisely as such demands an able man as editor responsible under press law. And when we consider Liunge from this standpoint, we still believe we dare maintain that he is not qualified for it, for on board the reforming ship that operates in our waters, he plays approximately the same role as *pius Aeneas* [the saintly Aeneas],[113] who once in a while raises his hands, palms upward, to heaven and prays for good weather. But because of that aforementioned competence, which can nevertheless be the presupposition for a certain independent activity, we have pointed out that he is in a certain respect too good to be editor for "anonymous reformers"[114] who merely need someone they can hang out in their stead, since, as an industrious collector, he would make a good editor of a *Politiven.*[115] And we hope that the readers will now think the same after a rather detailed exposition by *Fædrelandet.* Yet one thing more: *Fædrelandet* mentions as a proof of Liunge's competence that *Kjøbenhavnsposten* "has existed for a number of years, while various other similar papers have gone under after a short time."[116] This phenomenon can easily be explained, because the able editor, precisely when fighting for a cause, can more easily come to get the worst of it when the times are against him, whereas the weak, who follow the diagonal of the parallelogram of forces[117] given in life, can more easily keep going. This is a new proof that Liunge is not the right person to be editor for a reforming endeavor and that precisely his competence must be harmful to the reforming endeavor, because this competence sometimes depends on a yielding to the demands of the times.

XIII
25

We have now finished with the reasoned attempt by

Fædrelandet to refute our statement, and as we now look back over the whole exposition we could perhaps best describe it as an annual general meeting of assumptions, in which there is such confusion that we believe that, even if we were blindfolded and a stick put in our hand, we could smash one piece of Jylland-pottery[118] stupidity after the other.

We shall now go on to say a little more about the ethics of *Fædrelandet*. It is strange to see that a party that on the whole shouts so much about intelligence has so little of it. It is strange to see a paper that speaks excitedly against "ascribing bad motives to its opponents" (bottom of p. 646)[119] make itself guilty of the same fault. Now, where the first matter is concerned, it is indeed very evident that from that intelligent standpoint nothing more is required than to prove that the person concerned is wrong or has spoken falsely; it is not necessary to maintain that the author lacks a love of truth. But instead of this intelligent production of evidence, a certain ethical currying of favor, a certain Lafontaine-Kotzebue-like[120] blubbering, snuffling, sermonizing tone has of late crept into the polemic. Thus *Fædrelandet* also in the present no. 77 has chiefly made our piece the basis for its godly observations, and while it violently inveighs against us ("the *Flyvende Post* seeks to amuse its readers with witticisms without caring whether or not the truth suffers on that account";[121] "it makes shameless attacks";[122] "wit and dialectical skill that are not matched by love of truth but serve only to glorify his own little self"[123] etc.), it delivers a panegyric[124] on Liunge that could become at most an acceptable jubilee speech in a Vartov.[125] As we have said above, we would willingly refrain from analyzing this whole moralistic stewed kale more closely if we did not regard it as so characteristic that for this reason we ought not to pass over it in silence. As it has gone with thousands in life—when they could withstand life's dialectic no longer, they went into a monastery—so also has it gone here in the dispute with *Fædrelandet*. Because it cannot refute or conquer its opponents, it resorts to a jeremiad over the author's lack of a love of truth. Nothing very much is accomplished by this, except that the present age has such a great lack of intelligence that it

XIII
26

gives ear to invectives of this kind. When in a dispute the point is reached where the opponent says: I cannot understand you, although I have the best intentions—then that ends the dispute. And although we shall willingly leave outside the whole dispute the question of whether or not his intentions are the best, because until the opposite can be proved we remain ever convinced of this, one must always respect such a move by the opponent. But when instead he starts to attack the character of the person he is speaking to, accuses him of being a willful sophist etc., then it can at the most provoke a smile on the lips of the opponent, because the whole thing is nothing other than a comic despair. In our no. 76, we have not permitted ourselves one single attack on the opponent's character and intention. We therefore hoped to be exempted from that sort of attack, but in vain. The author in *Fædrelandet*, without further ado, reproaches us with lack of a love of truth, but no wonder, since with regard to intelligence the troops he commands are not especially well disciplined but seem rather to be a kind of motley militia. Whereas the author in *Fædrelandet* reproaches us with lack of a love of truth, he holds a eulogy over Liunge's, which we have never attacked, and which, when all is said and done, makes no difference to the matter, for Liunge could be a very truth-loving man and yet afford a counterpart to the foolish Gottlieb[126] in the story, especially according to the psychology of *Fædrelandet*, which fortifies a chasmic abyss between morality and intelligence without suspecting that they stand in an essential relation to each other, and that, if one wants to separate them in this way, one can finally speak about a bumblebee's love of truth and morality. And that *Fædrelandet* believes that the whole piece in no. 76 is written to amuse an "own little self,"[127] well, we hereby inform *Fædrelandet* that we do not play invitation[128] without having the king protected, and that we remain with the same color in which *Fædrelandet* in the present no. 77 has, so it seems, declared a blank suit, whereas in trumps it has shown great abundance (since by trumps we understand the "standing"[129] trump card of *Kjøbenhavnsposten* and, so it seems, also best color now adopted by *Fædrelandet*: moral invectives).

Finally, we owe it to the author in *Fædrelandet* to admit that of the two linguistic errors[130] he has found in our piece, one is a linguistic error.

B.

TO MR. ORLA LEHMANN[131]

> Quite right! You will see that I have thought of you.
> I have here medicine that is excellent.[132]

A change is as good as a rest, one usually says, but the kind of change that has fallen to my lot in my clash with *Kjøbenhavns-posten* [The Copenhagen Post] is not at all pleasant. When I write against *Kjøbenhavnsposten*, *Fædrelandet* [The Fatherland] replies, and when I write against *Fædrelandet*, *Kjøbenhavnsposten* replies, and God knows how long this antiphonal chanting will continue. To this must be added that I have to do with no fewer than four or more different persons: the author of the five articles about the press-freedom affair in *Kjøbenhavnsposten*,[133] the author in *Fædrelandet* (I have just learned that it is Mr. Hage[134]), the roundelay in no. 90 of *Kjøbenhavnsposten*,[135] and Mr. Orla Lehmann. This latest addition in a way makes the matter even more difficult, because I thus have to do with both named and unnamed authors. It seems, therefore, as if I had come to sit on the wonder stool[136] and the Liberals sometimes danced round in a great crowd (for example in no. 90 of *Kjøbenhavnsposten*) and sometimes stepped forward individually in order to say what they wondered about. Then, as for my position with respect to time, it is no less boring. If one were to calculate how far away the storm was by counting pulse-beats between lightning and thunder, one would certainly think that my adversary lived in Greenland at least. I trust the esteemed readers are convinced that I am not to blame for this dragging on of the conflict and the possibility conditioned by it of a thirty-years' war instead of a controversy, and I shall therefore merely add a mention of Mr. Lehmann's attempt to excuse himself in this respect. There can, of course, be no mention of the rejoinders that Mr. Lehmann "would have made even earlier,"[137] because they failed to appear; but for one who already over a month ago "would have

made rejoinders," it still seems somewhat late not to reply before the thirty-first, since the first section of my reply to Mr. Hage came on March 12. Yet Mr. Lehmann thinks "that there still might be time for this" and also, "that it does come *rather* late,"[138] and he adds, as the reason for its not coming before, that "earlier he had something better to do," for which reason we can do nothing other than regret that he has not done a somewhat better job of it now.

After these preliminary observations, we shall try to give reasons for an understanding of the whole of this article viewed in its essential relation to *Kjøbenhavnsposten* in general, an understanding that Mr. Lehmann will certainly accept since he "would have liked to maintain the fiction that the *Flyvende Post* [Flying Post] as the organ for a certain view, a certain party, was itself the source of its articles."[139] In return for this, we shall consider the name* as a means of indicating a certain shading of opinion in the common main direction taken by *Kjøbenhavnsposten.*** And we shall consider it a fortunate means, because Mr. Lehmann stands in total contradiction to the entire line taken by *Kjøbenhavnsposten*, for it actually seems to have made "a breach of the respect it owes its readers and itself" (as is written in that strange edict in *Kjøbenhavnsposten*, no. 90[141]) by "filling its columns"[142] with Mr. Lehmann's article, which is directed against a piece that can be regarded "on the whole as a stylistic exercise in the humoristic manner,"[143] the point of which consequently is not information about "an issue or a particular fact."[144]

XIII
30

---

* How "a mark"[140] can be a means of indicating "a certain shading" of opinion, as it is called, we cannot comprehend, because the mark is indeed something totally external and incidental and indicates a shading of opinion just as little as whether one wears boots or shoes, and only the article's own inner nature shows whether or not it is a shading. Yet the whole of this passage, "yet I regard such a mark" etc., is totally superfluous and is put in only in order to make an opportunity for invective against the editor of this paper, because Mr. Lehmann himself has, of course, sufficiently convinced himself from my article's "robust and energetic language" that "this comes from another hand than the rest."

** The main direction of *Kjøbenhavnsposten* is characterized by the individual staff members contradicting one another.

XIII
29
XIII
30

The situation is as follows. When *Kjøbenhavnsposten* was on
its way to bankruptcy, it did as all bankrupt people do: it lived
luxuriously (and the literary beggar-king piece in no. 90 is
best explained thus). However, it occurred to it that perhaps
the fairest thing to do was to enter into negotiations with its
creditors, and in this respect Mr. Lehmann kindly took it
upon himself to get hold of the, even if far from the most
important, yet at least, so it seems, most stiff-necked creditor,
and partly by assuring him that the claims of the other creditors were totally unimportant, partly by offering him apparently modest conditions, undertook to reduce him to silence.
I regard Mr. Lehmann as such an agent, who, while he is ne-
gotiating business with me, does not forget, in the manner of
a commercial traveler, to recommend the firm's goods.

We shall now go on to the point at issue, that is, what Mr.
Lehmann calls the point, for his statement that "he ignores all
irrelevant matters"[145] is surely neither here nor there, since
whether it is an irrelevant matter is, of course, not proved by
his saying that something else is the point. Likewise, whether
what he regards as the point is actually the point or is solely
the point is not proved by his declaring the rest irrelevant. In
this respect, it is a little suspicious that Mr. Hage, who, of
course, also keeps solely to the point, has discovered several
points. With regard to Mr. Lehmann's elucidation of the matter, it contains essentially nothing new but only the same as
what Mr. Hage has already said. Anything new in it reduces
itself to a defense of the reliability of Mr. Hage's summary and
the defense, linked to it, of the tone found in the accused article in no. 43 of *Kjøbenhavnsposten*, to which must be added a
couple of additions and improvements, each of which will be
elucidated in its proper place. With regard to the former, Mr.
Lehmann thinks[146] that it [reliability] is a strange requirement
for a summary of a couple of lines in which one ordinarily
looks for nothing other than "a faithful account of the [arti-
cle's] leading idea." This statement, however, seems more
than a little strange. That the summary is only a couple of lines
in length is, of course, none of my business, and neither do I
know whether any special obligation is incumbent upon Mr.

Hage in that respect. We have not complained that the summary was only a couple of lines long but that it was unreliable,
and we think we are justified in requiring, from a short as
much as from a long summary, that it be reliable. Where the
tone is concerned, it might be dangerous to admit that what
is wrong with the wording is a matter of taste in the sense
"that everyone must be permitted to have his own opinion."
In a certain sense, of course, no one will deny this last point,
because one cannot forever forbid a person to have his own
opinion about any subject whatsoever, but since this is probably as much as to say that one opinion is just as good as another, we must protest. This would of course lead to the most
absolute license in a stylistic sense, and to that extent be an
extremely profitable principle for *Kjøbenhavnsposten* and its
staff, since they seem completely at ease in that respect. And
since I see no essential boundary between the various intelligent expressions and moral invectives when one really thinks
that the form is a matter of taste in the before-mentioned
sense, and since, moreover, the logical confusion pointed out
by us in the aforementioned no. 43 is probably assigned to the
same category, then, if the principle were accepted, the rules
would indeed be entirely abandoned and the most complete
anarchy would set in in a literary respect.

Now, it is certainly strange to hear Mr. Lehmann speak in
this way about the form, since on another occasion he seems
to be precisely of the opinion that, for example, a form of
government is not a matter of taste in the sense pointed out
but is something of very great importance. Yet so it usually
goes with people who think about a given subject without
thinking out their view in a wider context. Neither could Mr.
Lehmann maintain this inconsistency, for otherwise he would
scarcely, at the same time as he bypasses the few "perhaps
somewhat strong words"[147] in the aforementioned no. 43 because it is a matter of taste, have undertaken to remark that in
my article I have let myself be led into "unseemly wantonness
or offensive injustice."[148] Nor could he have undertaken to remark "that others besides Mr. Hage have found my attack
shameless,"[149] unless Mr. Lehmann will perhaps supply an

XIII
32

amendment to the confusion-of-taste principle put forward, to wit, that everyone has his own opinion and that a majority of votes decides the matter. If this is the way Mr. Lehmann wants to have "science democratized,"[150] then this latter will certainly decline all such scientific carnival festivities.

—We now go on to the miscarried train of thought in the aforementioned no. 43 of *Kjøbenhavnsposten*, which is again served up for carving. Mr. Lehmann, probably through grief that Mr. Hage's summary was so short, has decided to supply a longer one, for something extra has appeared in it, so that while Mr. Hage summarizes too little, Mr. Lehmann summarizes too much. Because of this, one can also see that Mr. Lehmann does not reproduce the tone; so one learns that it is not merely a summary of a couple of lines but also summaries of twenty-four lines[151] that are exempted from being reliable. The new material added begins with these words: "In the last three decades of the previous century,"[152] and goes on to: "approximately at the beginning of this century." As a summary, these words refer to nothing in that immortal no. 43 of *Kjøbenhavnsposten*. The reason that they are added is, however, not difficult to discern. If that unknown author had wished (as is said in the present no. 96 of *Kjøbenhavnsposten*) only "to pursue a certain trend from its point of departure through its decay and to its resurrection,"[153] it would have been excusable if the author, fastening his attention on that "very promising development"[154] and the echo answering it in our time, had overlooked the intervening time a little. But the aforementioned no. 43 had "a somewhat polemical coloring,"[155] as Mr. Lehmann himself says, and does not mention at all that it is only as a transition point, that it deals with the recent past. However, he makes the contrast between the present and recent past and lets the comparison redound completely to the advantage of the present. For the rest, Mr. Lehmann's presentation of the matter is almost entirely Mr. Hage's, which we have adequately dismissed in the *Flyvende Post*, no. 82.[156] The attempt made to volatilize the conception of that time's competence by saying "that often a generally poor time can give birth to a few great talents, indeed, in certain isolated direc-

XIII
33

tions by concentrating its vigor—and no time is entirely barren—it can develop a *certain* competence"[157] does not signify
very much, for the statement certainly is not true of a genuine
national literary activity sprung from Danish vigor, and if Mr.
Lehmann (and with him the author of the five articles in
Kjøbenhavnsposten[158]) wants to apply it to the past, then, of
course, he is indeed charging the time with lack of competence on the whole, because he speaks of "a generally poor
time."

We shall not repeat what we have said before in the *Flyvende
Post*, chiefly out of fear that a new opponent will appear (for
example, the author of the five articles about the press freedom affair[159]) saying the same thing again that first Mr. Hage
and then Mr. Lehmann have already said and thereby forcing
us to repeat what we have expressed clearly enough, for such
a catechizing of every single staff member or friend of *Kjøbenhavnsposten* is not our affair. Yet [there is] still one more
thing concerning the first point in the matter. Mr. Lehmann
has embarked upon some chronological improvements. It appears, namely, to be very difficult to fix correctly the time
when that weak condition began. *Kjøbenhavnsposten*, no. 43,
says that it began at the end of the previous century, particularly with the decree of 1799.[160] Mr. Lehmann, referring to
the train of thought in that article, says that "in the last three
decades of the previous century Denmark found herself in
a lively and very promising condition."[161] He says, moreover, "that it was primarily the period 1807-27 that was intended"*[162] in no. 43, and Mr. Hage says[164] that it was a
number of years ago that the sad time began. A peculiar sort
of chronology is also that according to which "I am supposed
to have given up my complaint in reality, since in a way I acknowledge the opinions Mr. Hage puts forward as being the
train of thought in the attacked article."[165] The case is as follows: Mr. Hage wanted to defend the aforementioned no. 43
of *Kjøbenhavnsposten*, but this defense turned out so unfortu-

---

* Incidentally, I do not know whether Mr. Lehmann has any warrant from
the author of the five articles to make him contradict himself in this fashion.[163]

nately that on March 4 he said what I had said on February 18. According to Mr. Lehmann's chronology, this order has now been totally reversed. It seems, however, more correct to say that Mr. Hage has said the same thing as I have, than that I have said the same thing as Mr. Hage.

As to the other complaint concerning my grievance over the poor reforming endeavor of *Kjøbenhavnsposten*, Mr. Lehmann's defense reduces itself to the following: I am supposed to have "substituted the reformers of our time for the reforming endeavor of our time and then identified these with the publisher and staff of *Kjøbenhavnsposten*."[166] To this I reply that I have spoken solely about the reforming endeavor of *Kjøbenhavnsposten* and shall ask the reader to examine *Kjøbenhavnsposten*, no. 76. In considering the statement that "one can readily agree with me that our reformers lack vigor and manliness because one thinks that a more vigorous and more serious spirit is beginning to awaken among the people,"[167] one will notice on the one hand that it is difficult to maintain the conception of a vigorous time whose individual spokesmen lack vigor. On the other hand, and this is the main point here, one will notice that these words *more serious* and *more vigorous* are comparatives and that that with which the comparison is made is the past, which thus was not at all as serious and vigorous as a time whose individual spokesmen lack vigor and manliness. With regard to the end of Mr. Lehmann's discussion of the second complaint, which goes as follows,[168] "It is due to a misunderstanding, since he is certainly right that our political life and its reforming endeavor have not yet displayed any great vigor but is wrong in objecting that against an article that has asserted the selfsame thing," I must remind readers that I have never charged the article with having said that our time lacked vigor but censured it partly because it said that our enervated time was better than the past, partly because it itself was a poor reforming work. A poor article in a paper that presents itself as reforming, a poor article that is itself a reforming attempt, is indeed *eo ipso* [precisely thereby] a poor reforming product. And moreover, since Mr. Lehmann can readily agree with me that our time's reformers lack vigor and

XIII
35

manliness and *Kjøbenhavnsposten* forms a link in this chain (and probably does not belong to the exceptions of which Mr. Lehmann speaks) and that a reformer without vigor and manliness is really a nothing, a flower without color and scent, the parody of the true reformer, it seems to me that I have said with perfect justice that the conduct of *Kjøbenhavnsposten* was the parody of the reforming endeavor, for it relates to this as the Children's Crusade does to Gottfred of Bouillon's.[169]

I have now finished with what Mr. Lehmann calls the point. If more besides could be called the point, or if something quite different is the point, it might be difficult for *him* to decide, who comments that "the kernel is certainly hidden inside a very thick shell."[170] In this, however, may lie a proof that he has not cracked the nut, since he does not know how thick the shell is. I shall ask Mr. Lehmann to see a little courtesy in the fact that I have dwelt so long upon what he calls the point,[171] and so much the more because it has been a very boring dwelling, since it has gone with Mr. Lehmann in relation to Mr. Hage as with the deaf minister that Jean Paul tells us about, who at a royal banquet, when the queen had told a story, rose and told the same one.[172] The ambiguous praise[173] that has been bestowed upon my personage, I ignore.

On the other hand, we shall now go on to consider the attempt made by Mr. Lehmann to explain the genesis of our article. Because Mr. Hage could not go any further with our articles, the reader must receive with thanks what the house could provide, some moral buckwheat porridge[174] and an interesting table conversation about Mr. Liunge's love of truth. Mr. Lehmann is of course brighter, and because he cannot go any further, he suddenly becomes a psychologist and a searcher of hearts and in his discernment now finds out what my real intention has been with my articles in the *Flyvende Post*. We shall reprint the whole passage here in order to add our commentary on it. It goes as follows:[175] "On the whole, that attack seems chiefly to be only the vehicle for a number of more or less suitable jokes, and insofar as this gives well-founded reason for regarding the whole as a stylistic exercise in the humoristic manner, one certainly cannot deny it as such

XIII
36

a certain virtuosity, but since, in that case, the author's intention is not to give information about anything but only to
amuse—it is indifferent whether himself or others—one can
readily deny it a love of truth without thereby impugning
the author's morality. At least there are to be found such
palpable, although sometimes very amusing, distortions and
perversities that under another presupposition one must call
in question either the author's intelligence or his *bona fides*
[good faith]; but since there is no reason for doing the former
and the latter is something I cannot easily bring myself to do,
then the interpretation I have given is certainly the fairest of
all, namely, that the author thought he saw in the *Kjøbenhavnsposten* article an unjust disparagement of the previous time and
an unjust praising of the present, and opposing this presumed
one-sidedness, he has given his dialectical bent of mind and
satirical humor free rein with a poetic license that has certainly
sometimes led him into unseemly wantonness or offensive injustice."

XIII
37

From this we now learn that the intention of a stylistic exercise in the humoristic manner is not to throw light on anything but only to amuse. We must deny this, for the intention
of an exercise is always to achieve a certain proficiency: the
intention of an exercise in sermon delivery is not to edify but
to gain competence in the art of being able to edify. The intention of a stylistic exercise in the humoristic manner is thus not
"only to amuse." Yet for a moment we shall assume that the
intention of this so-called stylistic exercise in the humoristic
manner was only to amuse, in order to dwell on the next
proposition, "that one can readily deny it (presumably deny
the author) a love of truth without thereby impugning the author's morality." I do not know what that means, to deny me
a love of truth because I want to amuse, because to amuse is
indeed something perfectly innocent, and not until one tries
to amuse at the expense of truth can one be accused of a lack
of a love of truth. Consequently, the latter should be proved,
but if it is proved, it by no means follows from this that one
violates my morality by saying so, because in that case there
cannot be a question of my morality in the concrete instance
but only of my immorality. That I actually have had the inten-

tion of amusing, conscious that it happened at the expense of truth, the following sentence [Lehmann's] presumably intends to make clear. With regard to the aforementioned palpable, although at times very amusing, perversities, these words still do not attack my love of truth, but the term—*distortions*—seems to lay it in ruins.

Yet, since nothing is proved on that head, we reserve it to ourselves to answer this charge once the distortions are proved and now go on to the following words—that under another presupposition one must call in question either my intelligence or *bona fides*. From this one learns that under the presupposition "that a person wants to amuse" one does not need to call in question his *bona fides*, although "palpable distortions" are to be found in what he says. On the contrary, under another presupposition (for example, when one wants to be boring), one must on the basis of these same distortions call in question the author's *bona fides*.

We continue. Mr. Lehmann has, as we have seen, posed a dilemma, to wit, he must under another presupposition call in question either my intelligence or my *bona fides*, but what kind of presupposition is it that is opposed to this "other presupposition"? It is that my purpose has been merely to amuse, but under this presupposition it is impossible that any such dilemma can arise, since, as said before, to want to amuse is something perfectly innocent. Mr. Lehmann therefore has another presupposition as well, namely, to want to amuse at the expense of truth, and then the dilemma is correctly posed. Unfortunately, Mr. Lehmann has, however, remained standing like the scholastic donkey[176] of old (for there are no grounds to call my intelligence in question, and he cannot bring himself to call in question my *bona fides*), and however willing I am, I cannot help him out, because he does not wish it himself, and consequently I must let him remain standing. In what follows, a new interpretation used by Mr. Lehmann suddenly comes rushing to help, to wit, that my attack is due to the supposed one-sidedness of the aforementioned article.*

XIII
38

---

* This again places Mr. Lehmann in the same distressing situation, because here he has again put forward *another presupposition*.

How this interpretation is consistent with the foregoing, that the whole was an exercise in humoristic style merely to amuse, how these interpretations have come together in the same sentence and, it seems, in order to throw light on one another, is not easy to perceive.

—Now I have finished my comment and shall merely add that it has not surprised me at all that both Mr. Hage and Mr. Lehmann have assumed that my articles were merely to amuse, for the form certainly clashes with the solemn, funereal style one generally finds in *Kjøbenhavnsposten*. This [paper] can therefore say with Gert Westphaler, "I do not believe that any person, not even my enemies, will say that I at any time have started to talk nonsense . . . . . I carry on purely political and foreign discourse not to be found in many books and worth its weight in pure gold."[177] —And regarding its dispute with me, this paper can add, "Is it not incomprehensible that such a scoundrel as Jørgen Glovemaker dares to despise my speech and turn up his nose at it."

Mr. Lehmann says that he has signed his name in order to show me a little courtesy.[178] —I sign mine for the sake of consistency. And because Mr. Lehmann has apparently written a great deal before, since he says that he will sign his name under *these* lines, I cannot sufficiently rejoice at the change to what I, at least, regard as being for the better. I cannot sufficiently rejoice, I say, at this change, just as I cannot sufficiently congratulate *Kjøbenhavnsposten* on the butterfly developed out of its cocoon.

S. Kierkegaard.[179]

XIII
39

OUR JOURNALISTIC LITERATURE[180]

A STUDY FROM NATURE IN NOONDAY LIGHT

Paper Given to the Student Association
November 28, 1835[181]

Gentlemen!

Before I go into my subject proper, I must make a few prefatory observations.

When I as one of the younger members, perhaps unacquainted with many of the conventions, without a practiced eye for, may I say, the theory of perspective in oration, which promptly enables one to see how that which has been worked out in the study will look when it appears in a large assembly, how that which is spoken in a smaller circle must be modified when it lays claim to a wider audience—when I, I say, stand before you here, it is as much with confidence in your humanity as it is with the conviction that the person who mounts this podium is not thereby made assembly chaplain but, as an individual in the totality of the Student Association, perhaps expresses what is already shared by many other members, so that, without claiming to say anything new, he hopes he will not be unwelcome if he repeats something partially familiar, and so much the more so in this matter, since another member has recently attempted to stress and illuminate from another point of view something that is already in part given in the consciousness of most members—in any case I did not wish a point of view, if not the opposite of that position at least a modification of it, to lack a spokesman in this forum, where the subject has already been introduced. Therefore I must especially request the forbearance of *those* gentlemen present who perhaps *share my* point of view, insofar as my presentation may be faulty; the others can at most complain about a wasted hour and about the tediousness of such an indirect proof of the correctness of their point of view.

It is certainly not without reason that artists seldom or never paint a landscape by noonday light but more frequently by morning light. The distinctive freshness, the wonderful quivering, the exuberant changeableness of light and shadow evoke a particularly propitious total impression that does not permit any single point to be emphasized and, even though it were merely for the moment of discernment, to be divorced from the whole. Something similar happens in other spheres as well. We like to dwell on the first appearance of an idea in world history; we would like to have people from east and west come and worship it in its swaddling clothes,[182] and I by no means deny the significance of such a poetic consideration; but just as entire races as well as particular individuals eagerly turn from the perhaps somewhat Novemberish flowering of life to the fresh bud in order with the help of imagination to visualize the blossoms that were denied in life, so man also is inclined, when it is a matter of a new life that is supposed to break through, again to give imagination free rein and let a mighty tree spring forth from the factually given mustard seed.[183] Whether their hopes will put them to shame, only time will tell, but reflection can and ought to embark upon investigation of only the factually given and to inspect it in the noonday light. And if the result of these reflections should become a little frosty, one also knows—at this point I abandon the position of observation—that early frost does not harm the seed, that is, if it is winter seed and not the quick-to-shoot-up and just as quick-to-mature-for-harvest spring grain. On the whole, I believe that it is beneficial, as much for every form of individual life as for the individual man, to stop the wheel of development, to look back over the past, and to see how much progress has been made, whether dust and other such things have not caused detrimental frictional resistance to quicker progress. Although I heartily approve brisk action and also reflection, as that which collects and in the instant secures the often dissipated energies and thereby, like the significant silence before the battle, conditions new and vigorous activity,

I
B 2
159

I must, however, just as heartily disapprove of a phenomenon that often assumes the shape of reflection, a certain morbid imagining that hinders both action and true reflection, and if it does allow true reflection to break through for once, and then, if there has been any movement at all, true reflection reveals the past period more as an approach to caricature than to the ideal, the morbid imagination promptly lets a person fall into the same old daydreaming. It is certainly good and encouraging for a man to become conscious of having achieved something, but to fancy that one has achieved more than one really has is and remains harmful and easily leads to that kind of daydreaming.

Let us consider with whom we are comparing ourselves, and let the Liberal newspapers remember—I wish to say this here already—that even if they do more and better than the Conservative papers, this does not add up to very much, especially for the Liberals themselves, who so profoundly despise those papers. Just as I do not at present share many of our contemporaries' excessively sanguine hopes,[184] so I also advise against climbing Tabor[185] along with many hypochondriacs in order to assure people that they will not come into the promised land; I advise against both positions, because at least this evening I want to grant reflection the first voice. And even though I must disapprove of the daredevilry that boldly mounts Odin's throne and in the tranquillity of the gods' eternal contemplation smiles down on men's fighting and foolishness, and I must rejoice that, just as the time is long vanished that let people seek the company of wild animals instead of building and living among human beings, the time is also past that transformed men in the middle of life's clamorous noise into hermits—whether as moralists they were solely occupied every minute of their lives with drawing bills on heaven without paying any attention to what went on close at hand or whether as indifferentists they first felt the wall to see whether it was hot when they heard the fire alarm—so I must disapprove in practice of an abuse springing from the age's surely beautiful but also rather busy striving (to bring men to work jointly for one goal by setting aside the narrowminded bour-

geois mentality and moonlight family-sentimentality), an
abuse, namely, that one promptly has a party name at hand
for the one whose view somewhat approaches one or another
of the current views, without remembering the countless
number of shadings that must occur, since a natural and sound
life does not have its confession of faith all worked out, which
is usually a sign of one of the last stages of life—I must disapprove of it in practice, I say, because I stand here simply as a
réflecteur.

Moving on to my real subject, I shall first of all attempt a
historical recapitulation.*

Mr. Ostermann[187] begins his comments with Winther's
Raketten [The Rocket].[188] I completely share Mr. Ostermann's
appreciation of Winther's talent, the main characteristic of
which is, in my opinion, the distinctive style that marks his
pieces and gives every one of them its color. But when we
want to find *in it* one more seed of the later development, I
must protest. *Raketten*, with all its good and bad points, was
the most beautiful, most individual flower on the stem of *Politivennen* [The Policeman's Friend],[189] and it is certainly true
that most of his successors completely lacked his talent and
adopted his weak points. But the trend was nevertheless the
same. On the whole, *Raketten* was content with the existing
constitution; it criticized only the supposedly illegal conduct
of individual public officials: the Public Assistance Administrator devil, outpost skirmishing, and Hannibal Sehested.[190]
Its successors follow in its tracks, and I do not remember finding in a single paper of this kind an attack upon a larger func-
tion of the body politic, on the organization itself and not its
misuse by a concrete individual; perhaps the only exception is
Sandhedsfaklen [The Torch of Truth],[191] and it is also naive
enough to believe that in a way it walks hand in hand with
Kjøbenhavnsposten.[192] Or does Mr. Ostermann believe that
Raketten is to be regarded as the seed, inasmuch as it acted as
critic? Or did not *Raketten* coexist all this time with *Kjøben-*

I
B 2
161

I
B 2
162

I
B 2
161

* I owe it to myself to mention that part of the historical section was written
before I came into possession of Ostermann's manuscript.[186]

havnsposten without influencing the latter in any way? Or did not *Raketten* maintain its tone after the moment occurred[193] that changed the tone and character of *Kjøbenhavnsposten*? Or was there not some rather conspicuous reason for calling forth such a change in principle? I look upon Liberal journalism as a new development that no doubt may have many connections with a previous one—for example, by showing, as Mr. Ostermann himself points out, the extent to which the Freedom of the Press Ordinance permitted one to go in a certain direction polemically without necessarily designating the direction— but no doubt there are a number of new additional factors that have really made it what it is. In this respect, I need only cite as proof the acknowledged fact that, if I may put it this way, people greeted one another with a "Happy New Year" or, as the favorite poet of this new life says: "Denmark's May and Denmark's morning."[194]

And now I shall attempt to show where these new factors are to be found.

The *July Revolution* of 1830.[195] Revolutions follow the same course as illness. When cholera was endemic in Europe, the attacks were not very violent. The July Revolution was distinguished by, among other things, its elegance and refinement; it was a successful operation by an experienced surgeon. All the violent episodes that accompanied the Revolution of [17]89 were not present here, and thus the July Revolution stands as a remarkable example of a clean, pure revolution, free of extraneous elements. Meanwhile the rest of Europe stood like spectators and saw, to use an expression Börne uses, what time it was.[196] The news about it was played in every key, but since, however, there was nothing but the name, and so few here saw this, they saw only how smoothly it had come off, everything considered; naturally such a folk-recitative with choir could not fail to have an effect upon other governments and nations. Also here in Denmark it was not without effect, and although I cannot agree with a view expressed in the address of thanks[197]—a view that also makes it inexplicable how the order to the chancellery[198] concerning Provincial Consultative Assemblies could find the people fairly well pre-

pared—yet I may point out, since I am dealing only with journalistic literature here, that I am unaware that any Danish paper has expressed any wish or opinion on the matter *prior* to
the official announcement of the order to the chancellery concerning Provincial Consultative Assemblies. Whether a number of people prior to that time had clearly and explicitly
wanted such things or whether it was rather something vague
and obscure, one of those vibrations by which the French
Revolution agitated men in various places, I do not know, and
here it is not my concern, but I doubt that such a wish gained
journalistic expression *prior* to that order. From then on the
trail is clearer, in life—the Twenty-eighth of May Society[199]—
as well as in journalistic literature and in literature proper. But
just as we cannot deny here that the government was the active
agent and that that order was the sunshine that called forth the
flowers of literature, and just as, generally speaking, nothing
in the world appears without two factors, so also the Liberals,
as I call those in whom receptivity for such institutions had
been awakened, had their share in this; but I nevertheless believe that *prior* to that order the government and the Liberals
faced each other as two entities that, because of the July Revolution, had a great deal to say to each other but did not
rightly know how to begin until the government broke the
silence. To avoid misunderstanding, I repeat that I am speaking only about *literature*.

I
B 2
164

And now I am at the point where the new development has
its beginning, and therefore, in order not to interrupt my following exposition, I shall set up a milestone with the following inscription:

> By means of a natural elasticity, the July Revolution and its
> echoes in many places in Europe kept the people and the
> government apart in, if not a total, then at least a literary
> silence, until the government gave the signal.*

* Mr. Ostermann, of course, also emphasizes the government's step, and it
is to emphasize even more this element of time and the government's activity
that I permit myself this exposition.

Mr. Ostermann has made the transition to the genuinely new development by discussing the well-known publication by Lornsen[200] and the bold article in *Maanedsskrift for Litteratur* [Monthly Review of Literature].[201] As for the former, whereas I cannot refrain from pointing out that it does not immediately concern me since it is German and does not pertain to journalism, I do call attention to the fact that for one thing it must be regarded as a result of the July Revolution, mainly exerting an influence through the Polish ditto,[202] and for another—and this is the crux of the matter—that our journalistic literature (I have in mind *Kjøbenhavnsposten*) does not give it much of a recommendation* or draw any further conclusions from it. Thus you understand that this publication did not get a very favorable reception in the journals, and as far as other literature is concerned, you will remember that here as well as in Holstein, which really does not concern me, it evoked some counterblasts, even sermons against it, I believe. Apropos of that, may I point out that in *De slesvig-holsteenske Prælaters og Ridderskabets Adresse* [The Address from the Schleswig-Holstein Prelates and Nobility][204] it is stated that "also according to their most humble opinion (. . . . . 'while still being convinced that intrigues of individual malice by no means correspond with public opinion' . . . . .) the needs of the times require ever more insistently a consideration of expressed wishes." I must also point out that, if anything, the whole document must be regarded as a result of the influence of the July Revolution exerted mainly through the Polish Revolu-

I
B 2
165

---

* "Chancery Councilor Lornsen's Rebellion and Arrest" (*Kjøbenhavnsposten*,[203] no. 282, November 29, 1830). "From a publication printed and published in Kiel, *Ueber das Verfassungswerk in Schleswigholstein*, written by Councilor Lornsen, and several articles occasioned by the same that have come out in the duchy, all of which may be had along with Lornsen's book in the bookshops of the capital city, we have learned something of the rebellious aims and the proceedings that Councilor L., appointed a little over a month ago as sheriff of Sylt, disclosed not only by the publication and circulation of the above-mentioned book but also by other illegal actions." —His arrest and later his sentencing and imprisonment in Rendsborg Prison are reported quite briefly and baldly without even the exclamation and question marks the press customarily uses when it does not dare say more.

I
B 2
164

I
B 2
165

tion (my first thought), also that it is German, and finally that—my main point—the Danish journals quite baldly report the whole thing without a single side-glance. —As far as the latter (the article in *Maanedsskriftet*) is concerned, you will remember what Mr. Ostermann himself correctly pointed out, that it is even more recent than that order.[205]

For the sake of completeness, I shall, referring to the Danish journals, now do my best to give the reasons for the view concerning this *element of time*, a view resting until now, to a great extent, on a general consideration of the Danish development in relation to the European. I shall show, *for one thing*, that prior to that order no such wish was expressed in the journals (this then becomes the negative aspect), and *for another*, switching over to the positive aspect, I shall show that there can never be a mistake about the element of time, because of the remarkable fertility in contrast to the previous sterility.

I shall now go through *Kjøbenhavnsposten* for 1829,* 1830, and 1831 up to February 12, to substantiate my first point.

1829. It plays around with esthetics (Master Erik[206] is not to be seen) but does not ignore patriotic themes: praises the wedding ceremony of Prince Ferdinand and Princess Caroline and the illumination,[207] the smallpox service, also foreign news, although à la Riise's *Archiv*, for example, Mohammed II and Emperor Alexander, Turkish jurisprudence, Migueliana.[208] The news section[209] contains esthetic and cultural news, anecdotes, and other literary confection. Thus the paper is not political.

1830. Liunge continues to be an esthete and as such to attend Heiberg's confirmation classes; from September on,[210] special attention is paid to the remarkable volcanic eruptions all over Europe,[211] yet always theoretically, not practically.

1831. Up to February 12[212] it generally maintains the same tone. To indicate the contrast even more, I shall compare the first one and a half months of the year with a couple of the

I
B 2
166

---

* I need not pay any attention to 1827 and 1828, since Mr. Ostermann has himself correctly observed that during that period *Kjøbenhavnsposten* for the most part estheticized; I did not need 1829 either, but use it merely for the sake of completeness.

following months, up to May, for example. At the beginning
of the year (the first month and a half), there is some foreign
news, but it is dealt with simply as history. Material for
the news section is chosen from an artistic point of view.
From here on, the news section is more attentive to domestic
news—for example, in several numbers the comments about
the censorship, some taken from larger works, some from
foreign papers, and from March on a man who signs himself
T.[213] (and, please note, in the previous month and a half he
produced only one piece, and this a translation) begins to
write a lot almost every single day. In a series of articles under
the heading *Miscellany*, he tries to show what flattery is etc.—
elaborates on what a good heart is ("put up with everything,
let oneself be spit in the eye"), what it is to be "malicious," the
nature of egotism—he tries to arouse feelings by means of fa-
bles; he talks about the national economy, about the meaning
of the terms "aristocrats" and "democrats"[214]—and finally
gets started on the ordinance of April 14, 1831.[215] Here, however, there is surely a remarkable change; the pulse, which
previously was calm, now begins to speed up a little. A striking productivity appears outside the journals as well: writings
by David and by the two Tschernings[216] about the Provincial
Consultative Assemblies come out even before the end of
March. From now on, *Maanedsskrift for Litteratur* also begins
to carry some political articles, which, as the editor himself
observes in a note,[217] the times seem to require now.

I have thus tried to show that with respect to the origins of
the new development the government aroused the journalists,
not the journalistic literature the government. Here I owe it to
Mr. Ostermann to discuss in a few words his view of *Raketten*
as one more seed of the new development, which view I previously put aside. I looked upon it as an attempt to make journalism more *the active* factor in this whole development. I
hope what I have said previously helps answer the question as
to whether this is the case.

I now proceed further with my historical exposition of the
activity of our Liberal journalism—that it is only *this* I am
going to deal with ought to be suggested by the circumstances
of the times and be put beyond question by the relation be-

I
B 2
167

I
B 2
168

tween my presentation and Mr. Ostermann's, which deals almost solely with this. My previous remarks indicate my assumption that just as the government has set the tone for journalistic literature, it will also continue to do so. What has been said does not mean, as I have already suggested above, that journalism has not been active at all, but only that the government is the *primus motor*. Just as when two resilient bodies, one at rest and the other set in motion, collide, this collision occasions a reaction from the body previously at rest, and this reaction in turn produces a primary impact but in such a way that we always regard the reaction as conditioned by the initial primary impact—thus do I view this relationship, yet with the modification that sometimes it happens that the reaction was too weak and too momentary to call forth a new impulse from body no. 1, so that this body, if all activity is not to cease, must put itself in motion anew. To substantiate what I have said, I shall refer to the nodal points where, so to speak, the two powers come together and show whether the energy of journalism gives rise to action by the government or whether the government by its action causes journalistic activity, as much when it encourages and promotes the new development as when it repressively keeps the creek of journalism from becoming stagnant water and forces it to become a stream. However, that not much in the way of results can be expected before 1834 can probably to some extent be concluded from the fact that it is only in 1834 that a question of great significance for journalism arises, namely, freedom of the press, and instead of practical experiments in this respect, as one would have expected, theoretical investigations are undertaken.

I go on with my historical recapitulation.

In 1831, the government's next step was the provisional ordinance of May 28;[218] it does not create much of a stir in the journal. From now on[219] the news section is preoccupied with cholera and the paper itself with investigations into Denmark's national defense.[220]

In 1832 there is first the convocation of the wise men;[221] in April, I believe, there are a few items about the institution,[222] and later in May there is news about the Twenty-eighth of May Society,[223] which can be linked, not altogether incorrectly, to that convocation.

In 1833, the government takes no step. The influence of the Ordinance of April of that year[224] concerning censorship will be discussed later. Several items from the *Hamburger Korrespondent*, the *Kieler Korrespondent*, the *Zeitung für die elegante Welt*, the *Eremit*, etc. are to be found in the news section early that year. Research into the Latin language.[225] Tscherning goes abroad.[226] The king goes abroad; his illness.[227]

In 1834, investigations into the aforementioned Ordinance of April 1833 provoke a big fight,[228] and Algreen-Ussing proves fairly successfully that we do not have censorship at all.[229] Here follow the well-known articles about the Directorate of the Society for Moral Delinquents.[230] —The Ordinance of May 15 about the Provincial Consultative Assemblies.[231] From now on, the theoretically acknowledged freedom of the press begins to be used *in fact*. From now on, there is a constant battle between *Kjøbenhavnsposten* and the censor, beginning with the piece on political guarantees;[232] then comes the controversy about the Norwegian *Morgenpost*,[233] and finally formal legal proceedings are initiated against *Kjøbenhavnsposten*.[234] In connection with this, I am still bearing in mind, however, that the Ordinance of May 15 *precedes* this action. There also appears the first journalistic seed[235] of the Liberal chaos, but in the beginning an attempt was made to provide for the seedling the supporting stake of a few well-known theorems.

From now on the government's steps, as well as those of journalistic literature, which prior to this with suitable intervals had been somewhat *piano*, begin to be somewhat more *forte*. As I now approach the times in which we are living and thereby also must call attention to the enormous difficulties bound up with such a vivisection, I must mention—of the positive steps taken by the government, the elections[236] and the convening of the Provincial Consultative Assemblies[237] —of its repressive steps, the proceedings against Professor David,[238] the familiar recitative "We, we alone,"[239] and the ban on publicizing the proceedings of the Provincial Consultative

I
B 2
170

I
B 2
171

Assemblies.[240] I consider the petition[241] to be the most striking step coming from the side of the people, but at the same time I must point out that, regarded as a literary document, it floats without any anchor if one does not remember that it was occasioned by fear of a tightening up of the freedom of the press. But since it did not proceed from the journals, I shall not discuss it further. On the contrary, as is well known, it was that government's recitative that first set the journals in motion here and even in England.[242] Now both the government's repressive and positive steps speedily follow each other, and, as a result, the journalistic reaction as well; so a great deal of difficulty is involved in showing which side provided the primary thrust. But with regard to the government's positive steps, it should be recalled how large a role the elections and the convening of the Provincial Consultative Assemblies play, and with regard to the repressive steps, it should be recalled that the David case occasioned Haagen's contribution.[243] In drawing conclusions here, I want to say that just as the government provided the first impulse, so the relation between the government and journalistic literature on the whole can be described as follows: the government was active-passive (or affected through an activity); journalism was passive-active (or acting through a passivity).

Having finished my historical recapitulation, in which I have attempted to show what our journalism accomplished in relation to the government, I shall now consider more closely its weaker aspects. Since I am chiefly dealing with Mr. Ostermann, I shall discuss only *Kjøbenhavnsposten* and *Fædrelandet*.

I
B 2
172

Kjøbenhavnsposten. Our whole age is imbued with a formal striving. It was this that led us in daily life, with a disregard of cheerful atmosphere, to emphasize symmetrical beauty, to prefer conventional rather than sincere social relations. It is this whole striving that is sufficiently denoted by—to use the words of another author—the attempts of Fichte[244] and other philosophers to construct systems by sharpness of mind and Robespierre's[245] attempt to do it with the help of the guillotine; it is this that meets us in the butterfly-light, flowing verses of our poets and in Auber's music;[246] and, finally, it is this that produces the many revolutions in the political world. I agree completely with this whole effort to cling to form, insofar as it continues to be the medium through which we have the idea, but it should be remembered that it is the idea that is supposed to determine the form, not the form that is supposed to determine the idea.[247] One should keep in mind that life is not something abstract but something extremely individual. One should not forget that form, for example, from a poetic genius's position of immediacy, is nothing but the coming into existence of the idea in the world, and that the task of reflection is only to investigate whether or not the idea has acquired the properly corresponding form. It should always be remembered that life is not acquired through form, but form is acquired through life. If I imagined a man who had long been infatuated with the Greek mode of life and now, when he possessed the means, arranged for a building in the Greek style and a Grecian household establishment—it would still be highly problematic whether he would be satisfied or whether he would not soon prefer another form simply because he had not sufficiently tested himself and the stage of development in which he lived. But just as a leap backward is wrong (something the age, on the whole, is inclined to acknowledge), so also a leap forward is wrong—both of them because a natural development does not proceed by leaps, and life's earnestness will ironize over every such experiment, even if it succeeds momentarily.

Now, after these preliminary observations, as I look at the career of *Kjøbenhavnsposten*, I hope, inasmuch as I diligently tried to state the reasons behind *the whole striving in our time* because a single illustration here is futile, that you, gentlemen, will agree with me when I characterize it as one of bustling busyness. But I already hear some of you saying: You are contradicting yourself, since you previously maintained that the government had the active role. It merely seems so, however, for it is by no means my intention to deny that in *Kjøbenhavnsposten*, especially in the news section, a certain petty pin-pricking is to be found, but I did not want to discuss that earlier,

I
B 2
173

since at that point the discussion was simply about the progress of the new development through journalism and the merits of journalism in that connection, and I cannot regard such pin-pricking as any sort of step. It is this whole striving that I have tried to describe as one of bustling busyness, for bustling busyness is not action but a fitful fumbling. To use the words of a poet, words employed in another connection, bustling busyness is "a restless rambling—from castles in the air—to mousetraps—and home again."[248] Authentic action goes hand in hand with calm circumspection. Most likely you have all been in the situation of having traveled along a road in a stagecoach in which one does not arrive exactly sleeping at one's destination but, unfamiliar with the way, has to ask, and then a farmer says: "First turn right and then left and then left again at the willow lane by the village pond, and then you will have about half a mile left; then turn right, and you are there"—but you have all certainly experienced that one never arrives at one's destination that way. One must first drive to the nearest village and there inquire the way to the next one, and so on. And here, where the subject is a new development, here one should take heed and diligently pay attention to the compass. And although development and progress in other nations can help us considerably and teach us many precautionary measures, one should remember that it does not do to travel in Sjælland with a map of France.

I
B 2
174

There is always something Don Quixotic about such striving; one sounds the alarm every minute, gives Rosinante the spurs, and charges—at windmills; at the same time there is no lack of discernment to make one aware that some evil demon or other has changed the giants into windmills, although Sancho Panza most solemnly swears that they were, are, and will remain windmills.[249]

That a striving like this can easily unsettle life, I may dare assume to be *in confesso* [admitted], since common experience indicates that nervousness is something very harmful.

How this bustling busyness and the disturbing activity resulting from it can be inferred from the fundamental character of *Kjøbenhavnsposten*, I shall now attempt to show by pointing out that *Kjøbenhavnsposten* lacks unity. Scientists maintain that a heavenly body is formed from a cloud mass through the harmony of centrifugal and centripetal forces in combination with rotation on an axis—and to me *Kjøbenhavnsposten* seems to be just like such a fog mass, but one whose existence as a planet has still not been realized through the harmony of centrifugal and centripetal forces in combination with turning on an axis. It therefore does not surprise us that there has been a certain instability in the articles—as at one time the centrifugal and at another the centripetal tendency dominated—both during an earlier period and recently, when there has been an imbalance of the centrifugal tendency. That I understand a competent editor to be the axis on which the planet is to rotate, and that I have intended the centrifugal and centripetal tendencies to designate what people up to now have called by the so-popular party names Liberal and Conservative, scarcely needs to be pointed out. It is quite natural and can hardly be denied that *Kjøbenhavnsposten* has acquired a somewhat greater unity recently and that the center of our political solar system, the Assembly in Roskilde,[250] has exercised upon it some power of attraction and thereby helped it find its path and regulate its course, and that on the other hand the centrifugal force, which used to have the ascendancy, has done its best to keep it. However, to repeat, since the harmony of the forces has not taken place as yet, nor the rotation on the axis either, it easily runs the risk of being drawn into another solar system, since—seen from our solar system—the centrifugal direction in relation to another system must appear as centripetal.

I
B 2
175

Mr. Ostermann has also mentioned some complaints against *Kjøbenhavnsposten* and has tried to justify it. He divides them into two classes: (1) the charge of acrimony and unseemly tone, and (2) untruthfulness and dishonesty.[251] I shall venture to elucidate them a little more explicitly. After saying that he is by no means a blind worshiper of every utterance that bears the Liberal label and that, on the contrary, he frequently is compelled to concede what is true and justified in these complaints, and then, after examining the source of these charges and showing that they are advanced also by forthright, honorable, and truth-loving men, Mr. Ostermann proceeds to consider the charge in category no. 1.[252] He points out that an opposition party can hardly be expected "to sweeten the bitter pill";[253] he uses a metaphor to show how innocent abusive expressions can be. "It is a truth"—so go his words—"we must never forget, that where an energetic and forceful character speaks, his words acquire a special color because the thought is special, and however unimportant it may seem to many to omit a word here and there, yet one ought to consider how essential this little word, as one calls it, is for the writer, how totally and entirely the thought that lies in it lies in the individuality of the writer and how this word is precisely for him a major issue"[254] etc. I do not believe that the Danish ear is so spoiled that it is unable to bear some frank word; I do not believe that the Danes are so unfeeling that they do not know how to forgive some instance of acrimony spoken in indignation. But, gentlemen, I believe the discussion *is not about this!* When a writer heatedly and emotionally writes something that he perhaps is unable to substantiate, one is perhaps far more willing to be carried away by him than inclined to judge him harshly, for what comes from the heart as a rule goes to the heart. But it should be remembered that our authors have a battery that they must beware of—I mean the existing ordinance on the freedom of the press. The result of this is that, in the belief that one is right in what one says, one cuts as closely as possible to the ordinance on the freedom of the press, and the result of that, again, is that in order to avoid the punishment of the law, authors must use extreme caution so that the expression one previously could excuse because of emotion and blood circulation now comes out cool and premeditated. I do not blame an author at all for trying to say as much as he presumes he is permitted to say, but what is more natural for him, trying to dance on the narrow line between the legally permissible and impermissible, discouraged by some of his predecessor's desperate somersaults into the Siberia of freedom of the press, what is more natural for him than to move as adroitly as possible. Yes, if he stepped forward perhaps a bit rashly, yet for that very reason with fire and force, and let himself be carried away and ex-

I
B 2
176

posed himself to censure—well, then we would judge him otherwise. But recollect, too, that these tightrope walkers most often are also masked[255] (pseudonymous or anonymous[256]). And if it were in otherwise good and vigorous pieces that one allowed oneself such adroit acrimonies—well, it might be better that they were not there, but then one most likely would not really be so sensitive about the matter. It should be remembered, however, that these acrimonies actually are concealed in notes and footnotes, in questions and exclamation marks.

Mr. Ostermann now moves on to the heart of the matter and tries to show that a little acrimony in a daily paper is not so dangerous.[257] I do not think it is, either. But it is a mistake, all the same. I would never have discussed this whole abuse if attention had not already been drawn to it. I take exception to it first and foremost because it is not *action*, and next, because it is *cowardice*. That *Kjøbenhavnsposten* has more subscribers than *Fædrelandet* may be ascribed partly to the circumstance that it comes out every day, partly to the variety of its interests, and also to its practice of summarizing the most important domestic newspapers.

Mr. Ostermann now takes up the second charge, that of dishonesty and untruthfulness.[258] On this occasion, I must state that I have never heard *Kjøbenhavnsposten* categorically accused of dishonesty and untruthfulness; that it has been charged now and then with having spoken falsely in a particular article is quite a different matter. Mr. Ostermann attempts to show how someone who believes he has truth on his side, yet is lacking valid legal proof, has no trouble using the press to get his opinions expressed. Since Mr. Ostermann generally recommends great caution in this regard, I shall make only a few remarks. In the first place, every such accuser can very well be required to sign his name, because hardly anyone wants to appear before a secret court, and fairness also seems to demand that such an accuser must be branded a liar in public when the accused has cleared himself. In the next place, since on the one hand the charge must be expressive enough to be understood, and on the other hand not too expressive, lest he get a slander suit on his hands, the accuser

I
B 2
177

should recollect how easily he could hit *several people* and how inclined one is, if an innocent person actually replied and justified himself, to hint, if not to say directly, that *he* nevertheless just possibly feels himself the object of attack since *he* defends himself. He should remember that, in order to let himself be even more deterred from using such means.

I now go on to *Fædrelandet*, and here we have a happier situation. After withstanding the storm over the David trial, *Fædrelandet* got on its feet with rejuvenated energy and especially of late has achieved a vigorous and sound existence. *Fædrelandet* seems to have found the direction in which it wants to move and in a frank and honest editor[259] a hand that will prevent every kind of eccentricity. It seems to have understood that myth—I am almost tempted to call it that—about the battle of freedom of the press in this country, from which one learns among other things to investigate more closely what freedom of the press there is before sounding the alarm.

My presentation is now finished.

I have discussed our Liberal journalism and thereby dealt mainly with *Kjøbenhavnsposten* and *Fædrelandet* (of the other periodicals the one that perhaps most deserves mention is the *Dansk Ugeskrift*,[260] which, possibly more unobtrusive and quiet than others, has produced many interesting articles); I shall not, however, go into that further. I have attempted to show that on the whole it (Liberal journalism), perhaps with the exception of the most recent past, has *not* been *as active* as one is perhaps inclined to believe, that *Kjøbenhavnsposten* in particular has often used a substitute for genuine activity. —I have not discussed the Conservative papers since I did not believe that time permitted them to be included in one talk.

Whether my presentation has been successful, the honorable assembly can best judge—and however this judgment may turn out, it will always be a joy to me if the assembly will acknowledge my endeavor to stand this evening *solely* as a *réflecteur*.

II

From the Papers of One
Still Living

Published
Against His Will

by S. Kjerkegaard

A word in advance [*Forord*] breaks up [*bryde*] no quarrel,[1] one usually says, [but] this preface [*Forord*] at least breaks [*afbryde*] the continuity of a quarrel I have had for quite a long time with the actual author of this essay. Although I love him "with tongue and mouth and from the bottom of my heart"[2] and truly regard him as my sincere friend, my *alter ego* [other self],[3] I am still far from being able to describe our relationship by substituting another expression that might perhaps seem identical: *alter idem* [another of the same kind]. Our relationship, you see, is not a friendly *idem per idem* [the same with the same]; on the contrary, our opinions nearly always differ and we are perpetually in conflict with each other, although under it all we are united by the deepest, most sacred, indissoluble ties. Yes, although often diverging in magnetic repulsion,[4] we are still, in the strongest sense of the word, inseparable, even though our mutual friends have seldom, perhaps never, seen us together, albeit that someone or other may at times have been surprised that just as he has left one of us, he has, almost instantaneously, met the other. We are, therefore, so far from being able to rejoice as friends in the unity for which poets and orators in their repeated immortalizations have only a single expression—that it was as if one soul resided in two bodies[5]—that with respect to us it must rather seem as if two souls resided in one body.

What troubles we may have with each other, what domestic scenes sometimes occur—of this you, dear reader, will best be able to form a conception by permitting me to relate what has happened in the case of this present little essay, for from this trifle you can then easily infer the rest. The fact is that my friend suffers to a rather high degree from a sense of unfulfillment in the world, and this has often made me very worried about him and often made me fear that, if my good humor could not remedy things and dispel Saul's evil mood,[6] things would look bad for my friend, for me, and for our friendship. As is well known, the human soul does not need quite as much time as our globe does to turn upon its axis. This movement, however, is not only much faster, but the soul also passes through the various signs of the zodiac much more frequently, just as, for the same reason, the period of stay in each sign is naturally also considerably shorter in relation to the speed of rotation. Now, when the soul enters the sign of hope and longing, according to my understanding there awaken in him, during the attraction of the different constellations, vague presentiments that, as in antiphonal chanting, answer and are met by the distant tones that sound to us from our well-known, but also frequently forgotten, true home. In such moments, he closes himself up, silent and secretive in his ἄδυτον [inner sanctum],[7] so that he seems to avoid even me, in whom he otherwise usually completely confides, from whom he otherwise usually has no secrets, and it is only in a vanishing reflection, as it were, of what is moving in his soul that I, in a strangely sympathetic[8] way (explicable only by an incomprehensible *communicatio idiomatum* [communication of two natures]),[9] feel what is stirring inside him. And when he returns to me again, half-ashamed in case I should have noticed anything, and then after a little interval sadly exclaims:

XIII
47

> Es blies ein Jäger wohl in sein Horn,
> Wohl in sein Horn,
> Und alles was er blies das war verlorn
> [A hunter blew upon his horn,
> Upon his horn,
> And all that he blew was lost at once][10]

—he is actually close to casting a gloom over me. Although he succeeds now and again in seizing one or another of the fleeing ideas, he must also, as he says himself, struggle and strive with it. And although he forgets in the moment of blessing that he is limping,[11] he feels it only the more strongly when the idea departs from him. But should it happen that he secures and imprisons one of them in a fuller moment (you have surely also experienced, dear reader, that it is not only for our Lord that one day is as a thousand years[12] but also, though very rarely, for us men), he is often afraid that perhaps he has not had the thought christened in time and that nisses and trolls have thus acquired power to leave a changeling instead.

After many such difficulties, this present little essay was also finished, and I, as the medium through which he telegraphs with the world, had already taken charge of it in order to make the necessary arrangements for the attainment of its external destiny—to be printed. But what happens! He had strong objections to it. "You know very well," said he, "that I consider writing books to be the most ridiculous thing a person can do. One surrenders oneself entirely to the power of fate and circumstance, and how can one escape all the prejudices people bring with them to the reading of a book, which work no less disturbingly than the preconceived ideas most bring with them when they make someone's acquaintance, with the result that very few people really know what others look like? What hope can one entertain that one will fall into the hands of readers wholly *ex improviso* [without expectancy]?[13] Besides, I feel tied by the fixed form the essay has finally acquired and, in order to feel free again, will take it back into the womb once more, let it once again sink into the twilight from which it came, where the idea

> Shows itself and smiles and disappears
> Like the point of a desired headland in fog[14]

—maybe then it can emerge in a regenerated shape. Furthermore, I know very well what it is that blinds you. Author's vanity, my dear! 'Poor thing, can't you give up the vain hope of being an author of four sheets?' "[15] Amen! Ὡς ἔφατ᾿ αὐτὰρ ἐγώ μιν ἀμειβόμενος προσέειπον [So he spoke, but I answered him and said][16]: Stuff and nonsense. All you have said on the subject is of no weight and is neither here nor there, and since, as you well know, the chatter that is neither here nor there is

XIII
48

XIII
49

always more than enough, I will not hear another word. The essay is now in my power; I have the command. So, straight ahead, march. The order of the day is: What I have written, I have written.[17]

The Publisher.

———————

verte [p.t.o.]

Postscript for the readers who possibly could be XIII
harmed by reading the preface: they could skip
over it, and if they skipped far enough so that they
skipped over the essay as well, it is of no consequence.

Andersen as a Novelist

WITH CONTINUAL REFERENCE TO HIS LATEST WORK:
ONLY A FIDDLER[18]

Far from remembering with thankfulness the struggles and hardships the world has endured in order to become what it is, the whole newer development[19]—in order to begin again from the beginning[20]—has a great tendency even to forget, if possible, the results this development has gained in the sweat of its brow.[21] In uneasy foreboding of the perfect justice with which posterity could treat it in the same way, the development has a great tendency, on the one hand, to convince itself of its activity and significance and, on the other, to foist this acknowledgment upon posterity by making itself the true starting point of world history. It would like to do this by beginning, if it were possible, the positive era with itself and letting the previous existence [*Tilværelse*], if one is still reasonable enough to presuppose such, be a life serfdom, a piece of subtraction on which one must only regret that it has been necessary to spend so long a time. If we meet this phenomenon in its most respectable form, as it appears in Hegel's great attempt to begin with nothing,[22] it must both impress and please us: impress us, in view of the moral strength with which the idea is conceived, the intellectual energy and virtuosity with which it is carried out; please us, because the whole negation[23] is still only a movement inside the system's own limits, undertaken precisely in the interest of retrieving the *gediegne* [pure] abundance of existence. If we see the same phenomenon evoked by a genuinely original character's natural opposition to the whole modern phraseology, if we see such a one, raised high above the crowd by the deep artesian force belonging to genius, stand like an imposing statue, completely enveloped in the rich draperies of his homemade terminological cloak—but yet so egoistically enclosed in himself

that there is not the least rag the "gaping mob"[24] can clutch—
then we must indeed thank God that such a Simon Stylites[25]
reminds us of what self-reliance is but also regret that the mis-
direction of the age required such a sacrifice. As far, however,
as these two manifestations of the above-described inclination
to begin from the beginning are concerned, one must note
that they are advanced in order to show the relative truth that
can lie in this tendency, because, with regard to the first manifestation, it essentially rests with philosophy as a system to
reconsider continually its own premises, and this, if only by a
misunderstanding, has also been directed at existence itself.
And if we look at the second, this is in part compelled by the
more universal confusion covering entire nations and only dis-
tantly related to this tendency and is in part reformingly directed solely against abuses that have crept into the given positivity, without therefore wanting to eradicate even one word
originally given in the language. The extraordinary willing-
ness and readiness, the almost gracious obligingness, with
which thousands in our own day, as soon as a reasonable word
has been spoken, ever stand ready to misunderstand it, has
also been in tireless activity here. Its extent can easily be determined by everyone who has observed that the entire recent
literature is, on the one hand, so completely preoccupied with
prefacing and writing introductions. It has forgotten that the
beginning from nothing of which Hegel speaks was mastered
by himself in the system and was by no means a failure to
appreciate the great richness actuality*[26] has. On the other
hand, it is too greatly afflicted by these hysterical cases of brilliance.

---

* The Hegelians, however, must not be taken altogether literally when they
mention their relation to actuality, for when in this respect they refer to their
master's immortal work (his *Logic*[27]), it seems to me to be like the rules gov-
erning rank and precedence, in which, beginning with secretaries (*Seyn*, pure
being), one then through "other secretaries" (*das Andre, das Besondre, Nichts*
[the other, the particular, nothing]—therefore it is also said that other secretaries *sind so viel wie Nichts* [are just the same as nothing])—lets the category
"actual secretaries etc." appear, without therefore being entitled to conclude
that there is in actuality a single "actual secretary."

A sorrier form of the same delusion, actually the one we originally aimed at, is to be seen in the main trend of the age in the political sphere. This form misunderstands the deeper significance of a historical evolution* and clings curiously enough, as if in a fight for its life, to the cliché that the world always becomes wiser, understood, please note, with a logic favorable to this moment but parodic.** Either it appears as youthful arrogance too confident of powers untried in life (and this is its best form), notwithstanding that to the extent that the genuinely youthful, which was the integral element of truth in it, declines, to the same degree the phenomenon itself diminishes to giddiness, even though contemporaries should be infatuated enough to address themselves with their thanks to such a *klein Zaches genannt Zinnober* [little Zachary named Vermillion]***—or it appears as lack of patience to adapt oneself to the conditions of life, as powerlessness, when filling a particular position in the state, to share the burden of history, which is light and beneficent for the reasonable. But

---

*　　*Vernunft wird Unsinn, Wohlthat Plage*
　　　Weh Dir, dasz Du ein Enkel bist
　　　[Reason *becomes* a sham, Beneficence a worry:
　　　Thou art a grandchild, therefore woe to thee].[28]

The further away one is from the real crux of the development, the more curious this must obviously seem, and I do not doubt that a *Rana paradoxa* [paradoxical frog],[29] for example, could in a single sentence raise far more serious doubts about existence [*Tilværelse*] than *summa summarum* [the sum total] of all skeptics and freethinkers to date, for, as J. Paul says, "*Solchen Sekanten, Kosekanten, Tangenten, Kotangenten kommt alles excentrisch vor, besonders das Centrum* [To such secants, cosecants, tangents, cotangents, everything appears eccentric, especially the center]."[30]

**　　We on our forefathers' shoulders stand,
　　　We seem so tall—and are so small . . . .[31]

*** See *Hoffmanns Schriften*, IX, p. 45: "Seltsam war die Gruppe, die beide zusammenstehend bildeten. Gegen den herrlich gestalteten Gregor (this is the historically developed state) stach gar wunderlich das winzige Männlein ab, das mit hoch empor gereckter Nase sich kaum auf den dünnen (unhistorical) Beinchen zu erhalten vermochte [The two formed a strange group. Against the magnificently shaped Gregor . . . was contrasted, in a curious manner, the little manikin who, sticking up his nose, could scarcely keep himself upright on his thin little . . . legs]."[32]

XIII
56

in both forms, this tendency is guilty of an attack on the given actuality; its watchword is: Forget the actual (and this is already an attack), and insofar as the grandiose forms of government developed through the centuries do not let themselves be ignored, so must they, like the primeval forests of old, retreat before the plough of culture at the dawn of enlightenment, in order that on the cleared plains there cannot now be the slightest poetic shelter. But the few pure examples of normal people can, without being exposed to the least profane touch or falling for anything brindled, spotted, or striped,[33] sire, with an appalling monotony, a whole brood of select abstract *Cosmopolit-Gesichter* [cosmopolitan faces].[34] Like Hegel, it [the tendency] begins, not the system but existence, with nothing, and the negative element, through which and by virtue of which all the movements occur (Hegel's immanent negativity of the concept),[35] is distrust, which undeniably has such a negative force that it—and that is the good thing about it—must end by killing itself, something that surely will happen, for as soon as the *juste milieu* [happy medium],[36] the sole medium through which they cling to the state, gets it into its head for just a moment to say with the Molbo-man,[37] "Wait a bit, while I spit on me 'ands," they will tumble down, irretrievably lost.

After these more general observations, whose more intimate organic relationship to our project will, we hope, in the proper place become clear to readers, we shall try to orient ourselves a little in our novel and short-story literature, reminding readers that here, too, a similar attempt to begin from the beginning and from nothing has taken place, has actually been realized, for we do not know how to describe in any other way the cycle of short novels that began with *En Hverdags-Historie* [A Story of Everyday Life][38] (with nothing). This attempt, however, precisely by virtue of what was true in the trend, was in its negativity directed against an odious practice that had crept into this branch of literature, and, like all bad habits, had acquired a remarkably long tail, and, since every generation added its bit, had grown, like the well-known "Sip-Sip-Sipsippernip-Sipsippernip-Sippernip-Sipsip,"[39] and on its positive side unfolded such a great inner wealth and provided such a happy testimony to the poetic specific gravity of existence [*Tilværelse*] that it must inevitably encourage every subsequent novel or short-story writer to have such a beginning.

Drawing the readers' attention in as few words as possible to the cycle of short novels owed to the author of *En Hverdags-Historie*, we must remind readers that this is not done in order, after having paid the stories a certain amount of recognition-tribute, to raze this summit with modern philosophical bustling and transform it into a vanishing element in existence, beyond which various *homines novi* [new men][40] ("newborn earls, greenhorn journeymen"[41]) perhaps have already gone. Nor is it done in order to fix them in an absolute catholicity outside which there is no salvation;[42] it is done out of consideration for the life-view contained therein, which just as surely has had its corresponding element in existence [*Tilværelse*] for its presupposition as it has also an aroused element as its effect, a consideration that is by no means unimportant for our project and is carried through only to the extent that it has meaning for the same. However, we must in advance ask the honorable unknown author's pardon, that he—like those immortal classical writers, to whose interpretation, to the curse of these over the centuries, one generation after another has given its unfortunately often too large quota of insipid interpreters and thereby contributed to forming the disorderly mob that not infrequently has thrust itself between the authors and their most cherished readers—here again sees himself persecuted by a reviewer, who, however, just because he is conscious of this and in reliance only on the help of his good attendant spirit, will do his best *favere lingua* [to show favor to the language].[43]

The sublimate of joy in life, the battle-won confidence in the world, yielding a life dividend, a confidence that the spring of the poetry of life has not gone dry in the world even in poetry's most inferior forms, the confidence in people, that even in their most trivial manifestations there is to be found, if one will only seek properly, a fullness, a divine spark,

XIII
57

which, carefully tended, can make the whole of life glow—in short, the verified congruence of youth's demands and announcements with life's achievements, which here is not demonstrated *ex mathematica pura* [on the basis of pure mathematics] but is illustrated *de profundis* [out of the depths][44] by the entire inner boundlessness of a rich temperament and presented with youthful earnestness—all this gives these stories an evangelistic tinge that inevitably must assure them great importance (to everyone who has still not pledged himself to the devil in order to storm heaven or has not, in a thoroughly practical way, become deeply absorbed in his boots in order to find life's true reality there) and make their reading a truly upbuilding study.*[45] And even though we feel that the way leading to this joy undoubtedly goes over the Bridge of Sighs,[47] and even though one seems to hear a solitary sigh that has not yet found its complete cure, and even though in a single instance a certain well-being within the cozy walls of amiable domestic relationships therefore replaces the truly religious, a priori genius, the spirit going through these stories, in union with the objective attitude conditioned by artistic virtuosity, is nevertheless so gratifying, that even though their author, as he surveys the whole collection, is sometimes tempted to call it a "Benoni,"[48] the readers must necessarily call it a "Benjamin." Even though some of the younger ones dejectedly think that here, too, proof is given that it is only the Joshua of our life who enters the Promised Land and not its Moses,[49] and even though some youthful glance directs itself mournfully toward that mighty, long-since vanished past, and many a young person's ear listens for this

XIII
58

> Thundering** under horses' hoofs
> When the Danish knights ride in combat,[50]

---

* See *Ægtestand*, p. 198: "My dear young lady reader! You who perhaps have picked up this book to distract yourself from thoughts that you scarcely dare admit to yourself: to you especially this simple story is dedicated with an unknown friend's warm wishes for your victory!"[46]

** The modern substitute:

> Stamping on the floor with long legs
> Does not accomplish much.[51]

as if it could once again be experienced, as if, at the powerful urging of all youthful poetry's legitimate demands, it could not but rise up in its grave, like the fathers in its stories,[52] in order to hand its sons the sword with which it itself fought nisses and trolls—nevertheless this part of the younger generation will also join in when the author of these short novels rises up, like Palmer,* transfigured, and proposes a toast worth drinking: To genius, beauty, art, and the whole glorious world! To what we love and what we have loved! May it live a transfigured life here or hereafter as it lives in our recollection.

XIII
59

While these short novels must seek their truly sympathetic readers in the older generation, whose life-view is the premise for their coming into existence and is still unmistakably represented by a rather considerable number of significant, eminent individualities, their relation to the politicians** will not be worth talking about for the simple reason that it is still only to the one who has ears to hear[55] that the Gospel can be preached, and a resignation that is not a result of external pressure (and such flattened persons are not very rare phenomena) but a development of an internal elasticity, of the joy that has conquered the world,[56] seems all too intangible for political tangibilities—it will not be worth talking about, I say, except insofar as it provides a proof of the poetic specific gravity of these short novels, except insofar as it gives us occasion to rejoice that a vitality such as this has known how to survive in the "graduate-student prose"[57] of politics.

Yet among the younger generation that still stands making

---

* See *Extremerne*.[53]

** Although *Montanus den Yngre*[54] provides a remarkable proof of the earnestness and the love with which this author embraces every phenomenon in the actual world, and although the realistic-political development must to a great extent be obliged to him in that he has preferred to advance such a representative and, as it were, has not wished to heed all the invitations the development itself gave him to perceive its comic side, I nevertheless, despite all its [the story's] merits, cannot deny that it seems to me that in its structural finish it is inferior to the rest, since Montanus is more broken than transfigured through the development.

up its mind about the world, these short novels will also find attentive and grateful, albeit partially misunderstanding, readers, whether this misunderstanding arises because, in their youthful undulation (when they see how many sacrifices the minotaur of the labyrinth[58] of life demands), they will now admire, now almost despair of attaining, such a life-yield, or, although with a private admission that it is a proud dirge that this view of life is preparing for itself, they will still find that it does not quite go to the tune that they can in such moments clearly recollect was sung over their cradle. Or it [the misunderstanding] manifests itself in the fact that this generation, without as yet having developed the appropriate proficiency in life, now rather condenses a certain sum of propositions that are supposed to contain a guarantee of the requisite flexibility in life—in short, this generation comes to make what that author has by virtue of having lived through it its task and to dwell too much upon the consideration of it as such.

XIII
60

That these short novels have found attentive, yes, even talented readers in the younger generation, which as far as possible has avoided contact with the political, is amply and happily demonstrated by the so-called Bernhardian short novels.[59] That these latter, native to the younger generation since they totally lacked the viewpoint of the other novels, acquired a *moral* stamp instead of the *religious* character of the others, that instead of the serene levelheadedness of the others these at times developed a certain tendency to reminisce,* at least does not seem to disprove our assertion, and we shall therefore merely point out that the second kind of misunderstanding cannot so easily come to take shape in a similar manifestation, since, as an element in an assimilation process, it ought as much as possible to be kept free of self-reflection, and, as belonging to the most secret inner history of a youthful life, only under abnormal conditions can it manifest itself in other than more common lyrical outbursts.

We now turn from these short novels and their arena to that

---

* Were I to cite an example of this, I would mention *Børneballet*.[60]

voice* in the wilderness, Steen Steensen Blicher, who, however, and this is precisely what is remarkable, transformed it into a friendly place of refuge for the imagination exiled in life. Admittedly, here we do not encounter a world-view tried out in so very many lives, nor the life-gymnastic so characteristic of the aforementioned short novels, but a certain beginning from the beginning nevertheless takes place also here, undertaken, while the negative aspect is entirely latent, by virtue of a whole positivity that wakes up, so to speak, and makes itself heard and, youthfully fresh, renews and regenerates itself with autochthonic**[62] originality. Instead of the life-view contained in the short novels by the author of *En Hverdags-Historie*, which belongs to the individual who has finished the race and kept the faith,[63] there here appears a deep poetic mood, shrouded in the mist veil of spontaneity, the unity of an individual-popular poetic keynote, echoing in the soul's inner ear, and a popular-idyllic picture, spread out for the imagination, illuminated by mighty flashes of summer lightning. Instead of the masterly technique we must admire in those short novels, we are surprised here rather by solitary, dramatically charged speeches, which presuppose not so much the discernment of a Cuvier[64] in order to construct out of them a totality but rather nature's profundity as the reason for their genesis. In any case, there is also a unity here, which in its spontaneity significantly points to the future and which inevitably must grip the present age much more than it has done and thereby perhaps come to work beneficially on the prosaic manner in which politics have hitherto been handled.

Having in this way extended our telescope to the appropriate distances, we must ask the esteemed readers to let the eye follow as we point it in the direction of our actual object: the poet of a rather significant literary activity,[65] the not unfavorably known poet Mr. H. C. Andersen; we hope thereby to

---

*   Silent and dark-laden so is my heath,
     Though under heather top flowers will spring.
     Lark behind grave mound is building its nest
     And in the wilderness warbles away.[61]
** From the earth have you come!

secure ourselves against the illusory perception and the hallu-
cinations to which the naked eye is often exposed. Our telescope does not extend far enough to observe the few really
fine lyric productions of his early youth, but we hope that the
readers will concede to us the more general observation that
in his lyric poetry he is not characterized as a *Choragus* [choir
leader], authorized by a deep-feeling sensibility for a larger totality, or as a full-toned voice for a folk-consciousness, or, finally, as a personality sharply marked by nature who has no
other right to his peculiar outbursts and singular demands
upon the world than the *imprimatur* [let it be printed][66] of nature that history so often will not accept—but he is characterized rather as a possibility of a personality, wrapped up in such
a web of arbitrary moods and moving through an elegiac duo-
decimo-scale[67] of almost echoless, dying tones just as easily
roused as subdued, who, in order to become a personality,
needs a strong life-development.

As we now turn our attention to this story of Andersen's,
we find as good as no intimation whatever of the stage he
must normally run through after the lyric—the epic.[68] We
shall here refer only to the otherwise inexplicable lack—in the
course of such a frequent productivity as the Andersenian—of
any poetical works bearing the epic character in order to justify our assertion, which later considerations will substantiate
still more, that Andersen has skipped over* his epic [stage].
And although it might seem strange that such a skipping over
of the epic should happen precisely in our period, otherwise
so rich in epic material (a period in which, with a frugality that
calls to mind the economical union of poet and actor in one
person in the earliest development of the scenic art, each one
has his epic**[69] and his epic poet in himself), the phenomenon
is nevertheless undeniable and not uninteresting—yes, Ander-

---

* When I say "skipped over," it is here by way of an anticipation, since I
have not yet discussed his later activity and there would thus be a possibility
that he had not yet come to it.

** Therefore one does not so much speak in the situation where speech belongs as praise and discuss (*Dichtung und Wahrheit* [Poetry and Truth][70]) what
one has or would have said on a previous occasion.

sen's lyric self-absorption [*Selvfortabelse*] is both more interesting and more gratifying than the modern political-epic self-
admiration [*Selvforgabelse*].[71]

Without now embarking upon an extensive discussion of
the meaning of a proper epic development, we shall merely
remark that this must not be understood as a vociferous,
hoarse enthusiasm over some ephemeral culprit, or as a lan-
guishing staring at some chance individuality, or as a literary
paying of compliments, but as a deep and earnest embracing
of a given actuality, no matter how one loses oneself in it, as a
life-strengthening rest in it and admiration of it, without the
necessity of its ever coming to expression as such, but which
can never have anything but the highest importance for the
individual, even though it all went so unnoticed that the mood
itself seemed born in secrecy and buried in silence.

XIII
63

If we now take a closer look at how, for a temperament such
as the Andersenian, the transition from the lyric to the epic
would have to have been realized (here must be understood the
poetic mood that merits this name and is a necessary condition
for the following and corresponding epic action)—then we
can see that either this must have been done by Andersen's
having dedicated, with Pythagorean silence,[72] a period of his
life to a serious study, but already this would be rather unlike
him, or it could have been done if the age had, poetically pic-
turesque, gathered around a single hero, or if the age through
a colossal union of a large number of forces, each significant
in itself, amid the most motley profusion of these had pointed
absolutely undeviatingly to a single goal and had worked with
such energy toward it that such a striving must grip him for
some time and yield the life-supplement necessary for him.
Such a favor from the circumstances of time did not, however,
fall to Andersen's lot, because his life-development proper
falls in the so-called political period, and if we pay attention
for only a moment to what the politicians themselves say
about it, we will certainly be convinced as to how little this
period can fortify such a temperament. It is a period of fer-
mentation [*Gjærings-Periode*],[73] say the politicians; at any rate
it is not a period of action [*Gjernings-Periode*]. It is a period of

transition. —Quite right! At least, the formation of granite is already long past, the formation of sedimentary rock done with, and for a good while we have presumably been deeply absorbed in the formation of peat.* Or could the Annual General Meetings** of our time have caused such a transition in Andersen, these omnibuses of political life, these Brazilian ant-hills, which, according to a naturalist's account,[76] through a gathering of several millions present a striking resemblance to the ancient monuments put up over a man—a tumulus? Or how could he feel comfortable in the whole political school of gregarious*** whales that push and shove one another in order to spew out by turns a monologue? Or what, indeed, could there be for poetry to do in a time when the younger person who is striving after something higher must feel in a spiritual sense the same symptoms as the Frenchmen[78] on their march across the Russian steppes, where the eye vainly seeks a point on which it can rest, in a time when the older men, who still know what they want, with pain must see individuals trickle like dry sand through the fingers? What could poetry do in our time, when every day we encounter the most ridiculous combinations of individuals shaken together like bits of glass in a kaleidoscope, in our time, whose principle (*sit venia verbo* [pardon the expression]) is none other than Protestantism's profound and inward life-view now reduced *in absurdum* [to an absurd degree] *zum Gebrauch für Jedermann* [for use by everyone]. If we now let this development come in contact with Andersen as reading matter, it must (in its es-

XIII
64

XIII
63

---

* It is also rather noticeable that the newer development has distinguished itself in so many respects as the peat-formation period.[74]

** *Sed nimis arta premunt olidae convivia caprae* [But the reek of goats makes too crowded feasts unpleasant].[75]

*** "The pilot whale kept continually in a tight school, for it is, like certain kinds of birds, entirely gregarious. The school perpetually gamboled about, so that there were always several above water, first the head, then the tail, and thereupon immediately went under water again in order in turn to make room for others. As they came to the surface, they spouted great jets of water into the air, which some distance away could better be heard than seen, and were otherwise, as far as one could judge, fairly tranquil and submissive." See *Tidsskrift for Naturvidenskaberne*, edited by Ørsted, Hornemann, and Reinhardt, no. 11, p. 209.[77]

XIII
64

thetic abstract impotence, with its grandiose horizon, which, like that of the Jylland heath, is distinguished chiefly by the absence of a single twig to disturb the view) by its judgment—which is highly suited to the crystallization forms of these possibilities and "thoroughly parodies the creative 'Let there be' "[79] (this is an item from which something interesting could come; this would be splendid material, or infinitely *vice versa*[80])—of necessity affect our poet only rather discouragingly. If Andersen, therefore, early in life was wrapped up in himself, he also early in life felt thrown back on himself like a superfluous cornflower amid the useful grain.[81] And because he was thus continually thrust down in the funnel of his own personality, inasmuch as his original elegiac mood modified itself through such reflection to a certain gloom and bitterness against the world, his poetic powers, productive in their self-consuming activity, must manifest themselves as a low flame that again and again flares up rather than, as would be the case with a more significant personality, as an underground fire that by its eruptions terrifies the world.[82] A Heine[83] Andersen could never be; for that he lacks both his genius and his offense at Christianity. As for Andersen's relation to the philosophical development, this would either have to have directed him in its more significant form to a more serious study, or it could have taken him up into the endless succession of bricklayers' assistants who from Hegel onward throw philosophical bricks from hand to hand. On his retirement from this activity, it could have rewarded him with a hastily achieved result that for the sake of variety could become for a short time a rather piquant spice in the tedious enough social conversation. Whether to his loss or gain, he has not come in contact with this development at all.

As we now proceed further and trace Andersen in his relation to our recent short-novel literature, discussed above,[84] we shall provisionally make the general observation that the reason Andersen has not benefited as much from it as he could must be sought primarily in the fact that he has not entered into relation with it for the sake of his own individual life or out of any more general esthetic interest as a reader but for

reasons of prospective short-novel writing. As far as his relation to *En Hverdags-Historie* is concerned, we certainly may
justly reckon him among the misunderstanding readers mentioned earlier, who, also through these short novels among
other things, are brought to a certain degree of reflection,
which, however, is in no way carried through to any significant degree. And with regard to his relation to Blicher, we
may indeed with equal justification claim that the unreflective
folk poetry contained in Blicher's short novels, presumably
along with other things, has directed Andersen's attention to
folklore, except that this is not regained in poetic abundance
in Andersen. Instead, he has utilized it in a purely external
manner.* If we now add to this the temptation to produce
instead of developing himself, to hide an inner emptiness
under motley pictures, to let himself be absorbed in generation[85] without any reproduction, a temptation that reading
W. Scott[86] and such novelists necessarily must provide for
such a weakly developed temperament as Andersen's, then it
will certainly not surprise us that, instead of carrying through
his reflection, he on the contrary encloses himself in a very
small space of it. It will not surprise us that when we decline
Andersen in these different cases of life there appears a phenomenon that will supply a very good paradigm for a cycle of
phenomena.

As we now proceed to characterize Andersen more precisely as a novelist, we shall—encouraged by the surely undeniable fact that every observant reader of Andersen's short
novels will feel strangely disturbed by the double lighting
(*Zwielicht* [twilight]) that prevails in all Andersen's novels as it
does in the summer performances at our theater—make some
closer observations concerning how one must imagine these
novels to have come into being in a poetic sense. A host of
admittedly poetic wishes, longings, etc., after having been re-
pressed for a long time in Andersen's own interior by the pro-

---

* On the whole, it is sad to see the consumption, contingent upon spiritual
poverty, of poetry's assets (legends etc.), the perpetual repeating of these—
without any thought of intensely feeling the deeper poetry in them—so predominant in the newer literature.

saic world, seek namely to emigrate to that little world, accessible only to the poetic temperament, where the true poet amid life's adversities celebrates his Sabbath. But scarcely are these shipped to that world and incorporated there in new individuals before the nisse already loudly proclaims his arrival there, in other words, before the whole mob of depressing reflections about life—either in the form of a blind fate or in the form of the evil in the world (i.e. the actual world) that chokes the good—grow up, with a luxuriance like the thistles in the Gospel,[87] while Andersen sleeps. In vain Andersen works against them; yet sometimes he gives up these efforts, sometimes he turns to the opposite side, and, ruffled and discontented as he is with the actual world, in the faintheartedness of his own poetic creations he seeks a compensation, as it were, for his own faintheartedness. Therefore, like Lafontaine,[88] he sits and cries over his unfortunate heroes who must go under, and why?—because Andersen is the man he is. The same joyless battle Andersen himself fights in life now repeats itself in his poetry. But precisely because Andersen thus cannot separate the poetic from himself, because, so to speak, he cannot get rid of it, but as soon as a poetic mood has acquired freedom to act, this is immediately overwhelmed, with or without his will, by the prosaic—precisely therefore is it impossible to obtain a total impression from Andersen's short novels. Precisely therefore is it possible that readers are put into the most singular mood, very different from the one intended by Andersen, inasmuch as his fiction weighs one down like actuality because the whole collection of details, narrated as actuality, can surely have their interest, since one must presuppose the fundamental thought in the narrating individual's own consciousness going through all these, explaining everything, but this fundamental thought is first and foremost what the poet must make come alive. And his own actuality, his own person, volatilizes itself into fiction, so that sometimes one is actually tempted to believe that Andersen is a character who has run away from an as yet unfinished group composed by a poet. And certainly it is undeniable that Andersen could become a very poetic person in a poem, in which case all his

XIII
67

poetry would be understood in its fragmentary truth. Naturally the impression[89] repeats itself if one lets a reflection assist
as a perpetual *Memento* that it is the other way round, and with
an unshakable obstinacy, like that of Cartesian dolls,[90] it [the
impression] emerges victorious from every such battle with
reflection.

What we have developed here will afford the requisite inner
supplementary proof of the correctness of our statement, a
statement as much about Andersen's misrelation to an epic
development as about his indeclinability[91] in life. This indeclinability is conditioned by the misrelation, but seen from
another angle the indeclinability also demonstrates the misrelation in its shallowness. In the same way, when one reads
through one or several of Andersen's novels, what we have
developed here, kept *in mente* [in mind] as a provisional abstract result, will split up into such a quantity of isolated remarks with appurtenant *dicta probantia* [substantiating state-
ments] that we must resist as much as possible by not letting
these flutter round about as such, but, reminding ourselves of
the Latinists' significant *revocare ad leges artis* [conform to the
laws of art],[92] by letting them advance in closer formation so
that the reader, even when the isolated remarks are most dis-
persed, may still at times seem to hear the "call to assemble,"[93]
as it were, calling them back.

When we now say that Andersen totally lacks a life-view,
this statement is as much substantiated by the preceding as this
latter is substantiated by the statement itself verified in its
truth. For a life-view is more than a quintessence or a sum of
propositions maintained in its abstract neutrality;[94] it is more
than experience [*Erfaring*], which as such is always fragmentary. It is, namely, the transubstantiation of experience; it is an
unshakable certainty in oneself won from all experience [*Em-
pirie*], whether this has oriented itself only in all worldly relationships (a purely human standpoint, Stoicism, for example),
by which means it keeps itself from contact with a deeper experience—or whether in its heavenward direction (the religious) it has found therein the center as much for its heavenly
as its earthly existence, has won the true Christian conviction

"that neither death, nor life, nor angels, nor principalities, nor powers, nor the present, nor the future, nor height, nor depth, nor any other creation will be able to separate us from the love of God in Christ Jesus our Lord."[95] If we now look and see how things are with Andersen in this respect, we find the relationship to be just as we had expected. On the one hand, single propositions stick out like hieroglyphs* that at times are the object of a pious veneration. On the other, he dwells on the individual phenomena coming from his own experience, which at times are further elevated to propositions and are then to be subsumed under the previous class, and at times are brought out more as something experienced, without one's therefore being rightly able, as long as these remain in their bachelor state, to draw any further conclusions from them.

If one will now perhaps say that the life-view we have depicted is a standpoint one can approach only gradually and that it is unjust to make such great demands on so young a man as Andersen, then we shall, as far as the last point is concerned, although willingly admitting that Andersen is a young man, nevertheless remind readers that we are dealing with Andersen only as a novelist and, *anticipando* [anticipating],[96] add that such a life-view is, for a novelist of the class to which Andersen belongs, *conditio sine qua non* [a necessary condition]. With regard to the first point, we readily admit a certain approximation in the full sense of the word but also say stop in time, before we are saddled with the consequence, annulling our whole view, that the life-view proper commences first (*demum* [at last]) at the hour of one's death or perhaps even on one of the planets. If we now ask how such a life-view is brought about, then we answer that for the one who does not allow his life to fizzle out too much but seeks as far as possible to lead its single expressions back to himself again, there must necessarily come a moment in which a strange light spreads over life without one's therefore even remotely needing to

XIII
69

* This standpoint is very prevalent, and one can usually identify the species belonging to it by a tendency, even when the conversation is about the most insignificant subject, to begin with a "maxim."

XIII
68

have understood all possible particulars, to the progressive understanding of which, however, one now has the key. There
must come a moment, I say, when, as Daub observes, life is
understood backward through the idea.[97] If one has not yet
come this far, yes, even totally lacks understanding of what all
this means, then one comes to set oneself a life-task parodi-
cally, either by its already having been solved, if one can call it
that, though in another sense it has never been posed, or by its
never being able to be solved. In further corroboration of this,
we find both situations described in Andersen, since both
views are presented in borrowed maxims and also to a certain
extent are illustrated in individual poetic personalities. On the
one hand, it is taught that on every person there is written a
mene mene[98] etc. In analogy to this, individuals appear whose
actual task lies behind them, but this does not help them to
come into the right "backward" position for viewing life,
since this task is placed rather like a hump on their own
backs,* and therefore they never actually come to see it or
could never possibly become conscious of it in a spiritual
sense, unless for a change Andersen puts into them a consciousness that disturbs the whole conception—individuals
appear who, like other heavenly bodies, go their once-allotted
way with an undeviating precision. Or, on the other hand,
Andersen loses himself not so much in high-flown [*høitra-
vende*] as in long-winded [*langtravende*] observations, in which
the hero is a superb peripatetic[101] who, because he has no essential reason for stopping anywhere and because existence
[*Tilværelse*] on the contrary is always a circle, ends up going
in a circle, even though Andersen and others who have lived
for many years on the hill[102] believe he is walking straight
ahead because the earth is as flat as a pancake. In between, that
is to say in the unity of these standpoints, lies the happy medium, but from this it by no means follows that through a new
inconsistency, which, please note, does not annul the preced-

XIII
70

---

* For example, *O. T.*[99]
*Was ich nicht weisz, macht mich nicht heisz, so denkt der Ochse, wenn er vor dem
Kopf ein Brett hat* [What I do not know, I do not get heated about, thus thinks
the ox when it wears a blinder]. See Grabbe.[100]

ing (for that would be the most fortunate), new phenomena cannot appear, for example, that Andersen suddenly breaks off their undaunted wandering, sentences them to an arbitrary punishment, cuts off their noses and ears, and sends them to Siberia, and then our Lord, or whoever else wants to, must take care of them.—

But is it, then, absolutely necessary for a novelist to have such a life-view, or is there not a certain poetic mood that as such, in union with an animated portrayal, can achieve the same? Our reply to this lies for the most part in what we developed earlier with regard to Blicher, in which we have specifically sought to point out the significance of such a unity born of mood and, through a succession of modifications, understood by the readers as a whole picture. And furthermore, insofar as one wants to make a similar view valid for a countless number of given standpoints arrived at through reflection—and here one must remember that, where productivity is concerned, all these standpoints as such have a diminishing effect and increasingly allow the original mood to evaporate—we shall merely add that productivity is certainly possible from all these standpoints, but that when one is a little fastidious about one's designations, what is produced should be called studies for short novels etc. rather than short novels, since also at the level of studies productivity will be unsuccessful to the same extent as one really sets oneself the task of a short novel or novel.

Perhaps one wants to go further and—pleading that there is nevertheless one idea that continually appears in Andersen's novels (something I admit myself)—thereby salvage a life-view for Andersen and reproach me for my inconsistency. To this I must reply that I have never maintained that an idea as such (least of all a fixed idea) is to be regarded as a life-view, and furthermore, in order to embark upon this examination, I must have a little more detailed information about the content of this idea. If the idea is that life is not a process of development but a process of the downfall of the great and distinguished that would sprout up, then I think I can indeed justly protest against the application of the designation "life-

XIII
71

view"* to this, insofar as one will agree with me at all that skepticism as such is not a theory of knowledge or, to keep to my theme, that such a mistrust of life certainly contains a truth insofar as it leads to finding a trust (for example, when Solomon says that all is vanity[103]), but, on the other hand, at the same moment as it ends up as a final decision on life's questions it contains an untruth.

But to proceed. We shall for a moment assume that one could be right in calling such a view, arbitrarily brought to a standstill in reflection and now elevated to ultimate truth, a life-view. We shall imagine an individual who, greatly tossed about by an intensely agitated age, finally decides upon such a standpoint. We shall let him produce short novels. They will all receive a birthmark, but to the extent that he had experienced much, to the extent that he had really participated in life's vicissitudes, to the same extent he would also be able to develop in his short novels a great sequence of appalling consequences, all pointing to his hero's final downfall,** and to the same extent one would for a long time feel tempted to believe in the truth of his conception of life. But is this the case with Andersen? Surely no one will maintain this. On the contrary, Andersen skips over the actual development, sets an appropriate interval of time between, first shows as well as he can the great forces and natural capacities, and then shows their loss.*** Here, however, one will surely agree with us that it is no life-view. To clarify our opinion further, we shall merely add that such a loss-theory can emanate partly from a seriously undertaken but nevertheless abortive attempt to understand the world, in that the individual, depressed by the world, although long working against it, at last succumbs. Or

XIII
72

---

* In order to keep the question as clear as possible, I must remind readers that I do not seek to make one life-view valid, and Andersen another, but, uninterested in advancing any particular life-view, I seek only to combat this negative standpoint and its right to try to pass itself off as a life-view.

** How far this final downfall is poetically true, such an individual as a rule cannot judge, because he lacks the proper vantage point.[104]

*** One could almost be tempted to encourage him to demonstrate the identity of the character.

XIII
71

XIII
72

it can be brought about by this, that at the very first awakening of reflection one does not then look outward but instantaneously into oneself and in one's so-called contemplation of the world merely carries through accurately one's own suffering. The first is an abortive activity, the second an original passivity.* The first is a broken manliness, the second a consistent womanliness.

We return to our theme: to explain, through a brief suggestion of the necessity of a life-view for the novel and short-novel writer, how things stand with Andersen in this respect. A life-view is really providence in the novel; it is its deeper unity, which makes the novel have the center of gravity in itself. A life-view frees it from being arbitrary or purposeless, since the purpose is immanently present everywhere in the work of art. But when such a life-view is lacking, the novel either seeks to insinuate some theory (dogmatic, doctrinaire short novels) at the expense of poetry or it makes a finite and incidental contact with the author's flesh and blood. This latter, however, can take place through a great multiplicity of modifications, from an involuntary overflow of cleverness in the personality to the point where the author paints himself in, as landscape painters sometimes like to do; yes, they even forget that this could have significance only insofar as it is understood as situation, and therefore, totally forgetting the landscape, go on to paint themselves elaborately in their own vain Solomonic pomp and glory, which suits flowers[109] but not people. (When I contrast doctrinaire and subjective novels in this respect, I can very well see that it is indeed only through

XIII
73

---

* Andersen actually seems to regard such an original passivity as belonging to genius. See *Kun en Spillemand,* I, p. 161: "Genius is an egg that needs warmth for the fertilization of good fortune; otherwise[105] it becomes a wind-egg." I, p. 160: "He had intimations of the pearl in his soul, the glorious[106] pearl of art; he did not know that like the pearl in the sea it must await the diver who brings it up to the light or cling fast to mussels and oysters, the high fellowship of patrons, in order to come to view[107] in this way." This is a quite special kind of genius. Even in the classicism of the ancient world, they sprang in full armor from the head of Jupiter.[108] So genius needs warmth! Genius must use petticoat influence! Let us not be ungrateful to the geniuses we have, and let us not trouble the heads of the younger ones!

XIII
72

a subdivision that these become coordinated with each other, for the doctrinaire novels also stand in an incidental relation to the personality, because their authors, through an incidental resolution of will, rest satisfied with propositions that they have not yet sufficiently experienced.) Yet, although both classes of novels stand in a finite and wrong relation to the personality, I by no means think that the novel in a certain prosaic* sense should abstract from the personality or that one could from another standpoint justly exact as much from the novel as from rigorous speculation. Instead, the poet himself must first and foremost win a competent personality, and it is only this dead and transfigured personality that ought to and is able to produce, not the many-angled,[111] worldly, palpable one. How difficult it is to win oneself such a personality can also be seen from the fact that in many otherwise fine novels there is to be found a residue, as it were, of the author's finite character, which, like an impudent third person, like a badly brought-up child, often joins in the conversation at unseemly places. If we now apply this to Andersen, not so much arguing from as appealing to the rather prevalent judgment arising in conversation, "That is just like Andersen, he is always himself, etc.," we justly believe we might include him in the class of novelists who give an unpoetic surplus of their own merely phenomenological personality, without therefore wanting to attribute to him such a strong determination of will in this respect that it would prevent him from straying into the territory of doctrinaire short novels also, yet not as if he had some major theory he wanted to advance, but rather, as shown above, through a partiality for and an over-estimation of certain particular propositions, which, in so strict a celibacy as the author keeps them, have nothing much to say.

One will best convince oneself of how markedly Andersen's novels stand in a wrong relation to his person by reproducing the total impression his novels leave behind them. We

XIII
74

XIII
73

---

* As has happened with the word "impartiality," which in our lukewarm time more or less indicates what a man already long ago has expressed as his standpoint: to be neither partial nor impartial.[110]

by no means think that it is wrong that an individual succumbs in the novel, but then it must be a poetic truth, not, as
in some poets, a *pia fraus* [pious fraud][112] of upbringing or, as
in Andersen, his final will. We by no means require, in any
stricter understanding of the words, good sense and clarity
about life in every single one of his poetically created individuals. On the contrary, if the worst comes to the worst, we
shall grant him full authority to let them go out of their
minds, only it must not happen in such a way that a madness
in the third person is replaced by one in the first, that the author himself takes the mad person's role.[113] In a novel there
must be an immortal spirit that survives the whole. In Andersen, however, there is absolutely no grip on things: when the
hero dies, Andersen dies, too, and at most forces from the
reader a sigh over them both as the final impression.

Having thus referred several times here to Andersen's person and personality, I shall—in answer to an objection, although one possible only through misunderstanding and misinterpretation, as if by mentioning Andersen as a person I here
overstepped the limit of my esthetic jurisdiction and the competence admitted within this—I shall, without appealing to
the circumstance that I as good as do not know Andersen personally, merely state that the poetic production proper, especially in the domain of the short novel and novel, is nothing
but a copious second power, shaping itself in a freer world and
moving about in it, reproducing from what has already in various ways been poetically experienced to the first power.
Moreover, in Andersen's novels, on the one hand one misses
the consolidating total survey (a life-view), and on the other
one encounters again and again situations, comments, etc.
that are indeed undeniably poetic but in Andersen remain undigested and poetically (not commercially) unused, unappro-
priated, unfiltered. From this one could therefore justly draw
the conclusion that Andersen himself has not lived to the first*

XIII
75

* This note, for which I must here request some reader or other's attention,
is a genuine pleasure for me to compose because it contains the answer to a
question that only fairly attentive readers could ask. It could seem that when
I do not here use stronger expressions in mentioning Andersen's first power I

power with poetic clarity* since the poetic to the second power has not achieved greater consolidation in the whole and is not leached out enough in detail. One could draw this conclusion, I say, not that I therefore have drawn it or will draw it, but I shall merely point out to Andersen that if he should feel himself personally affected in any way (as a man resident in Copenhagen), the cause does not lie with me but with Andersen, whose novels stand in so physical a relation to him that their genesis is to be regarded more as an amputation than as a production** from himself. And it is well enough known that even if what is amputated is far away, one sometimes involuntarily feels a purely physical pain in it.

We shall now pursue the basic defect we have pointed out in Andersen through the consequences that present themselves when we do not so much look at the main structure of the novel, as we have principally done in the foregoing, but rather fix our eyes on the treatment of details, on the technique in the whole. We shall also endeavor to keep as much as possible to the middle way in the unity of the novel's consistency as such, which seeks its proof in details, and details that absorbed into the novel's consistency are thereby explained. Concerning the above we shall first observe that *Andersen understands things through their opposites or through something else.* As a

---

am then disagreeing with my earlier statement that Andersen himself could become a very poetic person if he were included in a poem. But to this I must reply that the reason I did not and could not possibly express myself in more detail concerning Andersen's first power was that I came to it from his second. On the other hand, as soon as I begin with Andersen as lyricist, I must nevertheless say that he could in many ways become a very good character in a novel, since the author would then behold with his eye the in many ways unconscious poetic power given Andersen in his somnambulist condition.

* Andersen's first power must rather be compared to the flowers with male and female on one stalk, which is most necessary as a transition stage, but not suitable for productions in the sphere of the novel and short novel, which demand a deeper unity and consequently also presuppose a marked cleavage.

** Just as there are people who like stone grow by external addition, so are there people who produce by an external fragmentation of the originally given, so that single thoughts are gradually lost just like teeth, leaving only a hole, and after a passage of time nothing else remains but a chewing on the stumps, a cud-chewing on the old, instead of a genuine poetic production that should make the poet inwardly freer, richer, more sure of himself.

greater manifestation of the same fault, we shall remind readers of the all-too-frequently occurring partiality of politicians
for guarantees, which, as replacement for an earlier supposed
exhaustion of the subject through one single staring glance
and for the in the long run rather boring apocalyptic reveries
flowing from this, is perhaps somewhat tempting. This partiality for guarantees, conditioned by the politicians' partici-
pation (without, however, finishing the race[114]) in a livelier
view entailed by a newer development, precisely in this partic-
ipation has its validity as relative truth, its total invalidity as
absolute truth. In seeing the subject, they actually understand
it only in its misuse, its opposite, and therefore demand a reassuring guarantee* and rest satisfied with it without having
carried through the dialectic implicit in this concept. This phenomenon will now appear everywhere, also in minor matters,
wherever either a train of thought or a life-development is not
completely carried through. Eternal youth—understood, not
as a foolish anxiety about development has imagined it, as the
age of youth bounded by childhood, manhood, and old age,
and fixed as such, but as that vigorous certainty in oneself that
is above all ages, thus also above youth as such—would be the
most desirable with regard to the intensity in writing the short
novel and novel. Likewise the standpoint corresponding to
this—and momentarily clear in truly great individualities, as
the rich present tense of childhood, youth, and manhood—is
the only one qualified to produce the writing in which a whole
development takes place. If we do not hold fast to this standpoint, then somehow one comes to make a particular age the
yardstick (which of course is wrong, since no age as such is

XIII
77

---

* *Omnia ad ostentationem, nihil ad conscientiam* [Everything is measured by
appearance, nothing by a good conscience].[115] This penchant for guarantees
in a similarly trivial sense appears also in the intellectual sphere, and everyone
who has merely a scrap of practical experience has certainly often encountered
individuals who justify their right to have arrived at the deepest results in
philosophy by the assurance that they have not been able to sleep for three
nights because of thinking over the matter, and this consideration is then the
introduction to a result that is not difficult to come by in some speculative
journal. The situation is this: like schoolboys they cheat their way to a result[116]
and then hide their theft by a guarantee like this.

XIII
76

the absolute, not even what one usually calls one's best years)
and is thus not able to give every age its due. Now, this is also
the case with Andersen.

We shall take a more specific example. If he is depicting
childhood, we do not encounter remarks that are as if taken
out of a completely childlike consciousness and worked out
according to the meridian of the zenith depicted by us. Instead, it often becomes either childishness, undigested reminiscences from a specific, concrete period of childhood, or,
what we particularly have in view here, one speaks as an adult
about the impression made by life and then adds at appropriate
intervals that one must remember childhood, the great creative power of childhood imagination;* in short, one furnishes
an external guarantee for the rightness of the understanding,
one puts a soprano clef before a tenor part.[118]

Or Andersen understands things through something else. With regard to this, we shall dedicate the following to the general
statement "that Andersen is always making comparisons." A
comparison has its significance, of course, only insofar as it
leads back to a deeper understanding of that for the sake of
which it appeared. Otherwise it ends with the overloading of
our memory and the leaving of a total deficit for perception.
Whether I say that a town[119] here, for example, is like a town
in Italy that I do not know or that a town in Italy is like a town
in Denmark, without describing them in more detail, I have
not thereby become the least bit wiser, except insofar as,
prompted by the author's naming them, I now find myself,

XIII
78

---

* See the first six chapters of *Kun en Spillemand*.[117] The question is, however, whether one should stop being a child in the sense that one is no longer
able to rejoice at little things because one has seen greater, which latter have
an unlimited relativity. I smile at the child because I have seen the Alps, but
should not Mohammed, then, when he had been in the seventh heaven, with
the same justice smile at a grown man who rejoices at the Alps? Does not this
view lead to pure materialism? It is another matter with the bourgeois mentality. The error is not that it rejoices like the child at little things but that
despite a contrast existing in its consciousness it clings to the little things and
claims that they are just as good as the great, clings to this proposition and
thereby forgets to enjoy the little things—and this latter feature is precisely
the error.

XIII
77

perhaps on the basis of my knowledge of them and with the help of my own poetic talent, in a position to take over the poet's role and poetically paint for myself a picture of their characteristics. I consider it useless to give an example of this. —Making comparisons is a convenience that has expressed itself earlier in literature, for example in the designation of contemporary poets and writers by names from classical antiquity, in the thought that these were thereby characterized in their distinctiveness. I shall, however, add that the reason for the comparisons is that Andersen, when he skipped over his epic stage, also skipped over the contemplation absolutely necessary for all description.

The occurrence of this mobility,[120] either perishing quickly in an equally wrong stagnation or expressing itself fictitiously in the direction of every real content, like merely marching on the spot, is so far from preventing relapses, however, that on the contrary it necessitates these with the usual deterioration belonging to relapses. In other words, this mobility is a fixed staring at a single object, as if all the world lay therein—a phenomenon that we would rather characterize as Andersen's *superstition as a surrogate for genuine poetry*. We shall not speak here of this superstition as it appears in the great situations in Andersen, since we have depicted it from another angle in the foregoing, inasmuch as by showing that Andersen lacked a life-view we actually had to seek the reason that his individuals come to nothing in the world in his lack of belief in the world. Yet this, seen from another angle, is precisely superstitious belief in the individuals, superstitious belief in his poetic heroes' genius and competence, although only, as we pointed out in the foregoing, insofar as it is manifest in the treatment, in the arrangement of details. This superstition is manifest in the weight he lays upon some depressing circumstance, a single little humiliation, even when the environment smiles upon one most, in the power he attributes to this [latter] to be able to crush even the true genius, which, to keep to *Kun en Spillemand*, Christian actually is.* This view implies a failure to

XIII
79

* I, p. 156.[121]

appreciate the power of genius and its relation to unfavorable circumstances (for genius is not a rush candle that goes out in a puff of air but a conflagration that the storm only incites[122]) and is due to Andersen's depicting not a genius in his struggle but rather a sniveler who is declared to be a genius, and the only thing he has in common with a genius is that he suffers a few trifling adversities to which, moreover, he succumbs. This superstition is manifest also in his ascribing to a single chance occurrence a meaning, pregnant with foreboding, for the whole of life. It is something that may well happen to this or that really gifted individual in his development as he, with a morbid irritability and without a survey of his course, is tempted to ascribe too much to chance occurrence. It is therefore something that can also have its significance in the poetic production and may well be true in the subjunctive but becomes untrue in the indicative, inasmuch as it then does not let itself be brought into harmony with the presentiment properly rectified poetically, which presentiment, precisely in the certainty of having the whole, can never become hypnotized by details.

Yet, before I pass on to the more specific discussion of *Kun en Spillemand*, I must ask my readers to give their attention to yet one more section, which I would like to head: "Andersen's Incidents." I do this not because the two preceding deviations observed from a more general esthetic standpoint are not bound to manifest themselves as incidents, but because these latter stand in such an essential relation to Andersen's entire stance that they can best be understood in this relation and thereby also provide the appropriate relativity, within which I can rightly describe as incidents the whole undergrowth of disturbing comments, which, for the tolerably attentive reader of Andersen's novels, makes the way in them impassable, I repeat, impassable, inasmuch as Andersen's novels, like other factory products, do not gain from microscopic observations but always lose. I am not hereby aiming at what could strictly be called episodes, for this point has been the subject of discussion by other people[123] and thus does not need to be considered further, and it has been touched upon in its place in the foregoing.[124] I am not hereby aiming at what one could include under the heading of episodes, a bringing in of some detail merely, it seems, to prolong time, since this no more enters into any kind of deeper organic relation to the principal character than it,* devoid of all elastic force, is able to appear before us in a flash, as it were, after a pressure on the hidden spring,[126] and for that reason merely has the disagreeable characteristic that one involuntarily comes to think of a secret record of around-the-clock observations.

I am aiming, rather, at the uncertainty, conditioned by the poet Andersen's misrelation to both his person and the fund of knowledge necessary for a novelist—at the conditioned shaking of the hand, which causes his pen not only to make blots but also to make gossip, and which characterizes his style to the extent that it thus becomes difficult to copy. And although, as I survey the mass presenting itself to me, I now feel in a singularly ironic manner at once so rich and so poor—so poor, I say, because I almost do not know where to begin or where to end—I do, however, catch a glimpse of a way out in the comment made earlier, that the whole has its origin in his misrelation to himself and to the necessary fund of knowledge. I shall follow this division and endeavor, when choosing, to take that which is fairly entertaining and, when substantiating my contention, to be as brief as possible. When I now describe the first misrelation as *incidental mood*, it will also be rather easy, according to our knowledge of Andersen's view, to find out how this incidental mood is constituted with regard to its content, since it must necessarily bear the stamp of Andersen's basic view: dissatisfaction with the world. Therefore, before I go on to baptize it with its correct name, I shall merely remind readers that the reason I call it incidental is by no means that it is essentially different from his other view but that I am dealing here particularly with the manifestations of it that intervene disturbingly in the presentation of

XIII
81

---

* (I wish to point out once and for all that I am taking my examples from *Kun en Spillemand*, since I have it at hand.) See I, pp. 146, 141.[125] One would think that the spiritual dress of the individuals in question was ordered from some poetical clothes-mender.

XIII
80

detail, which manifestations might well therefore have been avoided, however much one shared Andersen's dissatisfaction. Yes, probably Andersen himself would acknowledge them to be incidental.

In order to describe his dissatisfaction with the world in these, its incidental manifestations, I do not know of any other expression than *livid indignation*. The really talented novelist is able by one single oblique remark in the course of the narrative to remind the reader, as it were, so strongly of some character in the novel that he now suddenly appears once again as large as life before him and perhaps more clearly than at any time before—in short, from a single rib he is able to create the whole individual for us.[127] Andersen is far from doing this. Even when he himself introduces another person speaking where it is essential to keep oneself in the character of this other, he cannot guard himself against suddenly undercoating the particular utterance with his livid indignation against the world and giving it a tinge of his dissatisfaction with the world that is totally irrelevant to the poetic character. This kind of incidental mood, however, is more closely connected with the rest of his view than the one we shall now go on to describe, one, it seems to me, that is so curious that I only wish I might succeed in describing it in its entirety so that it could lie ready from my pen for acceptance by some museum of psychological curios. That is, it happens not once but many times that Andersen in the course of the narrative loses [*tabe*] his poetic balance and thereby drops [*tabe*] his poetic characters out of his poetic creator hand so that these even set themselves in opposition to him in a real existence just as valid as his own. As a result, a singular relationship now appears. With these individuals, who thus in every such moment cease to be merely poetic characters, Andersen now makes contact as he does with other beings on this, our earth. That is, on the one hand he conceives an entirely worldly love for some individual, who of course in most cases is his hero but whom he now treats more as a client he is interested in and at every opportunity seeks to push forward in the world. Likewise also, each

lack,* as it seems to Andersen, of dutiful attentiveness, even
in the case where attentiveness is so far from being dutiful that
it would even be unreasonable, does not go unpunished, because of the absolute power entrusted to Andersen as poet (to
do what he likes). —On the other hand, he becomes extremely incensed** with other characters appearing in his novels, and he is so outspoken against them that one would believe it was important to him to destroy their civic welfare in

* See *Kun en Spillemand*, I, p. 150, where Christian comes to the dance hall
for the first time; it says, "With hat in hand he bowed politely in all directions.
No one noticed it." It is not so strange, though (when a ship's boy joins sailors
at a dance hall, he perhaps rather runs the risk of being thrown out, and thus
far little Christian can be glad that he was not noticed); it is far more strange
that the reader's attention is drawn to it, and drawn to it not even through
Christian's own words—there would be some sense in that, for after all he is
a vain creature—but it is Andersen himself who makes the observation and
presumably wished that the people at the dance hall had spotted the great
genius at once (I, p. 156). He visits Steffen-Karreet,[128] and as he is going away
"a couple of other young women came in from the adjoining room; they were
scantily clad, as was she, and they heard the story and laughed, and looked at
the boy with foolish eyes." I shall say nothing of my fear that when the whole
story is over we shall all come to look at Christian with just as foolish eyes, if
by "foolish eyes" one understands eyes that cannot see that Christian was a
great genius. I would merely ask: Who makes this comment? It cannot possibly be Christian, because I do not think Christian was such a naughty boy
that, in a house where he had enjoyed attention (see I, p. 151), where also
Steffen-Karreet had laughed at him and made amends, where at most he could
be angry because they laughed, he would arrive at the thought that they
looked at him with "foolish eyes." It is again Andersen who has become angry. I am well aware how unconvincing any such isolated passage is, and I
must therefore on the whole think of readers who are very well versed in
Andersen.

** As is the case with poor Niels,[129] with whom Andersen several times
seems to become very irate, and I actually expected that one day, right in the
midst of his wrath, he would have exclaimed, just like many a worried pater-
familias, "That Niels is a blasted nuisance, he's always on one's hands, he
never lets Christian alone." Also, the manner in which he deals with His Rev-
erence Pastor Patermann[130] is, to put it mildly, very unseemly. And Naomi,
too, in compensation for the fact that Christian in the story, in accordance
with Andersen's idea, must go under in contrast to the so fortunate girl, is
not spared in particular outbursts and utterances against her,[131] when he seems
to become impatient, as it were, about the inconceivable good fortune that
has fallen to her lot.

the world where Andersen himself belongs but where they have absolutely no business to be.

Before I go on to describe the second misrelation, which I shall designate *incidental knowledge*, I wish to draw attention to a phase of incidents to be found that perhaps could appropriately form the transition from the foregoing. It is: *incidental association of ideas,** since these can be understood both from the angle of personality, seen as one who has no power over his thoughts, and from the angle of the object of thought, seen as that which governs the character in a rebellious manner.

We can now go on from this to discuss his incidental knowledge. That is, the mass of information that Andersen has gradually acquired has little by little conspired against him and started a revolution, with the result that, instead of deciding from his poet stall what shall or shall not be included, Andersen has been obliged to grant this mass of information a consultative vote.[138] The mass of information has, of course, simply looked upon this as the initiative for constituting itself as the sovereign power and making Andersen its proxy, who, obeying orders, puts its particular elements into print.

As everyone knows, Andersen usually divides his novels into chapters, and each chapter usually has an epigraph. Even if one does not share my view that an epigraph by its musical power, which to a certain extent it can well have without being verse, either ought to play a prelude, as it were, and thereby put the readers into a definite mood, into the rhythm in which the section is written (insofar as the epigraph is a verse, this is the thing about it that reminds one of vaudeville),

XIII
84

---

* For example, II, p. 113: "Her (Naomi's) delicate fingers turned the pages of a book . . ... Was it Balle's catechism[132] or the hymnbook, the new improved edition,[133] from which prosaic hands have plucked the scented leaves of poetry?" This last observation is completely irrelevant to the situation and arises because Andersen, in mentioning the hymnal, thereby comes to think of the variety of questions[134] that have arisen in this country on account of it. See III, p. 16. "But for Naomi it sounded like a sigh and mockery; it was the cold breeze from the damp prisons of Spiegelberg;[135] it was the oppressive heat from the lead chambers of Venice."[136] Here the association of ideas does not arise from the situation but is motivated by the circumstance that on the previous page Andersen has mentioned Silvio Pellico, *le mie Prigioni*[137] etc.

XIII
83

or it ought to relate piquantly to the whole section and not form a pun on one particular expression occurring once in the chapter or be an insipid general statement about the contents of the chapter. Even if one does not share my view, one will, however, surely grant me that it requires a good deal of taste, a high degree of inwardness in one's subject and in the temperature of the mood, to choose an epigraph that becomes a little more than an exclamation mark saying nothing or a figure like those the physicians usually write above their prescriptions.[139]

Now, Andersen does not possess these qualities. Through his long busying himself with poetry-making there is naturally at his disposal a large quantity of *loci communes* [commonplace remarks], of little verses etc., which, guided by a totally loose and exterior association of ideas, he now applies as best he can, and the only law I have been able to detect is this, to pay due regard to poets of second, third, and so on rank. After the epigraph the narrative begins, but Andersen as a writer has taken up the good old habit, now gradually gone out of use at the oral lecture, of beginning each section by clearing one's throat. That is, the chapter or section usually begins with some clever phrase.* The reason for this, however, is certainly not that Andersen thinks that these phrases really have much to say, but through long association with itself, such a phrase has, unperceived, developed such a great love of itself that it is continually seeking to fulfill its destiny, to be applied, and the reason it is not used even more often lies not in Andersen's mastery over it but in the circumstance that there is a variety of phrases that are the very spit and image of it. Yet this concerns more the incidental cleverness, which, however, like all secondary cleverness, is a matter of knowledge.

---

* I, p. 118: "The donkey often treads on the best flower, man on his brother's heart." II, p. 150: "The year 1820 held a great many events for Denmark. The national debt sprang a leak. Dr. Dampe,[140] with some hotheads, wanted to cause a leak in the ship of state. Conflicts of opinion developed in the religious sphere, and each party discovered a leak in its opponent. Among so many and such great leaks, we do not dare to speak of the ones that Ladislaus made in many a female heart" etc.

Finally, we shall merely draw the reader's attention to Andersen's incidental thoroughness.* The isolated historical, ge-
ographical, and statistical data, the isolated fragments of ex-
haustive knowledge, when they are not kept in check and
brought up in the fear of the Lord,[144] naturally begin to think
so highly of themselves that they no longer will let themselves
be used but want to be a *Selbstzweck* [goal in itself], and for
that reason, without regard to whether they apply in the context or not, they act with claim to absolute validity as truths
one can never say too often and therefore can never say in the
wrong place.

As an extension of what has been developed, we can now
add a special discussion of *Kun en Spillemand*, which will of
course essentially keep within the territory demarcated by the
foregoing and within the question about the poetically true,
limited not by an arbitrary papal demarcation line[145] but by the
indeed invisible, yet therefore all the more real, one given in
the concept. And it is only for the sake of appearances that we

---

* See I, p. 114. "Down there swam the pictures of the clouds, down there
flew the bird with outstretched wings, just as deep as it hovered above the
surface of the water." It is Christian, who is watching geese and sitting and
fantasizing, and in the middle of the boy's fantasy there now comes the clause:
just as deep etc. With this can be compared his entire investigation of Naomi's
attitude to religion. II, p. 119. "There began in her the Straussian evaporation
that dissolves everything historical into myths. There developed in her a view
on religious matters similar to the one that in our time is beginning to express
itself in certain individuals in Germany, a kind of freethinking . . . . ." II, p.
129. "Where religion was concerned, her view was neither ascetic nor
Hellenistic;[141] she was more a partisan for the Young Germany[142] flying ahead
of it." This whole investigation reminds one of a court case in which the question was raised as to how things stood with the defendant regarding religion,
on which occasion some village priests who had been sent for emptied out
with great thoroughness everything they had learned at school about:

> Deism, Theism
> Atheism, Pantheism.—

See III, p. 86, about the attitude to religion in France: "Paris at the moment
has no religion; they have forgotten the Madonna, indeed, almost forgotten
the Father and the Son; the Spirit alone is ruling. You see no monk in the
street, no procession. The poets preach Protestantism from the stage itself"(?). —See the whole of Naomi's journey[143] etc.

would construct a little outwork in order to keep an eye on a detachment of enemies, who are not actually enemies, however, since they agree with us in absolutely nothing, but who must rather be considered as some chatterers who, belonging nowhere, probably will not refrain from pointing out that what I say may indeed be true but that it by no means follows from this that the Andersenian position is untrue. These chatterers will probably repeat the same assertion even more loudly when the question is about the relation between the poetically true and the historically true and place Andersen in the dilemma of either having to insist that it is a historically actual event he is relating, whereby the whole standpoint becomes displaced, or having to try to vindicate the significance of his story as poetic truth in the face of the view that it is poetically untrue.

XIII
86

Here, then, the question is chiefly one of whether the principal character is actually represented as a genius by the author, and next, whether sufficient factors are then procured to bring about his ruination. And even if the latter point were cleared up, the question again arises as to whether the individual concerned actually was a genius. One certainly cannot deny that the idea that genius must win is an inheritance, as it were, from a previous better existence [*Tilværelse*], an idea that, when the human race is despoiled of it, must necessarily plunge mankind down into despondency. Now, when the actual principal character appears before us in all his development, it would be desirable if somewhere there could be found a point of rest, a resting place, where we could collect ourselves and look back. But in this respect his path of development is by no means perspective. On the one hand, Andersen himself at times stops at some insignificant event, as if we were now at a turning point (a circumstance by which we must not let ourselves be led astray); on the other, the path is full of will-o'-the-wisps, which sometimes induce one to believe that now the genius is awake, now he is matured, and which at other times are superseded by events that seem to witness to the contrary, until we again hear assurances that now the genius is matured etc. Yet, since there is a point

where Andersen with particular emphasis presents Christian's
life-dilemma, we shall stop at this in order to see, as we survey
the foregoing, if it can be justifiably presented or whether Andersen will fool us, or himself and us. This place is found in
Part I, page[s] 60[-62][146] and can be regarded as containing
rather briefly Andersen's entire passivity theory, his entire
view of a genius etc., and for this reason we reprint it here.

"It is popularly believed that barberry pollen is a poison to
grain, that the heavy head is spotted with the devouring rust.
The noblest, the most dazzlingly white poppy changes color
after a year when it stands among the colored ones. Environment is the name of the invisible hand that transforms the
basic element in its development.

XIII
87

"While the sculptor molds the soft clay, we do not grasp at
once what work will be created. It takes time and labor before
the plaster cast appears, and after this by a chisel blow the mar-
ble comes to life! How much more difficult, then, to conclude
from the person as child his development and fate as man. We
see here the poor boy in Svendborg; the instinct in him and
the influence from outside point like the needle of a magnet in
only two directions, totally opposite to each other. He must
become either an exceptional artist or a wretched, confused
being. The pollen from the environment already influences
him with its perfume and color.

"The god of music kissed him already in the cradle, but I
wonder whether the song of the fates will bring ecstasy or
madness? The boundary between them is only a thin wall.
Will he perhaps arouse the admiration of thousands, or perhaps in the wretched inn, with violin under his arm, as an old
man play for unruly, rough youths, be mocked as a half-wit
with his dreams, he whose soul invisibly received the baptism
of music?

"It is known that the Duke of Reichstadt was stillborn. In
vain every means was tried to bring him to life. Then the
hundred cannon shots thundered—he opened his eyes, the
pulse beat. He was the son of the great emperor; therefore the
world came to hear about it. Yet, no one knows a similar story
about the child of poverty. He also was a corpse, a newborn

corpse, already laid aside on the table by the shattered win-
dowpane. Then flutes and violins sounded outside where
wandering musicians played. A woman's voice was heard,
mournfully strong, and the little one opened his eyes, moved
his little hand. Was it the music that drove the soul back so
that it might be active here on earth, or only chance, the Solomonic sword[147] of the man of reason?

"He must become an exceptional artist or a poor wretch, a
sparrow with gold leaf on his wings, whom the other spar-
rows therefore peck until he bleeds. And what if he became
that? What consolation is there for him? What consolation is
there for a mankind with pride in its heart? Mankind is oblit-
erated and forgotten like the snowflakes that fall in the rapid[148]
current; only one individual's work and name go down to
new centuries. Enviable fate! But coming joys may await us
in our new existence [*Tilværelse*], where the happiness belonging to his fame is then far away in a world in which he
cannot appear, cannot take part. What does it matter how high
we stand if only we are standing well! That is the world's
incantation;[149] it is the booming self-consolation of the great
human wave as it surges along toward the coast of eternity.

"One can see from the knots on the trunk of a fir how many
years the tree has grown. A human life also has its visible
joints. This summer formed an important point of transition,
a kind of major factor in Christian's childhood, through the
acquaintanceship with Naomi, the instruction in music, and
the visit to Thorseng."*

We shall now for a moment make a survey of the foregoing.
Born in straitened circumstances of poor parents, Christian
had in his father the sort of man who is often found among
the common people—a man with some natural poetry who
had, however, found only moderate satisfaction through once
making a journey to foreign lands and had obtained for himself a bit of solace through the recollection of it, until this

XIII
88

---

* I must apologize to Andersen for almost making myself guilty of plagia-
rism by having such a large section reprinted, and I can say in my defense only
that what I have plagiarized is not what I consider to be the best.

overwhelmed him and again carried him off on his travels—a man, according to Andersen's description, with such deep, inexplicable, poetic longings that in order to portray him he needs must revive the Venusberg legend.[150] —In his godfather, Christian had such a unique musical genius that in order to describe him Andersen must resort to reminding the reader about Paganini, about "Ole Bull, Amphion of the North," about "these two masters in the art of Jubal,"[151] a genius who was certainly not in possession of "this perfection that these two masters of our time in the art of Jubal possess" but perhaps therefore in an even deeper sense was capable of inspiring and vitalizing what was slumbering in Christian—in short, his childhood is under conditions capable of stimulating him for the whole of his life.

If we now look at the closer contact he made with the musical in his childhood, we see this described by the relating of how the godfather's music made a deep impression on the boy—an impression it must of necessity make on almost every boy (since the music was as excellent as Andersen describes it), especially when his music had the unquestionably piquant, mysterious sounding board of sins hidden from the world,[152] regarding which childish innocence has just as much instinctive tact as horror. So far, nothing has occurred that discloses even a moderate aptitude for music. In the company of his godfather, however, he makes a little journey on which, in a singular manner to be sure, he is brought into a peculiar misrelation to the musical through getting himself positioned in a bell tower in the niche by the sound hole.[153] Yet this event, which someone or other might perhaps think contained a very significant hint for his whole future, Andersen construes with regard to the injurious effect it had upon his health, and here we are now at one of the main wheels: "the disastrous convulsions,"[154] to which, however, is also ascribed the merit of "making his ear more open to the language of music."[155] If we now add, *anticipando* [anticipating], the actual main feature of Christian's character, an indescribable vanity, then surely everyone will grant me that disastrous convulsions and what I would call a just-as-disastrous vanity are still not enough to

constitute the dilemma that he must become either a great artist or a poor wretch, or enough to set in motion such far-
fetched and high-flown observations as those found in Part I,
p. 20, on the occasion of the count's remark that the genius
must make his own way, as he gives him a rix-dollar[156] to encourage him: "It was the Icarus wings he bound on the genius's shoulders, daringly fashioned wings, but of lead. The
words, of course, were an old theme that from generation to
generation has sounded in the ear of the artist and will, with
variations, for thousands of years sound again and again, as
long as the world is the same as when it gave Socrates poison
and Christ a crown of thorns." Andersen should, however,
have added a *sans comparaison* [no comparison intended here]
in order to avoid being blasphemous. He was bound to become a "poor wretch" because he was one. The expression
itself seems to us very descriptive, since by "wretch" we think
chiefly of "the disastrous convulsions," and by "poor" chiefly
of his indescribable vanity. One of the things that usually
characterize the genius and give him his ascendancy over the
world is pride, which usually becomes stronger in adversity
and is therefore also often able to hold the individual's head
erect. With Christian, however, all is vanity.[157] What matters
to him is drawing attention to himself, being admired; yes, if
he can enjoy it for but a moment, he is content even with applause that he at heart nevertheless knows conceals mockery.[158] His vanity shows itself also in his relations with Luzie
and Naomi. With the first, that retiring, modest girl, he takes
delight[159] in letting all his vanity express itself in grandilo-
quent day-dreams, empties himself in admiration of himself
like Joseph[160] in his beautiful relationship with his brothers.
Toward Naomi, that proud but undeniably poetic girl, who is
the real object of his love, with whom he more often comes in
contact, he behaves so apprehensively (so vainly in the opposite direction), not because she is intellectually superior to
him, no, but because she is the aristocratic lady, surrounded
by liveried servants. He trembles like an aspen leaf whenever
he approaches her. And, finally, when we see him at the significant moment—when Naomi has done everything in order

XIII
90

to move him to a decisive step, when the whole of life's land-scape is burned down behind him, from the Jew's house to his stepfather's, when Naomi herself comes out disguised on horseback to say farewell to him—when we then[161] see him as a "poor wretch"[162] stay at home, we are certainly surprised that there has at any time been talk of anything else.

Yet the poet has reserved another chapter of his life for the third volume, and the few pages[163] dealing with this are also almost the only ones in the whole volume that actually have to do with the novel. The rest, containing almost nothing but bits and pieces of Andersen's reminiscences smuggled into Naomi's diary, could best be published separately, and if Mr. Andersen agrees, we could give the little book the epigraph (Andersen, *Kun en Spillemand*, Part I, p. 70): "At each re-minder of an older time, the tailor always came to think of what he had seen[164] like it, and he then made compari-sons. . . . . . What his heart thought, his mouth must gossip about, whether or not it amused the others." Twelve years[165] after we last heard anything about Christian, the author now has him appear before us as a poor fiddler who on Sundays eats with Luzie and her husband, the local schoolmaster, and who still thinks of Naomi and puts aside money to help her one day if her flight with Ladislaus should have plunged her into misfortune. In short, we find a person who seeks to con-sole himself as well as he can for the disappointment of mis-placed expectations. But it is quite certain that there is abso-lutely nothing in him to suggest an erstwhile genius. One does not even learn anything about his playing. As for his whole host of episodes, it is quite certain that not one of them, nor the whole lot together, would have been able to crush even a moderate genius. We learn that he belongs to the pietists.[166] To make him one of these is not difficult; for this Andersen needs only paper and pen, and it has, of course, become al-most a *Sprichwort* [saying] to become "religious" when one cannot make good in the world. From illustrating how he could become that and the most probable symptom of it, An-dersen has exempted himself. On the whole, he is better suited to rushing off in a coach and seeing Europe than to

looking into the history of hearts.[167] If we now add to this that
Andersen has the father suffer more or less the same fate as the
son, inasmuch as he makes him enter a monastery—(thus
modifying an old dodge—when one cannot get rid of someone in a suitable manner, one puts him in a monastery[168]—in
a rather singular fashion), although not in order to find consolation there for disappointed hopes, rest for his soul, as the
profundity of the Middle Ages imagined it (and it is as sure as
I write this that it is the Venusberg legend,[169] which always
has the monastery in the background, that has led Andersen
astray) but for fear otherwise of starving to death (III, p. 65),
a new and very poetic motive for becoming a Catholic. —If
we add to this that the godfather hangs himself,[170] then we can
with fair justice say that the whole family comes to an unnat-
ural end. On the other hand, the author of these lines is fortunate enough, so he thinks, to be able to finish his discussion
of *Kun en Spillemand* in a natural manner, insofar as the discussion should take place, and insofar as it could take place,
from the standpoint presented in the foregoing.

With regard to what I have to say in conclusion—prompted
by the misrelation, certainly on the whole conceded to be factual, between a reading and a criticizing world's judgment of
Andersen, insofar as this misrelation has also repeated itself in
my consciousness—I could wish that I might succeed in
speaking about this just as personally as I have tried to keep
the foregoing free of any oblique relation to my personality.
That is, as I reproduce the first stage [reading the book], the
recollection of a variety of poetical moods is brought to life,
moods with which every poetic life, even the most obscure
(and this, in a certain sense, perhaps most of all), must be in-
terwoven. And as I once again seek to retain every single one,
the one displaces the other so rapidly that the totality of them
assembles as if for departure in one single concentration, assembles in a present that nevertheless at the same moment
feels in itself the necessity of becoming a past and thereby
evokes from me a certain nostalgic smile as I consider them, a
feeling of thankfulness as I recollect the man to whom I owe
it all, a feeling that I would prefer to whisper in Andersen's

XIII
92

ear rather than confide to paper. Not that at any moment it has been anything but a joy for me to be able to give him what is his due and what, especially in our time, anyone who still has a little feeling for poetry in the *ecclesia pressa*[171] in which we live must almost be tempted to give more warmly than the truth perhaps could demand. Nor that such an utterance could not be brought into harmony with my whole earlier expressed view of Andersen, because in spite of all his tossing about, all his bending before every poetic breeze, it still always gives me joy that as yet he has not come under the all-embracing devil-may-care trade wind of politics. —I wished to say this to Andersen rather than write it because such an utterance is on the whole very exposed to misunderstanding, something, however, I hope that I shall be able to put up with if only Andersen, in order to avoid it, will hold what I have written with sympathetic ink[172] up to that light which alone makes the writing readable and the meaning clear.

III

---

*The Battle between the Old
and the New Soap-Cellars*

A heroic-patriotic-cosmopolitan-philanthropic-
fatalistic drama

in several episodes

This piece begins very merrily, progresses very dismally, yet
ends very joyfully.

With a frontispiece showing Luther sitting in a hazel tree
cutting switches for people who ask useless questions. Some
of them are to be seen lying on the ground; others will be
found scattered around in the book. The inexperienced will
perhaps mistake them for dashes.[1]

Dedicated to the four mad brothers in Claudius. The verse
is to be printed here.[2]

A concluding vignette should show Zacchaeus in the sycamore tree.[3]

Since the chosen title of the piece seems to imply a misplaced coquetry, it will be called:

The All-embracing Debate on Everything
against Everything

or

The Crazier the Better.[4]

From the Papers of One Still Living[5]
against his will published
by
S. Kierkegaard

Dedicated to the seven madmen of Europe, whom no city has
wanted to acknowledge.[6]

Characters:

Willibald,[7] a young man.

Echo,[8] his friend.

Mr. von Jumping-Jack,[9] a philosopher.

Mr. (Holla) Hurrison,[10] a provisional genius.

Mr. Phrase,[11] an adventurer, member of several learned societies and contributor to numerous journals. } maintained at public expense in the prytaneum.[12]

Mr. Ole Wadt,[13] acting military adviser, formerly writing-master.

A Fly,[14] who has wisely wintered for many years with the late Hegel and who has been so fortunate as to have sat on his immortal nose several times during the composition of his work: *Phänomenologie des Geistes*.[15]

II
B 1
286
A Ditto, nephew of the above-mentioned, a Hegelian.

A Horn, organ of public opinion, sometimes used for drinking patriotically, sometimes for blowing patriotically, on which everyone blows a piece when he gets the chance.

A Ventriloquist

A Pedestrian

A Fighter for Orthography[16]

Polytechnic Students

Wholesalers

II
B 7
287
Sallust. *Jugurtha*, Chapter IV: Profecto existimabunt me magis merito quam ignavia judicium animi mutavisse majusque commodum ex otio meo quam ex aliorum negotiis reipublicae venturum [They will surely be convinced that it is rather from justifiable motives than from indolence that I have changed my opinion, and that greater profit will accrue to our country from my inactivity than from others' activity].—[17]

However, in order that this piece will be useful for something, there follows a short compendium of conversation topics arranged *belieblich* [at pleasure] *zum Gebrauche für Jedermann* [for use by everyone], and a list of the abusive words one can use without becoming liable under the Freedom of the Press Ordinance of 1799.[18]

Postscript. Since I see, however, that a writer of verbiage at the office of *Kjøbenhavnsposten*[19] always steals a march on me, I must admit with pain that my book is entirely useless, indeed, not even suitable for hammering a nail in a wall. So I am compelled to omit this part in order to avoid being useless.

ACT I

After a brief monologue, Willibald is seen resolving to go to a tea party, where he meets Echo, who charms the entire company with his brilliance, his wit, and his ideas borrowed from Willibald. Willibald wants to leave, but his hostess detains him. Finally he escapes, hurries home to his room.[20]

In margin of Pap. II B 8:

One could also have Willibald sing: Rarely money, but many blows, etc.,[21] and have Echo sing: Oh, how bad, Oh, how sad, must one really not go mad?[22] (This latter aria resembles the former in music and idea as much as a milliner's despair by Auber can be compared to Leporello's by Mozart.)

Continuation of Pap. II B 8:

Scene

Willibald.

(Is sitting on the sofa in his study, pipe in mouth, surrounded by a large number of open books and pieces of paper on which he has noted various things.)
He is reading *Peter Schlemihl*.[23]

    What a strange work this *Schlemihl* is . . . . . or is it a work . . . . . is it not myself . . . . . yes, truly, I am one of Chamisso's fantasies . . . . . a shadow myself who therefore cannot cast any shadow . . . . . I collapse like Aurora's husband[24] and can soon entertain the hope of adorning a naturalist's study like a freak of nature under a glass bell . . . . . Oh, then one day I shall break the glass during an

II
B 8
287

II
B 8
288

II
B 9
288

II
B 10
288

II
B 10
289

erudite and very learned professor's lectures, and the hyper-
bola of my life will surpass all his decimal and algebraic cal-
culations . . . . . then my last fire-breathing gigantic sigh
will at least strike so much terror into the bourgeois that I
shall be freed from all condolences[25] . . . . . (puffing out a
cloud of tobacco smoke) and these fog masses—so that is
the kingdom where I belong. Oh, look how they condense
and seem to become figures . . . . . Well, now, if I am going
to be a shadow myself, I will at least compose a new one, I
will create one . . . . . (with great feeling) Let there be a
person . . . . . (at that very moment the cloud assumes the
form of Echo) What do I see? Is it not my tormentor—my
other self [26] . . . . . but am I then I . . . . . no matter (he
grasps his sword), come forth you most conscientious
bookkeeper of all my words . . . . . face me, and the whole
flock of parrots with you—would that all your heads sat on
one neck[27] (he slashes, but nothing is there) . . . . . nothing
is there . . . . . what if I tried the same experiment on myself
. . . . . (points the sword at himself but just then happens to
cough violently) is it possible that I have in my throat a bit of
the quill pen I was playing with earlier . . . . . I can already
feel it going down into my windpipe (coughs, takes the
light and looks in the mirror) . . . . . I am unusually pale
(coughs) (someone outside is heard clearing his throat; there
is a knock at the door) . . . . . it is my friend; when I cough,
he clears his throat . . . . . I am ready to bet that he, too,
has swallowed a quill pen . . . . . *herein* [come in]!
Echo enters with a respectful compliment.

W. *Wo komst du her geritten* [Whence have you ridden]?[28] (embraces him in a very friendly manner).

E. To continue as you have begun: *Wir satteln nur um Mitter-
nacht* [We don't saddle up before midnight].

W. Bravo . . . . . but then I'm sorry to say your time is now
up; the clock is just on the stroke of one.

E. Oh! in such excellent company . . . . . (he becomes aware
of the sword that Willibald is still holding in his hand) What
do I see, why the weapon?

II
B 10
290

W. At the request of a compassionate devil,[29] I was just killing a grasshopper[30] so that it could at least fall at the hand of its only friend (lays down the sword).

E. I don't understand you.

W. Well said.

E. Explain yourself; you are in an excited state . . . . . why did you leave the party so early . . . . . everyone rushed up to me and asked me the reason; what could I answer?

W. I don't know . . . . . whatever they liked.

E. Oh, unburden your heart to me . . . . . to me, with whom you went to school, me, who have been initiated into so many of your plans.

W. (interrupting him) Yes, you, you who have also been caned together with me by the headmaster . . . . . you, my best, my only friend.

E. (continuing) me, to whom you are united by so deep a sympathy.[31] I feel the same way as you do . . . . . You are bored by parties, so am I.

W. Oh, no, I think they are amusing.

E. Of course, many of them . . . . . You seek solitude.

W. You do, too.

E. Oh, how sad it is to be misunderstood, not to dare to open one's whole heart, yes, misunderstanding, yes, misunderstanding.

W. (with an ironic smile) Yes, but there are cases in which the person concerned can be well served by it.

E. I do not deny *that* . . . . . up to a point.

In margin of Pap. II B 10:

W. All novels lie.

E. I, too, have noticed that. For example, the other day I read a novel that began with the words: "The yellow tiled place on the corner of Kronprindsensgade and Store Kjøbmager-gade[32] has surely often caught the attention of the passers-by." Strange, I thought, that you have never noticed it. At once I hurried down there in order to make myself even more familiar with the novel through the contemplation of it and if possible, by peeping in at the window, to come to

II
B 11
290

II
B 11
291

know the family described. But, despite every effort, it was impossible to find such a place.

W. Strange, but have you also noticed to what year the novel belongs, or at least in which year the novel takes place; perhaps the place has been repainted.

E. Could it be possible? Yes, I will indeed make proper inquiries.

W. But just suppose that it had never been yellow; in that case it is indeed strange that you, who write novels yourself, have not noticed that device and have not used it yourself.

E. Of course I have used it, but it would never occur to me that others used the same one.

W. So the next time you make use of such a device, you will have to bring into the novel the reflection that you know very well there are some authors who use this device in order to deceive the reader, but that what you say is so true that they are welcome to apply to the rent office and inquire whether such a house is not to be found at the place described.

Continuation of Pap. II B 10*:*

II
B 12
291

nonnulla desunt [something lacking][33]

W. Right now I am standing and investigating the condition of my lungs and heart. My breathing is wheezy; I can feel exactly how a bit of quill pen I have swallowed is slowly going down in order to do away with me.

E. You should eat a piece of bread or drink something. The other day I, too, had a crumb go down the wrong way.

W. I am spitting blood[34]—run for a physician.
                    (E. rushes off as fast as possible)

W. God be with you—(as Echo closes the door) the devil be with you. Finally I got rid of him. Oh, why have I become a social animal,[35] a human being, why not an owl or a bittern, then I would be free from the worst torment—from friends.

II
B 12
292

He runs out of the house bareheaded, faster and faster, and nothing is heard except, far away, the faint music of a drum, cymbals, and an out-of-tune clarinet that is rendering the well-known theme from *Muurmesteren*, "No, never give up, never give up; friends are always close to us";[36] whereupon Willibald becomes even more despairing and rushes off in a rage.

Echo returns with the physician.

Continuation of Pap. II B 12:

His surprise at not finding Willibald is soon replaced by a somewhat solemn mood evoked by contemplation of the room now abandoned by its animating principle.

II
B 13
292

E. I see a great deal of him, an extremely odd person, an eccentric character full of the most curious ideas, which flutter about, since like the goddess he writes on leaves that he lets the wind blow away. I once took the liberty of speaking this way in a short story, of which a reviewer has been kind enough to say that in my old age I would certainly marvel that I could have had such great genius in my youth.

P. Oh, if you have not entirely lost your memory by then, it probably could indeed give you the appropriate information.

E. He is a man I keep my eye on just as the police do with suspicious persons, as I have expressed it in a short story, and in my double-entry bookkeeping of ideas he is given a book to himself. If I would not injure myself, particularly my royalties, as much as I could benefit the general public, I would publish a separate work on the organization of such bookkeeping. I shall, however, tell *you* about it.

P. Remember, though, that it is of course the first step.

E. Don't be afraid at all; I am convinced that your practice will prevent you from making use of it. By the way, it cost me a lot of time before I found the correct way both of calculating the sequence in this literary crop rotation[37] and of chemically analyzing the marl[38] I use and its relation to the nature of my own crop.

II
B 13
293

P. However much I would like to hear about it, you will nevertheless see an adequate reason in the same reason that conditioned your kindness in telling me this . . . . . per-

haps a later, more favorable moment will again bring us together, and then perhaps you will have the goodness . . . . .
unless in this concession of time you should see a reason for
silence. So, goodbye.

E. Who knows whether it was not a happy dispensation of
providence that stopped me when I was just about to betray
my secret for the first time, although I shall not, however,
deny that I do wish that someone would speak to people
about the great secret in my possession.

We return, however, to Willibald. Despairing, as we saw
him at the friendly last farewell song, he rushed further on in
the hope of avoiding friends for once. This, however, was to
happen to him only all too soon. In his confusion, he ran into
a man who, as he now discovered, was walking along deep in
a conversation with two others. After having made his apol-
ogies, he received the reply that he need not make any apology, for the man well knew he was a great sinner, and it would
only please him if he might meet with the good fortune of
suffering something for the sake of Christ.[39]

In margin of Pap. II B 13:

II
B 14
293
N.B. In this book only the train of thought will be indicated
for what follows; the rest will have to be gradually worked
out on pieces of paper.

In margin of Pap. II B 13:

Great contest between three revivalists [*opvakte*] as to who
is the greatest sinner.[40]

II
B 15
294

Continuation of Pap. II B 13:

II
B 16
294
Willibald has scarcely taken leave of them before he hurries
on in the greatest haste, lacking a destination, reciting aloud
to himself: Before, my honor was like a mirror-bright shield
of polished steel, ... now there is a stain of bloody rust

on it[41] . . . . . This talking aloud is enough to attract the attention of a police agent sent out to arrest some revivalists,[42] and this talk of "bloody rust" is more than sufficient to make him highly suspect. In the meantime Willibald has gone out of sight, and since, despite their most zealous efforts, the police have failed to arrest him, the readers will perceive the necessity that he is no longer to be found on earth.

ACT II

A fantastic region. The prytaneum—in which the previously mentioned persons are maintained at public expense. Everything is arranged triangularly. Three Card[43] is being played etc.

Scene 1

Ole Wadt   Holla Hurrison

O. Wadt. As I say, I by no means disapprove of your general direction; on the contrary, I am very willing to acknowledge your immortal services in the affairs of the fatherland, but regarding style, regarding expression, there is always something that jars—your pen is not soft enough, if I may say so.

H. So you think it is because I use steel pens?[44]

W. Quite right! You have made a much profounder observation there than perhaps you yourself thought. There is nothing that spoils hand and heart as much as steel pens. What would a love letter be like if it were to be written with steel?

II
B 16
295

H. It has certainly a profound practical meaning, a symbolic significance, that steel has been transferred in this way from lances and spears to pens.

W. I already feel, I'm sorry to say, that time's sword has passed through my heart, that the present has lost the soft, flexible, elastic loveliness in which the past rejoiced.

H. Am I now to be plagued with the old story about the past? It was an idyllic state of innocence, but now we are men.

Now we must with earnestness intervene in things, arm
ourselves with steel gauntlets.

W. You mean with steel pens.

H. Oh, go to hell with your goose quills; you have no high-
minded feelings; there is as much soul in you as in a goose
quill. (goes away in a rage)

Scene 2

The same   Phrase   von Jumping-Jack

(Mr. von Jumping-Jack is a little unimpressive man, whose
one leg is a good six inches shorter than the other, and, in
order to illustrate his philosophical ideas, after first having
raised himself on the longer leg,[45] he used to desert this illusory standpoint, as he usually expressed it, to win the deeper
reality.)

Phrase stops Hurrison.

P. Let me halt your winged and urgent step, Mr. Hurrison. A
matter of great importance has filled my soul for a long
time, a matter in the execution of which I hope I may count
on your favorable assistance. We should by no means strive
to isolate the great stock of knowledge each of us possesses,
but, working hand-in-hand, we should realize great aims.
But not only that, we should also strive to make the great
results of scholarship accessible to the people; our time's development ought to gain in extensity what it loses in intensity.[46]

II
B 16
296

v. *J*. Yes, that's all very fine with the popular, but my doubt
is by no means popular; it is not a doubt about this, that, or
the other, about this thing or that thing; no, it is an infinite
doubt.[47] Yes, sometimes I have been troubled by a truly
scholarly doubt as to whether I have indeed doubted
enough, for doubt is the specific character of modern philosophy,[48] which, said *in parenthesi*, began with Descartes,
who said *de omnibus disputandum est* [everything must be dis-
puted],[49] by which he totally destroyed the proposition that
was formerly valid as an axiom: *de gustibus non est disputan-*

dum [there is no disputing about tastes].[50] You must see that such great scholarly problems could not possibly be imparted to the ordinary man in the street.

P. Neither is it my opinion that one should actually write for peasants; no, one should write for the educated middle class, for wholesalers, polytechnic students, for capitalists, and if one modified the style a little more . . . . .

Wadt. Excuse me, that is just what I have expounded for Mr. Hurrison; yes, the style, the style of writing, that is what counts. Remove some of the sharpness, the angularity,[51] the excessive spikiness, from the many-sidedness of modern philosophy, round off the forms a little more, and there will be no doubt that it will succeed, that we shall write the new development from that date.

Hurrison. Philosophy, fiddlesticks! It is not philosophy that counts. It is the practical questions, questions of life—in short, life.

v. J. Yes, what is life?

P. Life is a going out from itself returning to itself.[52]

v. J. Etc. etc. It was only to show Mr. Hurrison that it is exceedingly difficult to become popular that I made this objection. Also at stake here is the newer philosophy's profound requirement δός μοι ποῦ στῶ [give me a place on which to stand].[53] But where shall I find a foothold in the vulgar sphere of reasoning? δός μοι που στῶ.

H. Yes, you must certainly always find it difficult to find a foothold, and that is the case with almost all philosophers who are as poor on foot as you are, Mr. Jumping-Jack.

v. J. That's a low attack.

Wadt. Yes, he lacks form. The offensive shows up so very strongly in his every utterance.

II
B 16
297

In margin of Pap. II B 16:

When von Jumping-Jack was really expounding his skepticism, he used to lay his finger significantly on his nose in order, as Hurrison observed, to have at least one fixed point amid the infinite doubt.—

II
B 17
297

Continuation of Pap. II B 16:

II
B 18
297

nonnulla desunt [something lacking]

Scene 3

Willibald.

(Somewhat confused in appearance, he looks around him surprised, becomes aware of the inscription "prytaneum," in joy
casts himself on the ground and kisses it. He cries out joyfully
at being freed from the whole of that life in which he hitherto
toiled like a slave and at finding himself transported to a region
where wisdom must necessarily dwell. Catching sight of
Jumping-Jack, he goes with deep respect to meet him.)

Willibald (approaching Jumping-Jack). Without actually
knowing where I have arrived, it is nevertheless always a
comfort to me that we,[54] that I, have left the home of all my
afflictions. The external environment, the total impression,
has awakened in me a joyful notion, a happy presentiment,
that wisdom must be found here, that here I can be healed
of all the abominable relativity under which I hitherto have
suffered.

v. J. My dear fellow! I fully perceive what ails you. It is the
Faustian problem;[55] it is what modern philosophy, which,
said *in parenthesi*, began with Descartes, has suffered from
to a great extent. (During these lines, the other members of
the prytaneum appear on stage talking) (Jumping-Jack ad-
dressing the other members) . . . . . since I am just in the
process of giving a short account of modern philosophy
since Descartes, I can perhaps oblige the rest of those present by speaking about it publicly so all can hear.

II
B 18
298

Phrase. Is this the same exposition of which I have already appropriated a great deal? Oh, then you would do me, at least,
a great service in enabling me by such repetition to survey
the historical incarnations of the great ideas from speculation's Mount of Ascension.

v. J. Oh, what joy to have such a disciple, what indefatigabil-
ity—yes, even though you will not have such a wide influ-

ence as your master, you will nevertheless soon be able to hold a docent's post in the northern lands with honor and dispel the Hyperborean[56] gloom.

Gentlemen:

Thus it was from Descartes—who was persecuted in life (whether he really was persecuted I don't know, but, as it is several centuries since he lived, he has reverted to mythology, and seen in its light he must of necessity have been persecuted), forgotten after his death, but is now immortalized forever—that the whole of modern philosophy dates. I am well aware that unfortunately there have crept into our society some ignorant men who, mundanely occupied with the most inferior interests, assume that the world began last year and do not, gentlemen, celebrate with us intuition's Great Day of Prayer[57] now world-historically begun, on which day, man, that is, the philosopher, after having returned from the state of immediate paradisiac innocence to the immediate through life's dialectic, precisely for this reason should not work but should relive in intuitive enjoyment the world-drama already experienced. I am sure, however, that nothing will disturb me in my contemplative tranquillity. I see the opposite view as a vanishing element, if for no other reason than that otherwise, of course, mine would not be the fixed one. It was Descartes, then, who uttered the remarkable, eternally unforgettable words *cogito ergo sum* [I think therefore I am] and *de omnibus disputandum est*[58]—words that in every well-ordered speculative state really ought to be learned in confirmation instruction, words of which no theological graduate, at least, ought to be ignorant, since no speculative spiritual adviser can hope to carry out his difficult call successfully without them. Yes, what a great thought—someday it will go so far that one will regard these words, I repeat them, *cogito ergo sum* and *de omnibus disputandum est*, as the state's scholarly order of the day, as a palladium[59] that will eliminate all heresy, as words that, like the word "Adam," will remind us of the creation of our intellectual life.

II
B 18
299

Continuation of Pap. II B 18:

II
B 19
299

nonnulla desunt [something lacking]

The President. Since holding such long monologues violates
our rules as well as the dramatic decorum we have hitherto
observed in our society, I must, by virtue of my office, interrupt you.

v. J. I would be sorry if I should in any way have been so
transported by my eloquence as to transgress the accepted
conventions of our society. And if this is actually the case,
then the reason must be found solely in the freer discourse
in which I have indulged with regard to our catechumen,
whom I wished to initiate into the correct standpoint also
concerning the nature of our society. With the greatest tranquillity, I venture to call several of the gentlemen present to
witness that the short discourse I otherwise usually hold on
modern philosophy since Descartes, or more correctly, on
modern philosophy, would in no way be too long even in
the best constructed drama. Indeed, Mr. President, I will
wager that it does not last more than one-and-a-half min-
utes, because I have prepared it precisely with regard to our
society's requirements.

President. I am obliged once again to call you to order and call
for silence.

v. J. It was Descartes who said *cogito ergo sum* and *de omnibus
dubitandum* [everything must be doubted].

President. *Silentium* [Silence].

v. J. Spinoza now carried through this standpoint purely objectively, so that all existence [*Tilværelse*] became undula-
tions of the absolute.

II
B 19
300

President. Beadles, step forward!

v. J. This objectivity, however, was entirely distilled out in the
critical development, and whereas Kant carried through this
skepticism only to a certain extent, it was reserved for
Fichte to look this Medusa[60] in the face in the night of criticism and abstraction.

President. Arrest him and take him away.

v. J. Since I see that force will be used, I cannot do the piece on Schleiermacher, but it was Hegel who speculatively drew together the previous systems, and therefore with him knowledge has reached its proper dogmatic peak.

(The beadles make as if to seize him.)

Now I have finished, and with Hegel world history is over; you can just as well take me away, for now there is nothing but mythology left,[61] and I shall myself become a mythological figure.

Phrase. This is a totally one-sided standpoint (clears his throat). Gentlemen, I have gone beyond Hegel; where to, I cannot yet say very precisely, but I have gone beyond him.

v. J. What do I hear—serpent! Judas! Release me; or must then the eternal idea always succumb to the mass?

President. Take him away to prison.

(They lead him away.)

Phrase. I repeat, gentlemen, I have gone beyond Hegel. It was, namely, modern philosophy, which began with Descartes, that said: *cogito ergo sum* and *de omnibus dubitandum est.*

The President. (interrupting him) Since Mr. von Jumping-Jack has been the occasion of some unpleasant scenes and thereby caused some tension, I am compelled to adjourn the meeting. Everyone leave. —What pains me most, however, is that we could not at once secure an opportunity to hear Mr. von Jumping-Jack's opinion about a very difficult question that has arisen in our society. It will, however, be taken up tomorrow at the general meeting, *cui vos ut frequentes adsitis etiam atque etiam rogamus* [to which we most emphatically ask you to come in full strength].

Missa est ecclesia [The meeting is over].—

Meanwhile, no one in the prytaneum knew at all what to do with Willibald, who had not found himself much edified or satisfied by von Jumping-Jack's philosophical lectures. It was finally decided to refer him to the academic institute founded by the prytaneum—the *World-Historical College*. This, however, was not yet completed, and only the atrium could be used, but this was so large that four professors lectured there simultaneously without disturbing one another.

Indeed, it was so large that the audience could not even hear what the lecturers were expounding, although these were incessantly wiping the sweat from brows softened by their efforts. Two of these four professors were saying the same thing verbatim, and when finished they turned round with an air as if no one in the world could say anything like it.

Here Willibald, through personal contact, was gradually won over to the views current and recognized in the prytaneum, and so he had already regretted an idea that in his indignation against von Jumping-Jack he had sent to the President, a question, namely, why it was that the sun in the prytaneum never changed its position at all, as a result of which the light was always the same, a question that now disturbed the prytaneum very much and was the occasion for the general meeting about to be held.

General Meeting

President   v. J.   Phrase   Ole Wadt   Holla Hurrison
          Polytechnic Students   Philologists etc.

The President presents the matter, which had already become known, and hopes therefore that the debate could be more balanced.

Holla Hurrison. I request permission to speak. The phenomenon to whose explanation attention will now be directed is of great importance, although for anyone who with watchful eye has followed the gigantic steps of the modern period to emancipate the sciences and scholarship and macadamize[62] them, it is easy to explain that it is the light of morning—it is the solemn break of day; it is the sun's struggle with the final efforts of darkness; it is, as a poet has said, the prytaneum's May and the prytaneum's morning.[63] Not until these efforts of darkness are defeated shall we have our eyes opened to the results of the great birth-pangs of our time. Then we shall herald a golden year,[64] the true New Year time, when all the old leaven[65] and all the old pedantry, all Jesuitism and popery, will be swept away.

In margin of Pap. II B 19:

(This speech should naturally be worked out in far greater detail, but I will now merely give a suggestion of it.)

II
B 20
302

Continuation of Pap. II B 19:

v. J. I by no means fail to appreciate the honorable speaker's efforts to make the outlook for the future as bright as possible, but I must say that he has a tendency to hurry forward far too much, to go *gerade aus* [straight ahead] far too much. I, on the contrary, feel within me the dialectical pulse; I move in the true speculative zigzag. Just as we see that the common fish, the common bird, the common animal, in their mode of travel always move in a simple straight line following the nose, whereas the noble bird of prey, the dignified predator fish, the proud beast of prey, are seen to seize their quarry with a leap, so it goes with the genuine speculative movement when we carry through the profound meaning of this genuine speculative metaphor. Therefore, in the conception of world conditions there can be no question of an outlook, least of all not *gerade aus,* as in Mr. Hurrison's enchanting "out-views." Instead, what remains for the speculative observation might be called "insights," just as a snake that bites its own tail (that inexhaustible metaphor for speculation) certainly cannot be said to look out, but to look in, so that finally it looks into its own eyes from behind, looks, so to speak, out of and into its own eyes and from its own eyes at the same time.

II
B 21
302

Hurrison. I have listened to Mr. von Jumping-Jack's prolixities long enough. They are indeed nothing but Hegel's famous *perpetuum-mobile* thinking. But we who are working for life, we who have graduated from the school for life,[66] truly cannot be content with driving round and round the horse[67] without going any further on life's way, and we cannot let ourselves be fobbed off with Mr. von Jumping-Jack's inexhaustible, or, as it seems, indestructible, snake metaphors, and with all the ideas that can arise only in the brain of a

II
B 21
303

man born, as Mr. von Jumping-Jack probably was, under the sign of Capricorn.[68] Indeed, we are surely right to leap over all his leaps.

v. J. Without letting myself be disturbed by Mr. Hurrison's misunderstanding, which deprives me of part of my joy at seeing that he nevertheless has grasped one idea properly, the transition-category by which one goes beyond one's predecessor, I shall go on to solve the problem before us. The phenomenon can be explained as the light of evening. In other words, philosophy is the evening of life, and with Hegel, who speculatively drew together the previous rational systems, this evening has world-historically begun.[69]

Phrase. I have gone beyond Hegel.

Hurrison. I demand that there be a vote.

President. Is it to be by ballot or by show of hands?

v. J. I demand to speak. It seems to me unreasonable to want to decide such a question by voting, and it is my humble opinion that the finitude of discussion achieved by voting is actually no finitude but rather the spurious infinity.[70]

(Several speaking at once)

A. It is a matter of the utmost importance.

B. It is a question of life.

C. It is a question of principle.

D. It is a principle of life.

A Polytechnic Student. The state is a galvanic apparatus.

v. J. The state is an organism.

Phrase. Mr. President, I call upon you to declare whether I am the one speaking; otherwise I demand to be given the floor.

Hurrison. I demand that there be a vote on whether there is to be a vote. I am fighting for freedom. We will no longer let ourselves be oppressed by these tyrannical philosophers.

Ole Wadt. Friends, how sad it would be if such a question were to destroy the harmony of our ancient society.

President. The difficulty is whether our rules permit voting in such a case.

A Philologist. I request that a committee of people expert in the study of the past be appointed in order to find out through sound criticism the meaning of the rules.

President. The honorable speaker's proposal seems to be su-perfluous, because the rules are only one year old.[71]

During this noisy discussion, Willibald appears. In the pry-taneum's World-Historical College, he has in the meantime been won over to the Society's ideas. He assures them that it was not at all the case that the sun did not move, but that the sun, the physical sun, that is, actually changed its position, but that by it all he had only wanted to suggest the poetic, philo-sophical, cosmopolitan eternity that in a spiritual sense had already entered the prytaneum.

This soothes feelings, and the meeting is adjourned.

ACT III

Willibald.

(He is walking in a fantastic region near the prytaneum.) (With rising pathos) You infinite one, you . . . . . what shall I call you, how shall I name you, you infinite denom-inator of all human numerators, you absolute spirit who are no longer a secret to me but whose hidden depths I can now plumb. Yes, it is good to be here; wisdom's native land is here; here is where I found my immortal teacher von Jump-ing-Jack. Yes, now the light has dawned on me about everything. (As he is saying this, a fly buzzes past him recit-ing some Hegelian propositions, and the horn can be heard sounding out some political axioms.) And this too, only this, was lacking—assuredly world history is now over, for now nature itself can grasp the concept.[72]

Ole Wadt appears.

O. W. My dear young friend, you ought to do everything to bring about unity in the society, for the latest incident has left behind some tension that makes me very anxious.

W. I will hasten to do so. I will do everything, everything that lies in my power.

          (They go off stage arm-in-arm.)

Willibald, von Jumping-Jack, Holla Hurrison, Ole Wadt, Phrase, etc.

II
B 21
305

W. Although I believe that the real point of contention has been removed by my withdrawal of my petition, I do think that we ought to intimate in some way or other that peace is restored. I think that we should begin a new era and, also to that end, give our Society a new name under which it will nevertheless remain the same. I therefore propose that for the future we call it the New-and-the-Old-Prytaneum, written, please note, with hyphens.

Hurrison. For my part, I am not at all interested in such logical decisions. Only insofar as one thereby intimates a new development do I approve of it.

v. J. The proposal itself seems to me to be highly speculative. One might well believe that by effacing the old inscription "prytaneum," and thereupon inscribing "prytaneum" again, one achieved the same thing, but it would, however, be only to return to the immediate, where the dialectical oppositions had not yet developed themselves and speculatively penetrated one another. But this is incorrect. Besides this, the entire incident sheds a remarkable light on a myth that is surely known to everyone present, namely, the battle between the old and the new soap-cellars,[73] and hence the speculative significance of myth is also absolutely evident, that it contains an anticipation of history, a preliminary run, so to speak, to becoming history.

O. Wadt. However much I approve of what Mr. von Jumping-Jack has said, I really think that we also ought to preserve the memory of this unforgettable day in a more concrete fashion by erecting a memorial, a monument. That rewards, both money prizes and official praise, are very beneficial, I have experienced in my time as writing master at Efterslægten.[74]

II
B 22
306

Thereupon a monument is erected, on which occasion several enthusiastic toasts are proposed, especially by Willibald.

The End

SUPPLEMENT

KEY TO REFERENCES

Marginal references alongside the text are to volume and page [I 100] in *Søren Kierkegaards samlede Værker*, I–XIV, edited by A. B. Drachmann, J. L. Heiberg, and H. O. Lange (1 ed., Copenhagen: Gyldendal, 1901-06). The same marginal references are used in Sören Kierkegaard, *Gesammelte Werke, Abt.* 1-36 (Düsseldorf: Diederichs Verlag, 1952-69).

References to Kierkegaard's works in English are to this edition, *Kierkegaard's Writings* [*KW*], I–XXVI (Princeton: Princeton University Press, 1978–). Specific references to the *Writings* are given by English title and the standard Danish pagination referred to above [*Either/Or*, I, p. 120, *KW* III (*SV* I 100)].

References to the *Papirer* [*Pap.* I A 100; note the differentiating letter A, B, or C, used only in references to the *Papirer*] are to *Søren Kierkegaards Papirer*, I–XI³, edited by P. A. Heiberg, V. Kuhr, and E. Torsting (1 ed., Copenhagen: Gyldendal, 1909-48), and 2 ed., photo-offset with two supplemental volumes, I–XIII, edited by Niels Thulstrup (Copenhagen: Gyldendal, 1968-70), and with index, XIV–XVI (1975-78), edited by N. J. Cappelørn. References to the *Papirer* in English [*JP* II 1500] are to the volume and serial entry number in *Søren Kierkegaard's Journals and Papers*, I–VII, edited and translated (and amended in the Supplement) by Howard V. Hong and Edna H. Hong, assisted by Gregor Malantschuk (Bloomington: Indiana University Press, 1967-78).

References to correspondence are to the serial numbers in *Breve og Aktstykker vedrørende Søren Kierkegaard*, I–II, edited by Niels Thulstrup (Copenhagen: Munksgaard, 1953-54), and to the corresponding serial numbers in *Kierkegaard: Letters and Documents*, translated by Henrik Rosenmeier, *Kierkegaard's Writings*, XXV [*Letters*, Letter 100, *KW* XXV].

References to books in Kierkegaard's own library [*ASKB* 100] are based on the serial numbering system of *Auktionspro-*

tokol over Søren Kierkegaards Bogsamling (Auction-catalog of Søren Kierkegaard's Book-collection), edited by H. P. Rohde (Copenhagen: Royal Library, 1967).

In the Supplement, references to page and lines in the text are given as: 100:1-10.

In the notes, internal references to the present work are given as: p. 100.

Three periods indicate an omission by the editors; five periods indicate a hiatus or fragmentariness in the text.

BACKGROUND MATERIAL
PERTAINING TO ARTICLES, ADDENDUM,
AND *FROM THE PAPERS OF ONE*
STILL LIVING

In Defense of Woman's Higher Origin[1]

[PETER ENGEL LIND]

Taking our stand on the proposition advanced and defended by Jean Paul and several others, that the greatest poet is the greatest philosopher,[2] and inferring from it according to mathematical principles that a great poet is a great philosopher, we have arrived at the conviction, through reading the works of many poets who in their enthusiasm betray a gift for prophetic vision, that woman's origin is not earthly but ethereal, a conviction, which, having rooted itself in us (partly through the assertions of many young men in love, partly through our own observation of the delicacy of the female structure and the charm and beauty the female life-principle shows in its formations), has become all the more confirmed by the fact that woman herself seems to intuit her higher origin (as also Plato says, of course, that all learning is recollection[3]), inasmuch as her light clothing, gait, and manner of speech suggest an imprisoned soul on the point of spreading its wings to fly away.[4]

The view of woman's nature contained in ancient history should not be objected against the principle I now want to put forward. The treatment of woman in Paradise (insofar as Genesis contains actual history) can be excused only by the evident barbarity of the past, which manifests itself especially in Cain's fratricide.[5] That later times and a large part of the present treat woman as a useful chattel rather than contemplate her as a work of art may well be explained partly by an envy with which Adam regarded Eve (just as the devil regarded Adam with envy, according to the teaching of Mohammed and the rabbis[6]) and partly by a misunderstanding of the truth that woman is created from man, since the latter, instead of seeing in woman the phoenix rising from its ashes, believed that because of this creation he had a right to command woman as his lawful property. We thus confidently put forward the principle that woman is a superterrestrial being, as such only an object for veneration, and that she ought to act only to display herself in her glory.

Now, although our age seems in the main to agree with us, there are several phenomena that here require closer examination. Some men in particular, following Basilius's[7] incorrect principle, which is the basis of his teaching, "that at the resurrection women will arise as men," do not seem to appreciate this truth, notably those who, by encouraging woman to participate in scholarly tasks, seem to want to set themselves above her. We shall not enlarge upon this further but, to their honor, believe that women themselves regard this enterprise as wrong. Instead, we shall go on to investigate whether or not woman, by responding to such invitations, has failed to appreciate her higher origin.

Not long ago, woman began to appear frequently in a form borrowed from man, namely, in trousers,[8] and thus seemed to set man above her, by analogy to the proposition "*a potiori fit denominatio* [designation is given by the stronger one]."[9] And this, her acceptance of man's superiority, became even more convincing when we saw her sex attending lectures in such large numbers. Yet this does not refute our proposition but, on the contrary, seems on closer investigation to substantiate it even more. As for the first phenomenon, it arises, as do all the variations of fashion, from the desire of a higher being to appear in changing form; and as for the second, without doubt woman will display herself in her glory in this way only for those other creatures who rejoice at the sight.

But woman nevertheless ought also to observe the show of consistency.

Therefore, (1) we shall not say, as does Jean Paul, that women (and children) must not stretch their cord of profundity lest it break (for this man proceeded from an incorrect principle, as his *Grönländische Processe*[10] shows), but ask them to stretch it tighter and to lecture to one another, in which respect a well-known copperplate engraving by Chodowiecky in Claudius's works[11] will be illuminating.

Neither (2) shall we therefore demand that they should stay away from lectures in order to seek chemical knowledge in the cookbook and to observe how a realization of reason develops in the saucepan, but exhort them to teach the menfolk the ability they possess in consequence of their higher nature, namely, that of living on little or nothing, since the men will otherwise soon experience most perceptibly what hunger is and thus, according to a well-known proverb, be deprived of their heroic strength.[12]

Finally, (3) neither is it our opinion that "they ought to do honest work with their hands," as the apostle says,[13] but we ask them to use the time they spend in the lecture rooms in cultivating the arts they have hitherto cultivated with great consistency, notably embroidery and beadwork, since by thus damaging their eyes they have clearly exposed their hatred of the material world to the light of day and thereby their elevation above it.

P. E. [Lind]

[ORLA LEHMANN]

It was acrimony we were talking about last time, [15] and although this accusation is probably rather insignificant and although it appeared to us that it has been almost entirely dropped since the draft of the enactment has become known, [16] it will surely be worthwhile to dwell for a moment on the question of what may lie behind this complaint.

People will of course remember how already at the end of the previous century, especially since the Ordinance of 1799, [17] the progressive spirit that had been in evidence among us in the two previous decades came to a standstill. Later, war, defeat, humiliation, bankruptcy, and crop failure [18] stormed in on the unfortunate people, and the public spirit, still weak, succumbed to all these hard blows. While domestic cares thus weighed down the people's courage, the external conditions were of a nature that—far from being able to yield any refreshment or uplift to the weak—they were bound to dishearten even the strongest soul: the Napoleonic military tyranny, which under the warlike conditions of the time was copied almost everywhere, the Restoration, [19] the Holy Alliance, [20] the Second Peace of Paris, [21] the Vienna *Schlussacte* [Conclusion], [22] Carlsbad, [23] Verona, [24] etc. —In short, if everything that happened to us could not produce anything other than powerlessness, despondency, then courage must utterly collapse when one looked at the direction things seemed to be taking throughout the rest of Europe. In these cheerless times during and after the war, the memory of which we recall here only in order to enjoy all the more the gladness that they are over, the exhausted people now sought consolation wherever they thought they could find it. The present offered nothing but degradation and wretchedness; no wonder, then, that they turned their glance away from the same and fled to the dim figures of antiquity[25] in order, in the contemplation of a supposed past greatness, to forget the littleness of the present. Public life was shrouded in the night of sorrow; no wonder, then, that all social activity narrowed itself down to family life and that behind well-closed doors one tried to make things as warm and cozy as one could and to amuse oneself in the best way possible. There thus arose a sort of "still life" in which one estheticized, played with "old Denmark" and "the Dannebrog," or, when one wished for once to keep to actuality, flirted with "Sjælland's beech groves" and "Kodan's billows,"[26] but among all these baubles forgot or lacked the courage to get down briskly to what it was really all about: with strength and wisdom to restore what all the storms that had swept over Denmark had demolished. Yet, through the—if we dare to express ourselves thus—vegetative vigor dwelling in every people, the country's wounds little by little healed,* and, as the recovery gradually proceeded, courage grew and confidence in a better future, and as each individual began to feel better, so also increased the desire to think about and work for the good of the whole. This awakening sense of citizenship, this so often unappreciated something that comes to mind when we hear the so often misused expression "public spirit," is that from which Denmark can expect its rebirth; but, although this public spirit, through the July Revolution,[28] through the introduction and first activity of the Provincial Consultative Assemblies,[29] and through the continuing freedom of the press crisis, has received a powerful and fruitful thrust, no one will be able to deny that with us it is still in its early childhood and in addition until now has had to fight too many adversities for it to have been able to develop itself with any particular strength.

It is this dawn of the life and freedom of the people in which we find ourselves at the moment, and if we look at this condition in its natural connection with the preceding time, the

---

* If Mr. Nathanson[27] will admit to us that this happened *quoique* [in spite of] rather than *parceque* [because], we can readily grant that he is right about the rest.

complaints we tried to explain appear as something quite natural, we could almost say necessary. During the last twenty years of enfeeblement, a certain sentimental-idyllic mood had spread over the people, probably a natural consequence of the universal faintheartedness, but hardly at all matching the serious reforming spirit one otherwise regards as the salient feature of our time. On the contrary, it stood in strange contrast to the indeed not very cozy or cheerful condition in which the whole, as much as each individual, found itself. We were like children who sing in the dark in order to banish or at least drown their anxiety; it was as if the secret consciousness of how unstable the ground was on which one stood caused people with uneasy merriment to cling tightly to the common center, as if at every moment one feared that the whole thing would fall apart. The less satisfactory the state of the country, the more eager one became to impute to it falsely the lacking glory. There has lately been much talk among us about a narrowminded Norwegianness, by which one thinks of the odious self-importance and stupid boasting of individual Norwegians. In approximately the same way with us there developed a truly no less unpleasant Danishness, whose bragging and self-praise originated precisely from, but on the other hand also strangely contrasted with, our actual condition.* This Danishness, as different from true patriotism as day is from night, which found everything as it was with us here divine and glorious, has, however, little by little had to give way to a greater love of truth in people's thinking and talking, but yet it is still not very long ago that it was almost the sole spokesman, and that it has not quite died out is shown by the small reminders we still receive every moment.**

---

* The kinship between the Norwegian ultra-Democrats and the Danish ultra-Royalists, and between the Norwegian Royalists and the Danish Liberals, has been especially demonstrated in a review of Welhaven's *"Norges Dæmring"* in *Literaturtidenden* for last year.[30]

** Who does not in this connection think, for example, of Blicher's *"Om Danmarks nærværende Tilstand"*[31] or of Møller's *"Danmarks Stolthed"*[32] and Garbrecht's incense factory in the late monthly periodical *Skjold*[33] in Copenhagen, or the Odensian *Hempeldom*,[34] the Aarhusian *"Søn af gamle Dan-*

On the whole, however, this barrel-organ music begins to go out of fashion, for the people's entire way of life has taken a far more dignified, more serious, and more positive direction. We have now come so far that we have the courage to examine our condition because we feel the strength to improve it. Attention is therefore chiefly directed toward the things that should be put right, but it is also natural that one cannot praise what one wants changed. As it goes with the individual, so it goes with an entire people. If it wishes to advance to a greater perfection, then it must first recognize its faults; indeed, it must feel pain at its imperfection before the desire and strength for improvement can awaken. But those who felt at ease in the delusion in which they flattered themselves and others with vain delight in a fancied glory and bliss of course become uneasy when the rays of truth dispel their vague phantoms; those who had taken pleasure in or perhaps taken advantage of this patriotic jingle of Danishness of course see a lack of patriotism when a more serious and better time casts away these fool's bells; and those whose ear was accustomed to perpetual hymns find it both unesthetic and tone-deaf to speak of making the national finances public and of the abolition of villeinage[37]—all this is quite in order, but that it is not these people who can be valid witnesses against, or even lawful judges of, the strivings of our existing press is surely just as evident. We are speaking here only about those whose complaints actually spring from a certainly unclear and perhaps half-unconscious but yet honest and respectable feeling. That the royal stable horse, for example, must find it very insulting when the amount of money spent on the royal stable is compared with the amount used for scholarship and science and that those who live from abuse are very bitter when someone wants to take the means of abuse away from them is presumably quite in order also, but against such witnesses and such judges we scarcely need to make an explicit protest.

But if anyone now asks us where all this is going, then we

---

mark,"[35] or the Ribensian patriot[36] who recommended to us animal skins and bread and water.

think it will be evident from the above that it lies entirely in the nature of the case that as yet many may be unable to tolerate or really gain pleasure from the change that has taken place in the press, but this still does not imply that there is any real and well-founded reproach against it. We can well account for it if there are those who with a kind of longing reflect upon the good time when one lived merrily and luxuriously—"*in den Tag hinein* [without thought for the morrow]"[38]—ate and drank, cared about nothing, or at the most, at a L'Hombre[39] table in a club, coined a little witticism against "the adjutant regiment."[40] It was a jolly time, when privateering went with a vengeance,[41] when one could get a hundred-dollar bill for a specie[42] and a royal bond for a score of dollars. —We can well account for it that many a person dwells with pleasure on the peaceful, cozy time when one was so well satisfied with everything, when everyone took care of his own business and let the government take care of the rest, when one went on picnics or to comedies, rejoiced over every forget-me-not one found in Danavang[43] and let oneself be carried away by N. T. Bruun.[44]

We can well account for it, we said—No! It is impossible, impossible that any honest soul can seriously think of his time of degradation or this *misère générale* [general distress] without contrition and pain, impossible that anyone can look upon the seriousness and honesty with which everything now is striving forward without looking with joy and gladness into the future that one day will harvest what the present sows. But if one wants all the narrowmindedness and egotism that previously oppressed the soul and choked every higher striving to perish in order to be reborn to a purer and higher existence [*Tilværelse*], in order to be merged and transfigured into a nobler activity; if one wants all the slumbering powers to be awakened to life and to joy in life, to be set in motion and movement in order to work themselves forward to freedom and well-being; if one wants the great garden in which we all live and build to be cleared of all the weeds that have so luxuriantly grown up in the same, so that the good seed can flourish and yield a rich harvest—then one must also rejoice over and praise the direction that the people have taken, then one must rejoice over the more forceful style our press is beginning to use. If one wants the end, then one must also want the means to it; but it takes a plough to clear a fallow field, and the plough is sharp; and it takes medicine to purge the sick body of unhealthy fluids, and it is often very bitter; and, we repeat, if one wants the end, then one must also want the means to it. How unfair, therefore, one is toward the press! How self-contradictory are most of the judgments heard at the moment about the same! One wants it to strengthen the people but forgets that what is to be able to give others strength must itself be strong. One wants it to be honest and sober and yet wishes to force it to flatter and be hypocritical. One wants it to expose abuse and criticize deficiencies and does not want to hear anything but sweet, pandering words. One wants it to prune away all corrupting growths and does not bear in mind that pruning takes a knife and not a peacock-feather fan. All manly, forceful speech is called intrusive; any expression of indignation or merely of disapproval is decried as acrimony. In short, we believe that the complaints that are in fashion at the moment—or at least were so a short time ago, and to which we have attributed far greater weight and extent than they actually have in order not to seem to take the matter all too lightly—originate, in our opinion, for the greater part from reminiscences from a vanished time that half unconsciously still slink about in the new time, or they originate from sheer misunderstanding.

But is, then, the press entirely guiltless? Has it not committed any error? —But, good Lord, who has made this assertion, and, we add, who thinks himself entitled to make such a claim? Here below where everything is imperfect, how could *this* alone be perfect? And how precisely *this*, which is still young and inexperienced? How precisely *this*, which has to fight with so many adversities—with an ambiguous and hard press law that is bound to make it apprehensive with every step it takes, and forces it, often through indirect writing, hints, and implications, to say what nevertheless ought to be said but cannot safely be said with the openness and impartiality with which all parties would best be served—with a system of secrecy that at every moment cuts the thread of investigation and leaves the writer in perplexity where he most needs information and makes him irresolute and unsure even where he with laborious diligence and conscientious effort has collected everything that could be obtained—and, finally, with a public that certainly loves freedom of the press but with an apprehensiveness as if it were a guilty love, with a scrupulousness that often degenerates into ungratefulness and unfairness. And what is it, then, that is most often complained about? Some trifling expression in an article with which one is otherwise very satisfied, a word that one finds not entirely felicitous or to which one certainly has no personal objection but which someone could possibly misunderstand in such a way that it came to contain something that could possibly be offensive to someone. God have mercy on every tongue in all the king's realms and dominions if it has to be answerable in this way for every single little word! Does one never reflect that another person may find this selfsame word very appropriate, a third even far too weak? Does one never reflect that it is impossible to please all, so that everyone must be satisfied if only he is gratified in essentials?

And it is precisely with journalistic literature that one is most severe, and yet it is that which can claim the greatest forbearance. If one applied here the Horatian *nonum in annum* [keep it back till the ninth year],[45] if only one were to let every work, every little item of news, lie aside for three days in order to think carefully over every word, then one would hear a complaining. If anything of common interest occurs without being mentioned by journalism—then that is wrong. If it is certainly mentioned but not exactly in the way in which each had thought it should be mentioned, then that is wrong, too. Indeed, sometimes it happens that one hears people complain about something said that they themselves have said in the selfsame, possibly even far stronger, words. What is to be done about this? —What Hage[46] recommends: not bother too apprehensively about the tiresome *qu'en dira-t-on* [what will people say about it] but trustfully follow the path dictated by honor and conscience. And what if the press made far worse mistakes than it does? Does the government never make mistakes? And does one therefore then promptly condemn it? And what entitles people to a severity with the press that nobody would allow with regard to judgment of himself? —We cannot view the whole matter as anything but a little indisposition, which, moreover, already seems to have passed its crisis.

After rain, sunshine—this is the eternal order of nature. If reproaches rain down on the press—then it must put up its umbrella until the sun shines again, and if a thunderstorm is in the offing, then it goes into a gateway until the bad weather is over. Perhaps the time is not far distant when the tide will turn, and then one will appreciate the striving that one now feels entitled to reject with an air of superiority, which only ill becomes most people. That the press will then gain not only in vigor and activity but also in dignity and bearing, that it will itself benefit very much from the, if too strong yet educative, discipline under which one now wants to keep it, is easy to foresee.

On the Polemic of the *Flyvende Post*[47]

[JOHANNES HAGE]

A long time ago we made some comments about the view of the *Flyvende Post* [Flying Post][48] on publicizing the affairs of the Provincial Consultative Assemblies.[49] People will hardly be surprised that for a long time we have not replied to the attacks the *Flyvende Post* has repeatedly made on this paper. Only rarely does it contain factual information. For the most part, its polemic consists of emphasizing particular phrases or words, with which it then amuses itself by putting them in a ridiculous light. The editor of the *Flyvende Post* strives to bring down his opponent with mockery and witticisms, and certainly this is easier than laboriously collecting data in order to embark on discussions about reality. It is easy enough to detect some deficiency in the form of the articles in *Fædrelandet* [The Fatherland]; a statement is not made strongly enough; a word is unfortunately chosen—in this there lies a convenient opportunity to fill the paper at a bargain price. We shall here contribute an article about our opponent's polemic, without therefore having any intention of replying to everything he may advance against us in the future . . .[50]

We have become acquainted with the nature of the factual information the *Flyvende Post* communicates[51] and its petty hunt to find phrases that in some way or other should be stated more precisely. But not rarely it also uses other weapons in seeking to amuse its readers with witticisms without caring whether or not the truth suffers on that account. To make its opponent ridiculous, to show its own cleverness—that seems to be the clear aim of several articles, for example, no. 73 (take a look at the vocabulary[52]) and 76. We shall discuss the latter in a little more detail. It is aimed against no. 43 of *Kjøbenhavnsposten* [The Copenhagen Post], "Press Freedom Affair V."[53] In this on the whole well-written article, it is shown how a num-

ber of years ago Europe's general as well as Denmark's particular fate had weakened the public spirit and driven the citizens
back into the narrower circle of family life, how the national
feeling expressed itself more in a nostalgic dwelling on past
events or in a misplaced patriotism than in a vigorous striving
to improve our condition. The author also shows how the
freer utterances of the press must be received under such circumstances, how they must grate upon many an ear that was
accustomed only to perpetual praise, and explains historically
the cause of the indignation with which particular excesses of
the press have been one-sidedly received. On this article the
Flyvende Post has exercised its wit; how far this has happened
at the cost of truth, readers will judge from the following.

First, the author in *Kjøbenhavnsposten*, whom we shall denote by a K.,[54] is accused of conveying to himself some of the
praise generally bestowed upon *Fædrelandet* and of shoving a
good deal of the blame from himself onto *Fædrelandet*. In K.'s
article we cannot find the least thing to justify this accusation.
Is it perhaps the fact that K. mentions the press in general, not
Kjøbenhavnsposten in particular, that has provoked this accusation? Or is it because K., against unjust critics, recommends
what we once said—not anxiously to pay attention to gossip?
But in both cases the groundlessness of the accusation is glaring. —Next, the *Flyvende Post* wants to find in some of K.'s
comments a censure of the dwelling on past events in which
compensation is sought for the bad present and adds, "I certainly know that it goes with the state as it does with individual people, and that an individual who has never been any
good at anything is always in a terrible hurry to rush into the
future and never dares to look back."[55] But this censure does
not touch the author in *Kjøbenhavnsposten*. He has not blamed
the past in general; he has presented only its lack of interest in
common affairs and presented it as something that must of
necessity follow from the course of events. And now with regard to that looking back at the vanished past—it is natural
enough that one dwells on it, but this must not, however,
weaken the vigor with which we are going to meet the future,
for, first and foremost, we have to do with this, and if it is

wrong to be, as the *Flyvende Post* descriptively expresses it, in a terrible hurry to rush into the future, then it is certainly just as wrong to move sluggishly and faintheartedly with the times.

We shall disregard what the *Flyvende Post* says about "little dogs that always yap and in the moment of danger creep into hiding"[56] and leave it to the readers themselves to decide how far the comparison fits the staff of *Kjøbenhavnsposten*. On the other hand, we will say a couple of words about the shameless stab at Liunge, "who," it is said, "in a certain respect is too good to be editor of *Kjøbenhavnsposten*, since its staff might prefer to have a perfect nothing instead."[57] We would not think of mentioning this passage if we had not often had opportunity to wonder at the distorted judgments pronounced over the editor of *Kjøbenhavnsposten*. Already the fact that this paper has existed for a number of years while various other similar papers have gone under in the course of a short time and that it is now recognized even by its bitterest enemies as being the most indispensable domestic paper, already this fact ought, we say, to permit the assumption that Liunge possesses the necessary qualities essential for an editor. Nor is this assumption without foundation. Anyone knowing the editor of *Kjøbenhavnsposten* will be unable to deny him zeal in gathering materials, industry in working them up, a high degree of discretion and deep respect for truth without petty, egotistic motivation—qualities that we for our part place high above wit and dialectical skill when these are not matched by a love of truth but serve only to glorify one's own little self. Liunge is reproached for lack of criticism with regard to the contributions he accepts. We shall merely ask how a daily paper could survive if the editor with great severity were to reject the contributions he receives. And yet the conditions now are very different from what they were some years ago. Had Liunge not been lenient in this respect, he would have had to have stopped the paper long ago. The mass of materials needed to publish a daily paper—and such a thing is after all just as necessary as daily bread—is scarcely fully comprehended by those who rant against that lack of severity. He is further reproached for often accepting in one number what he must correct in the next. But how is he to be certain that all the contributions he accepts are perfectly accurate? If he accepted only those of whose complete accuracy he was certain, the majority of contributions would have to be excluded, and then the paper would totally fail in its aim. The main point in publicizing affairs is, of course, to work against abuses and deficiencies; the errors that easily slip into such accounts are soon corrected through the discussions that arise, and even if they are not always corrected, it is still better that cases of that nature are aired in a deficient manner than that they should be totally left on one side.

In no. 75, 78, and 79 of the *Flyvende Post* are to be found "Some Comments about the So-called Liberal Journalists in Denmark."[58] With respect to the wish expressed by both ourselves and others that a Conservative paper would arise in opposition to the Liberal, the author comments that the complaint about the lack of papers of that color is not justified, because in Denmark there are not two sharply opposed parties, since the government promotes anything new that is expedient and beneficial, and the reasonable Liberals recognize the good in the establishment and want the new brought in only with caution. This one can admit insofar as the government on the whole has paid attention to the demands of the time and the opposition party has paid attention to the establishment; also we admit that both the parties mentioned here have essentially the same goal, but nevertheless a considerable difference remains, on which the author in the *Flyvende Post* lays far too little weight. There it is said, "And although it may seem even to these (the reasonable Liberals) that the government in particular instances proceeds too slowly, just as on the other hand the government in particular instances may find that even the reasonable Liberals go too far in the demands of the moment, this is a difference of opinion that is leveled out in the passage of time, without there being any tension to fear in this respect."[59] This "difference of opinion" is, however, of such significant weight that it forms a partition wall between the reasonable members of both parties. I can be in full agreement with a Conservative when reforms are discussed in general, but as soon as the question arises as to when they are to be carried out, then the difference manifests itself, in that the Conservative asserts that the time for them has not yet come or that the time is certainly suitable but the obstacles are too great, that reform can easily lead to greater evils, to an overthrow of all established order; I, on the other hand, think that the time has come, that the obstacles are not insurmountable, that the fear of possible bad consequences of the reforms is exaggerated.

A reasonable Conservative paper would not, of course, make it its task to defend all the government's measures, just as the Liberal papers do not defend all the opinions and actions of the Liberal party, but it would, when a provision was attacked, emphasize what could be said for it, what had been the reason for its being made or for its not immediately being abolished when it appeared that it should be abolished; it would shed light on errors made in the Liberal papers through lack of expert knowledge and thus contribute significantly to promoting exactly the reforms we need or to working against the discontent that easily arises when improvements regarded as necessary are not carried out. Consequently, we do not want—as the *Flyvende Post* says elsewhere—an opponent who one-sidedly defends everything the government does and who therefore would be easy to overcome, but that we do not find that the *Flyvende Post* meets the need is, after what we have said in the foregoing, surely understandable.

Although the article in question is written in a more dignified tone than most things in the *Flyvende Post*, it is nevertheless not entirely free from one-sidedness and partiality. Thus in no. 75 it is said, "But what is especially frequent: in many articles there appears an inclination to view everything concerning the government's measures from the dark side alone, a desire to disparage these, an eagerness to expose the class of government officials to hate, which by no means can lead to anything good."[60] As proof of this striving, as the author calls it, "to expose the class of government officials to hate," a quotation is given from *Fædrelandet*, no. 72,[61] where regarding the

Provincial Consultative Assemblies it is said, "Even if one wanted to regard the allowances as salaries—then even the grossest and most material calculation would find them better allocated than the salaries of most government officials." When we accepted this little piece, we certainly saw that the above quotation could, if it was read with evil eyes, give rise to misunderstanding. The statement, however, is quite true, whether one considers the time the deputies have had to use each day for their business or the benefit that one can with good reason expect from their work. In this matter, the *Flyvende Post* appears to be very sensitive, since it raises objections against one of the reasons A. Ussing[62] had given for commercial schools, namely, that in making provision for the education of the middle class one must create a "counterbalance to the predominating influence of the aristocracy of government officials." But who, then, doubts that the influence of the class of government officials is all too one-sidedly predominant, that there is a lack of a class of independent, informed citizens outside the class of government officials? And is it a degradation of the class of government officials when one says that by being almost alone in the possession of a solid education it gains all too predominant an influence?

That the Liberal papers in their fight against the Conservative ones take refuge in assigning ignoble motives to their opponents is an accusation we certainly read in no. 78,[63] but we find it more applicable to the opposite party. For how often are not the Liberals charged with acting out of vanity, ambition, lust for revenge?

Calculating people cannot easily grasp why one wants to put oneself to all that inconvenience and expose oneself to all the unpleasantness bound up with this kind of writing, and they so easily hit upon the belief that there must be something or other at the bottom of it. How precisely the author of the aforesaid number makes himself guilty of attributing ignoble motives to the Liberals is shown by the quotation given above[64] (about the desire to make the class of government officials hated, etc.).

In no. 80, the *Flyvende Post* has with great sophistry gone through Professor Clausen's article "The Church and the Provincial Consultative Assembly."[65] About the first point in Bishop Mynster's declaration, that he regards it as his official duty, when he has proposals to make for the good of the Church, to present them in another way (than through the Provincial Consultative Assemblies), the *Flyvende Post* comments that for the one who wants to join in the complaints of the nine pastors, it must be of importance to refute this point. No—not for the one who wants to join in the pastors' complaints but for the one who wants to work against that statement, which, through the bishop's authority, could easily, if in itself it did not have it, gain a general application—it is important to refute this point. Later on, the *Flyvende Post* comments that the highest spiritual and secular authorities stand in such a close connection with the government that their position does not allow them to act except in agreement and cooperation with the government, and that he [the author in the *Flyvende Post*] would find it unsuitable if a bishop or county councilor presented petitions. Neither the bishop nor the county councilor is the highest spiritual or secular authority: the Board of Justice is that in its entirety. If the entire Board of Justice presented some petition to the king through the Provincial Consultative Assemblies, it could seem unsuitable, but if a particular county deputy was elected a member of the Provincial Consultative Assemblies and then presented a petition, we would find this in order.

And with this, enough about the *Flyvende Post*, to which for the future we shall reply only when it produces well-founded objections.

On the Anonymous Reform Service of
Kjøbenhavnsposten[66]

[ANONYMOUS]

Heiberg has written several witty things but scarcely anything better than the article in *Flyveposten* [The Flying Post],[67] in which he speaks about the anonymous reformers in *Kjøbenhavnsposten* [The Copenhagen Post], who probably one day will awaken from their deep morning sleep[68] and then, as in that famous German poem, discover that they "are cutting the noses off one another";[69] further, he speaks about their perpetual "cockcrow,"[70] which suits the dawn so well, about their "broker's business"[71] with the newspaper *Fædrenelandet* [The Fathers' Land] [*sic*], about "little dogs that yap the most but are the least regarded,"[72] about the "journalistic juggling tricks"[73] in that striking article in no. 43 where one tried, to the best of one's ability, to demolish the nation's glories, about "this Liunge who is fattened up and well fed in order at last to fall like a sacrificial lamb under censorship's razor,"[74] etc. etc. Wit and an exquisite humor pervade the entire article; if Rahbek[75] still lived among us he would call it priceless.

It would be a remarkable phenomenon if in the history of reforms an account were to be found about anonymous reformation preachers; therein would lie an even more decisive proof that they were uncalled. But it is inconceivable that it has been possible to give weight to the arguments lately advanced about the freedom to write, that is, a freedom to write freed from every restraint and disregarding every consideration, or that any member of a consultative assembly, even of rather poor spirit and intelligence, should let such arguments influence him, as the thousand-tongued rumor has tried to spread it abroad.

There are articles in the paper that do not originate from full-time staff members and really do have merit, but these are rare, because they do not agree with the publisher's[76] interest, which especially requires pieces that coincide with the taste of the masses and are intelligible to them. But its better pieces are at times handled in a strange manner in that sometimes, probably when the censor demands publication under a name, they are supplied with an "ed.," which signifies the acting editor, whose name is said to be very similar to one of the euphemisms for death;[77] under him is the editor in name, who functions merely as daily assistant messenger boy. Other pieces have something *Rocket*-like[78] about them; although they do not exactly elevate and recommend Winther's unbridled gutter paper, they nevertheless will eventually provoke the same result as this paper brought about in 1833,[79] namely, a greater sharpening of the press law. Some articles seem intended solely to show what clever dialectical fellows the authors are and that they understand how to turn a thing around in a hundred ways without, however, achieving at the end a better argumentation or clearer view than at the beginning. Such pieces are very far from having an actual reforming spirit and aim; neither can one trace in them true love for the good of the fatherland, zeal for truth and right, a thoroughgoing spirit of investigation, temperate and beneficial proposals, or versatilely devised reform plans. They consist for the most part only of carelessly thrown-out aphorisms with some brilliant point, acrimonious language, a very pronounced urge to admonish the king and his men, and a manner of speaking that cannot be used toward other cultivated people but is considered good enough for the rulers of the state—for example, the king should not in his old age issue such an enactment (like the new press law,[80] which is to set a limit to such indecent and immodest forms of writing); it would cause bad blood (a pet expression of one of these writers).[81] At times there are also manifest distortions, sophisms, false perceptions that come from superficial and undigested reading, or biting jests. That this last has often actually been the aim is shown by a remarkable admission in no. 49, p. 95, where it says: "To censure, to give vent to *acrimony*, to use improper and unseemly expressions, is already forbidden; does that which lies outside these limits merit attention—this *ambiguously wanton, acrimo-nious* tone, or whatever one wants to call it, is it really so dangerous that one needs to upset the entire people for the sake of such *trifles?*"[82] —So, then, is it a trifle when an author writes with ambiguity and wantonness, or even with acrimony, about the most important affairs of the nation? If the subject were not so serious, one would be tempted to call the author laugh-man [*Leemand*] or laughter man,[83] although the laughter, just as much as a just indignation, recoils on himself in that he sets the Danish people's common affairs and its leaders at such a low level that they merely serve him and likeminded people as a vehicle for venting his *wantonness*, *acrimony*, and ambiguous wit. Nor is it probable that anyone will allow himself to be hoodwinked into believing that the people "are upset" because bounds are set to such an odious practice, unless those in question demand that they be regarded as the entire nation.

Reply to Mr. B. of the **Flyvende Post**[84]

ORLA LEHMANN

Lately the wish has often been expressed that in the press itself there might arise an opposition to the one-sided direction our time's craze for reform has threatened to give our daily papers, for it was recognized that it is not only the government that needs a competent opposition, but that this opposition, too, precisely in order to be competent, must find a counterbalance that not only holds it in check but also by counterbalancing its necessary one-sidedness makes its own contribution, so that the product of all the intersecting factors comes as near the truth as possible. It may therefore have surprised many that now when the *Flyvende Post* [The Flying Post] might seem to have fulfilled this wish, the friends of reform have not, at least until now, embarked to any great extent upon any polemic against this certainly not dangerous opponent. But with this, it must be remembered that, for one thing, that aim by no means requires an actual direct conflict between the organs of the different intellectual trends, since this debate ought rather to take place in the individual readers themselves; for another, that hitherto the editorial policy of the *Flyvende Post* has been rather unsuitable for the production of a fruitful discussion. I am not hereby aiming at the really improper ignorance that was manifested in, for example, several of its finance articles, not at the often bad and sometimes plainly indecent witticisms with which it has tried to amuse its readers at the expense of its opponents, not at the not very brilliant hair-splitting that is a part of its polemic; but what I have in mind by the above statement is the system of taking particular articles, sometimes even particular phrases, from an article, in order to point out particular actual or supposed contradictions without ever coming forward with a policy of its own, new facts, or better information. It can easily be seen that a conflict that could lead to little more than whether a particular article is well written or not is without real interest to the public, and that if such bickering, such a conflict for the sake of conflict, were to be perpetuated, the press would waste away without advancing a single step.

There was more of an invitation to reply in an article written by Mr. B.,* "The Morning Observations in *Kjøbenhavnsposten*," which attacks an article printed in this paper about the "Press Freedom Affair," and, since I agree with the views expressed in it,[88] I would have made some rejoinders even earlier if I had not known that a reply would come elsewhere. But since the writer in question [Mr. B.] has not been pleased with that reply, there may still be time for this.

Corpus delicti [The body of evidence][89] is, as was said, an article about the Press Freedom Affair that appears in five numbers of *Kjøbenhavnsposten*.[90] The first three tried to explain with legal precision the somewhat veiled mention of the content of the enactment in the parliamentary gazette[91] and to point to all the considerable restrictions on our freedom of the press that it would entail if it were passed, something that was all the more necessary to point out since in the first few days it was regarded in many places as being of little significance.

---

* I would like to have maintained the fiction that the *Flyvende Post*, as the organ for a certain view, a certain party, was itself the source of its articles, without any disturbing consideration as to which person in each particular instance is incidentally the spokesman for this party. Neither would I in this respect let myself be disturbed by the B. put under the article, for although it is probably to indicate that this comes from another hand than the rest, which is also amply demonstrated by its robust and energetic language, yet I regard such a mark as an entirely permissible means of indicating a certain shading of opinion in the common main direction, and therefore could so much the less take offense at it in a paper whose editor[85] on previous occasions has taken the liberty in this respect—to put it mildly—to the most extreme limit of what is permissible. But after this same B. has replied to an article in *Fædrelandet* [The Fatherland], "On the Polemic of the *Flyvende Post*"—in which his article was mentioned only as one of several[86] examples of error that regularly are to be found in this paper whose mode of action was to be described—has replied saying that *he*[87] had nothing to do with *Fædrelandet* (with which the *Flyvende Post* undeniably has much to do), then it becomes necessary here especially to keep to Mr. B.

The last two parts of the article discussed the complaints that might have given occasion to the momentary reaction against the press, and among them also the charge of acrimony. As the cause of this charge, that article mentioned, for one thing, an ill-timed concession[92] from our *juste-milieu* [happy-medium] people[93] and a momentary fashion among the imitators of these, and for another, the plain self-seeking of those whose interest is bound up with the attacked abuses; but since one did not want to stop with these more external reasons, the ultimate source of those complaints was sought in a certain coddling in the preceding time that allowed many to regard the natural expressions of the reawakening life of the people as dangerous deviations; furthermore, at the end of the article it was noted that by no means did the article intend to attribute all the complaints made against the press solely to the people's being unaccustomed to see it treat public affairs with liveliness and independence, but that nevertheless its *actual* mistakes could not justify any condemnation such as that contained in the draft of the enactment. What in this series of observations has given offense to Mr. B. of the *Flyvende Post* is what was said about the preceding period in Denmark's history. The train of thought here is approximately this: in the last three decades of the previous century, Denmark found herself in a lively and very promising development, which revealed itself in important reforms in our legislation, in a fruitful industrial and commercial activity, and in a vigorously budding life in the people; approximately at the beginning of this century a deplorable situation arose, and a series of heavy misfortunes later brought the country into a very sorry plight; on top of all these sufferings followed a period of enfeeblement that with the general mood of the people must entail a certain soft sentimentality, but gradually the people have somewhat recovered their strength, and the natural result of this is that instead of the previous faintheartedness there appears a more vigorous striving forward, that the people's spirit again turns to public affairs, whereas formerly it withdrew into family life, again directs itself toward its future, into which it previously did not dare to look. That this change must displease many, the article in *Kjøbenhavnsposten* found very natural and saw in it an essential contributing factor to a discontent that it tried to explain by viewing the phenomena of the present time in their natural connection with the conditions by which they were determined, in their necessary connection with the whole development of the time.

If we now ask what Mr. B. of the *Flyvende Post* finds in this to complain about, then I hope I have rightly grasped his meaning when I assume it is this: that the article in *Kjøbenhavnsposten* was one-sided and unjust in making too low an evaluation of the past and too high an evaluation of our present. The former is said to lie in the emphasis on only the dark side of this epoch, while its bright side, namely its literary, especially esthetic, ability and the endurance with which the people bore all their misfortunes, was viewed as transient; the latter is said to lie in there wrongly being attributed to the reforming endeavor of our time a vigor that it does not possess. But when the article under complaint is read in its context, one will find that it speaks only about the movements in political life, and in this respect scarcely anyone will deny that the time described was a wretched time, and that the freer and more able development begun earlier has only recently begun to make progress again after a long pause. Thus there was not the least reason for talking about Grundtvig's and Oehlenschläger's poetry, the direction of which may very well have been determined by the disgust of the more powerful natures with the badness of that time, or about the Baggesenian polemic,[94] whose radical and lasting effect is perhaps the greatest proof of the sense of lostness of that time, or about the legislative activity of Ørsted,[95] who with all his ability nevertheless stands as an isolated phenomenon. How that article was supposed to manage to mention the recent Church disputes,[96] for the ignoring of which it has been reproached in another quarter, I have not been able to fathom at all. For here there was no question of maintaining an all-embracing characteristic of a certain time, but only of pursuing a certain trend from its point of departure through its decay and to its resurrection. Incidentally, one need not fail to appreciate the ability lying in that literary productivity because one thinks that the period from 1807 to 1827, which was primarily intended, was not merely a deplorable time but downright bad, and one need so much the less fail to appreciate it as history teaches us that a poor time in general often can give birth to a few great talents, indeed, in certain isolated directions by concentrating its vigor—and no time is entirely barren—can even develop a certain virtuosity. That the endurance with which the people bore their misfortunes witnesses to the fact that they still possessed the ability to make a better future is certain, but this was surely never called in question by anyone. I will even add that it is easy to detect in this torpor of the national spirit the seeds of the new development that now appears to be beginning, but all this lay outside the scope of the article under complaint.

Thus, to the best of my judgment, the first charge is groundless. Indeed, Mr. B. himself seems to have given it up in reality, since in a way he acknowledges the opinions Mr. Hage puts forward as the train of thought of the attacked article and complains only that he has not also reproduced the style that prevailed in *Kjøbenhavnsposten*. Now, this is indeed a strange requirement for a summary consisting of a couple of lines from which one usually seeks no more than a faithful account of the leading idea, but if the entire complaint collapses into a mere dissatisfaction with the form, perhaps even merely with a few somewhat strong words, then this is a matter of taste about which everyone must be permitted to have his own opinion. Moreover, the author of the accused article[97] has shown in the earlier sections of the same that when he has given the conclusion a somewhat polemical coloring this was not because he could not write with objective ease and dialectical coolness, and it is always strange to hear this complaint from an author whose sole merit—insofar as this is documented by that article in the *Flyvende Post*—consists of an admittedly unmistakable talent in the use of powerful words and bold metaphors.

As for the second complaint, I am in agreement with the author in regretting that the work of reform here at home still cannot boast any O'Connell, let alone any Luther or Moses; on the other hand he goes totally astray when he first substitutes *our reformers* for the *reforming endeavor* of our time, and then identifies these with *the publisher and staff of Kjøbenhavnsposten*. When he pronounces our reformers destitute of vigor and manliness, one can readily agree with him in that—naturally with exceptions, which he probably will recognize of course—because one thinks that a more serious and more vigorous spirit is beginning to awaken among the people—and the article in *Kjøbenhavnsposten* has never said anything else. But when he clears the path for an attack against the "sacrificial lamb" and "yapping little dogs" of *Kjøbenhavnsposten*, an attack that surely others besides Hage have found "shameless,"[98] he will certainly find, after calmer reflection, that even if everything that he says about it was true, it still would not contain any argument against the assertions of the accused article. That our political life is still in its childhood, about that I am in total agreement both with the article in *Kjøbenhavnsposten* and with its opponent, but that it will grow in vigor and ability, that I hope every right-minded man will wish, and if I have not misunderstood the two opposing articles, then it is also their intention to contribute to this, each in its own way. Furthermore, that our reforming endeavor has still not become flesh, as it were, in particular great individuals cannot surprise anyone who with understanding has observed the entire direction of our time, for this tends to democratize everything, wealth, science, yes, even character, and thus it is easily explicable that even if the sum of material well-being, of insight and vigor, is now greater than at any time before, yet all this is not to be found united in particular prominent individualities in the same way as previously; moreover, it must still also be remembered that the concept of such prominence is totally relative and that much, therefore, of what has previously been raised high above the populace can now be lost in the mass. Thus the second complaint might also be due to a misunderstanding, since Mr. B. is certainly right that our political life and its reforming tendency have not yet displayed any great vigor but is wrong in objecting this against an article that has asserted the selfsame thing.

I have tried to the best of my understanding to find out what Mr. B.'s opposition to the attacked article actually consists of in *reality*, but I am, of course, far from being sure that I have seen the point, since the kernel is certainly hidden inside a very thick shell. On the whole, that attack seems chiefly to be only the vehicle for a number of more or less suitable jokes, and insofar as this gives well-founded reason for regarding the whole as a stylistic exercise in the humoristic manner, one certainly cannot deny it as such a certain virtuosity, but since, in that case, the author's intention is not to give information about anything but only to amuse—it is indifferent whether himself or others—one can readily deny it a love of truth without thereby impugning the author's morality. At least there are to be found such palpable, although at times very amusing, distortions and perversities that under another presupposition one must call in question either the author's intelligence or his *bona fides* [good faith]; but since there is no reason for doing the former, and the latter is something that I cannot easily bring myself to do, then the interpretation I have given is certainly the fairest of all, namely, that the author thought he saw in the *Kjøbenhavnsposten* article an unjust disparagement of the previous time and an unjust praising of the present, and opposing this presumed one-sidedness he has given his dialectical bent of mind and satirical humor free rein with a poetic license that has certainly sometimes led him into unseemly wantonness or offensive injustice.

What I have replied to here is the only point I could discover in Mr. B.'s article that was pertinent to the issue, and it is only the issue that is important to me. I therefore do not need any excuse for ignoring all irrelevant matters. On the other hand, I must apologize to my honorable opponent that my reply comes somewhat late, but earlier I had something better to do. When I put my name to these lines, I hope Mr. B. will regard it as a little courtesy toward him, since I see that it pleases him to know with whom he has to do, but I must also ask him not to let it prevent him from preserving his own anonymity, since it is totally immaterial to me what my opponent is called.

Orla Lehmann

[PSEUDONYMOUS]

The heat begins to stream down from heaven; the earth emancipates itself from the chains of winter; the ice melts around its breast and dissolves into juicy liquids and fertilizing vapor, from which the bud of spring develops with a host of summer-green shoots. The rain clouds blow over our heads like migrating birds and bedewingly sink over field and meadow—in short, a humoristic tendency is pervading the whole season and spreading itself to the smallest parts, to the tiniest particle of the work of creation—why should not man, then, follow the directive of nature, melt the ice about his heart and let the healthy humor stream through his mind and stream out again from it? That means: he is not to make his humor nature's but nature's his own—mere liquid[100] is not enough, but if everyone puts a little intelligence into it like malt[101] in alcohol, then the whole keeps better and through this union conditions its own existence. —Lo! In these few words already lie sufficient grounds both for the existence of these papers and for their name: to unite *utile dulci* [the useful with the agreeable][102] has been, ever since the days of Horace and his daughter Mette,*[103] a worthy task for young and old of all ages and both sexes; yet let no one expect to see us like Wessel: "At the end of our work distributing moral saws."[104] —We detest the moral here just as we do wherever it shows itself solely in its inexcusable nakedness, and to that extent we are in fashion, for it is beyond all doubt that if the same person went from door to door and every time he was asked, "Who's knocking?" said, "I am the moral"—then the reply in most cases would be, "There is no one at home" or "We don't want anything today" or the like. So the reader need not harbor any

* See Wessel.

fear on that account; if he does not here and there trip over the moral or it over him, he need not fear any kind of ambush; and we are pleased to inform him that he has the right of way[105] wherever and whenever he meets it, just as he is of course at liberty to step aside wherever he may think it justified. We owed to the reader, as well as to ourselves, openness on this point and can now continue with a relieved heart. So, we have shown that the child is both lawfully born and baptized; if it should now occur to anyone to ask what the child will be, whether it will be apprenticed to some definite trade—for what can there not be asked about in our inquisitive times—then the answer would undeniably embarrass us. There are enough indeed in the arts and crafts, also in the military both on land and at sea; yes, even the field of politics and diplomacy is occupied—all roads are full; probably the best thing, then, is to let the little one go its own way and so, in that case, leave it to time to answer the question. With this, all presumptive questioners must now be satisfied insofar as they cannot as yet deduce the child's coming fate from its physiognomy. On the other hand, those who do not ask but say straight out, "Humor! What good is that? It is water, you know—and how much of our literature, how many of our journals are not swimming in pure water, 'which is even rather muddy'?"—those we shall first refer to what we have already observed, that humor is not mere liquid;[106] next, we shall remind them of the power of water, which is by no means weak, and Zetlitz's words, "Water strengthens, quenches, cheers";[107] and finally we shall leave it to them to consider whether this same liquid does not play a rather significant role in life, in which respect a picture taken straight from life must take the place of a long explanation. Imagine a beautiful summer day! The sun shines clear and bright above the landscape, which only now and then is fleetingly overcast by a whitish cloud passing over the shining orb. On the earth everything is life and movement; the young ladies trip lightly, the gentlemen strut, the lame walk, the blind warm themselves in the light of the sun; a thousand thoughts pass each other, a thousand glances meet in the clear air. Suddenly the sun is darkened, the white cloud has become gray; like a humorist *en Gros* [wholesale], it expands itself across the meadow and lets its mood stream out in a sudden shower of rain. What haste comes over the people! What groups disperse, what groups form! What visions are conjured up for the eye! Here a dress that *has been* white, there a black hat that *has become* gray, here an amaryllis[108] with goat's feet raising skirts high, there a springing satyr in pantaloons, here under an ethereal[109] parasol a fat matron whose husband tries in vain to save his new hat with sandwich paper from *Statsvennen* [Friend of the State][110]—there the three Graces[111] and a midwife under a family umbrella[112] that a blast of wind has turned inside out so it points with cup toward heaven like a newly opened tulip. And all this is the humorist's work! This entire hullabaloo, in which all follow the diagonal of the parallelogram of forces given in life,*[113] is provoked by a bit of humor from a rain cloud! We could say: When such a thing is possible for such a foggy and unclear character, what cannot, then—— — — —but our modesty forbids us to go further. We think we have said enough in defense of humor; and if we are thought to have asserted that the humorist's call is the most important in the whole world, then in asserting that we have not gone further than so many great men whose example we have before us and who from the school and high-school teacher's desk or at the bar of the people have, each one, protested that their call and efforts certainly took the prize even if they led only to a systematic theory of old people's nightcaps or the younger people's attempts in the art of sewing gloves from old stocking-legs.[115]

So much for the introduction, dear reader! I think we have understood each other. Here outside stands a person who asks to be admitted in order to pay you his respects. If you agree, then we will take a chair and sit down, giving him permission to speak and some moments' attention.

* By the way, this sally is not by us; as far as we remember, it is "by a head clerk."[114]

A FEW WORDS ON THE CURRENT JOURNALISTIC POLEMIC,
WITH SPECIAL REFERENCE TO A PIECE IN THE *FLYVENDE
POST* TITLED "ON THE POLEMIC OF *FÆDRELANDET*."[116]

It cannot have escaped anyone's notice that almost all our journals and daily papers have recently put on armor and, mail-clad, make a stand against each other, in that they, just like the Homeric heroes of glorious memory, as a matter of form first let fly a stream of abuse at each other as rapid and agitated as* can be produced under the circumstances. If anyone were to find a resemblance between the noise caused by this and the croaking of frogs in the marsh when they all stick their mouths above the surface of the water and try to make their voices heard, or were to compare the battle to that of the Greeks and Trojans at the taking of Troy, when friends and enemies fought each other without respect to persons—then one would certainly have to find all such comparisons highly indecent; on the contrary, this state of war, this *bellum omnium contra omnes* [war of everyone against everyone],[118] seems to us so very interesting, indeed, picturesquely beautiful in that a mass of powers thereby unfolds and the entire muscle power of the combatants is developed and is evident to the eye, that we would much rather compare the conflict to one of the tournaments of the Middle Ages,[119] where knights, with and without closed visor, unhorsed each other for the honor of their lady's color, whether she is *tricolor* or one color or rainbow-colored, and whether the knight wears the cloak on one shoulder or on both shoulders[120] or wears no cloak at all, perhaps in the hope of winning his opponent's etc. In this connection, we would even suggest to the combatants that they adopt certain fixed names and shield devices such as: Knight of the Flying Dragon with Charles V's shield device, the Pillars of Hercules and its inscription "*Plus ultra* [Further for-

---

* The publication of the present communication has been significantly delayed because of accidental circumstances, but this delay could be so much the less a reason for us to keep it back, since eulogies about people never come too late, not even if they come after their death.[117]

ward],"*[121] and above this a flying dragon; Knight of the Two Days, with the motto "*Noli me tangere* [Do not touch me]!"[123] or something like that, etc.; by this not only would much be gained for social life—since in daily speech one could now indicate one's meaning far more briefly, for example, "Dragon and the Knight of the Days have got hold of each other by the forelock" or "The former has given the latter a proper box on the ear" etc.—but also it would perhaps be the most successful way of arousing the ladies' interest in the conflict and drawing them into it, so to speak, when it was made completely clear to them that what they saw and heard was an actual tournament with actual knights whom their charm and beauty could animate and whose bravery would find its sweetest reward in receiving the prize from their hands.

It is, however, by no means our opinion that such a measure should be necessary in order to give the whole thing the stamp of chivalry; everyone who has watched the conflict, for however short a time, surely will have easily detected in the combatants' knightly bearing and gracious warfare that this is not a matter of a hostile rendezvous of rough prize-fighters[124] or a Kjøge-encounter[125] of Sjælland's "cattle-rich sons." But cast a glance at, for example, the polemic in *Dagen* [The Day],[126] at the series of combatants who have visited its arena lately. What dignity! What beautifully maintained Conservative grace! What knightly faith, built on the gospel of the *Nordisk Kirke-Tidende* [Northern Church Times]![127] What a collection of knightly virtues! In truth, it is of them a well-known author speaks in that much-read newspaper *Selskab i Eensomhed* [Company in Solitude][128]: "They encourage the most beautiful, the most dignifying virtues of the human race, not only by the most powerful ideas but also by their own example, since their whole life is a chain of noble and useful undertakings." For a long time *Dagen* has occupied an honorable place

---

* It is conceivable that several knights could unite under one shield device but with different mottoes; for example, under the dragon another could put "*Non plus ultra* [No further]" or, freely translated, "Stay, my fine Count, for I want you to learn that I, though poor," etc.[122]

in our periodical literature; even if it did not provide any satisfactory witness to the external and internal polemic of the state, it bore so much the more brilliant witness to the polemic of its editors and correspondents. For a long time it has been its honest task, together with *Adresse-Avisen* [The Advertiser],[129] to praise the dead; and it is primarily because of the paper's greater tendency toward expansion and the editors' discernment of late that it has extended its activity also to censuring the living, presumably in the conviction that it will of course later make full compensation to them once they are dead. It would, however, be unfair if our interest in this paper should cause us to forget the other ephemeras,[130] who deserve well of the good cause especially by acting for the material interests; one need only follow one's nose in our literature in order to stumble upon a row of such, in all of which an energetic spirit stirs, and which all present a more or less excellent foundation for the pearls of science and art.

But in this place and in this connection it would certainly betray above all an unforgivable forgetfulness not to mention the *Flyvende Post*,[131] which, especially lately, after it has assumed a firm and threatening position against the "so-called Liberal" papers,[132] has shown more than at any time before noble dignity and rare dexterity in the use of all kinds of weapons that distinguished to such a great extent the vanished age of chivalry. We feel that our warmth on this point would lead us into a labyrinth of panegyric and eulogy at which even the *Flyvende Post* would have to blush, although *Kjøbenhavnsposten* would not find it exaggerated, and it is then in order to give our praise a more special direction and thus to be able to motivate and defend it more easily that we wish to draw attention to a particular article, yet without therefore characterizing it as *primus inter pares* [first among equals], and to make it the subject of a more detailed consideration. But to all the combatants one can, as is also evident from the foregoing, more or less apply the poet's words when he says:

"Is anyone wounded, let him remember, the conflict
    Is only a feast;

Smile at the wound, then unsheathe his sword,
  And saddle his horse!
For if we have peace, yet in camps of war
  Is the feast to be held:
Always jousting and festive victories
  Best have glorified peace!"[133]

In no. 82 of the *Flyvende Post*, an author[134] (in an article with the title "On the Polemic of *Fædrelandet*"), after having stated about *Kjøbenhavnsposten* in a previous number[135] that it is "a parody of the reforming endeavor,"[136] "reminds one of Don Quixote"[137] etc., has further informed us that *Fædrelandet stammers*.[138] Although there is every probability that the aforesaid author, who, of course, like the *Flyvende Post* in general, preaches the gospel to the poor and moreover speaks so clearly that the blind must see and so loudly that the deaf must hear,[139] will also easily be able to cause the stammerers to speak and thus also heal *Fædrelandet* of the errors and weaknesses from which it may suffer, we have nevertheless—under the assumption of the aforesaid paper's helpless condition, and especially encouraged by the strongly castigating tone in which the aforesaid author speaks, and which shows that there actually is danger afoot—regarded it as our duty to come to his assistance, also by attempting to appease the wrath of the severe one with a few friendly words. We are, then, so free as to follow Mr. Author's own instructions by putting his article "On the Polemic of *Fædrelandet*" in front of us and emphasizing in it what can especially serve *Fædrelandet* for instruction and warning. After a number of powerful expressions as appropriate as they are significant, of which two at most would be enough for a blacksmith and in which, by the way, the author exerts so great a force that his pace in the language seems to us to be a kind of hornpipe dance or Scottish jig, in which at every other step one taps the heel and stamps on the floor, he tells us that in the article by *Fædrelandet* that has occasioned his own he has his place in the middle and has been involved there in a terrible hullabaloo, "since nearly all winds—morality's northeast and intelligence's southwest, grammar's east and compassion's south—blow all at once,"[140] and so he fears being drowned by "this journalistic Niagara Falls."[141] We would not have emphasized these words if we had not found in them the most unmistakable proof of the author's imagination and flowing wit, since through all these winds he sees in all kinds of directions a roaring Niagara Falls, quite naturally because his entire head is full of it, which even better explains the flowing wit we have noted above as an advantage possessed by our author. Thus already at this point we can describe him by using an expression, which we once heard used by a Danish theologian, that he is not only extravagantly imaginative but, what is more, he is really and truly a genius.

Thereupon the author goes on to wonder and amazement that *Fædrelandet* has concerned itself with an article "aimed exclusively at *Kjøbenhavnsposten* and trying specifically to isolate *Fædrelandet* from this paper."[142] If the author, as he says, along with "many" has been amazed at this, we, on the contrary, have been so much the less so at his amazement. The old saying: *nil humanum a me alienum puto*,*[143] which in Horace's time may have been quite good but soon is so old that the year and date have worn away, he, along with many, does not understand, and this again shows a correct view of the matter. Moreover, he hereby discloses to us his principles about the system of intervention[144] in general, somewhat like the Romans when, at the beginning of the First Punic War, they reproached the Carthaginians for their interference in the conflict between Mamertines and Messinese. It is to be assumed, however, that it was not the above-mentioned saying alone that motivated the utterances in *Fædrelandet* on behalf of *Kjøbenhavnsposten*, but, just as on the one hand it regarded the article under attack in *Kjøbenhavnsposten* as being "on the whole well-written,"[145] so on the other hand it must regard a product that presupposed the opposite view as on the whole reprehensible and the direction it followed as dangerous for the good cause in general; indeed, it must regard the opinions and views expressed in it as an indirect attack upon its own, insofar as

---

* I regard no human affair as irrelevant to me.

these in the main harmonized with those expressed in *Kjø-benhavnsposten*. To what extent, however, we want to make these opinions in *Fædrelandet* ours, about this we regard it as superfluous to make any declaration to the honorable author. This accepted, one does not need to explain the phenomenon according to Jewish laws,[146] even though one readily admits a certain not very distant kinship between *Fædrelandet* and *Kjø-benhavnsposten*.*[147] Neither need one wonder so very much that these comments by *Fædrelandet* are found in a piece that calls the *Flyvende Post* "our opponent"[151] and speaks of the repeated attacks by the *Flyvende Post* on *Fædrelandet* etc.; for just as it was of course possible that this paper regarded the *Flyvende Post* and everything therein as the opposite of itself, as representing a direction in the development of the political opinions that were in total opposition to its own and consequently on the whole must also have a definite color, so can it also be supposed that *Fædrelandet*, through a certainly unforgivable carelessness, has overlooked our author's considerable breadth and cubic capacity[152] in literature, and above all his "lion's share" in the war ammunition and entire polemical stock of the *Flyvende Post*, and has lumped him together with the rest, without first having assessed the size of his mighty shadow and thereafter assessed the width of the back that must correspond to such a very extensive mouth.

---

* Since the subject is about family connections, we seize this opportunity to comment on a word that suggests our author's relation to the *Flyvende Post*. He says, namely, that *Fædrelandet* in its criticism of the *Flyvende Post* has allowed him the "lion's share [*Broderpart*]."[148] The brother's share of an inheritance, according to Christian laws, usually falls to a brother, and moreover this is questioned only when a sister or the descendants of the same are alive. Consequently, we assume that the author is here thinking of the *Flyvende Post*, and we heartily congratulate him on the manly sister who, as the elder, will also be able to have a very beneficial influence on his wandering through literature. On the other hand, it seems to us that the author, with a certain impetuosity and self-esteem that do not betray the genuine brotherly spirit, claims his right to the greatest share of the inheritance during the reading of the will at which the guardian of *Kjøbenhavnsposten*[149] functioned as executor, and we cannot help thinking of Jacob von Tyboe, who asks Jesper whether he [Jacob] has to stand drinks first, and when Jesper replies that he has the preference, replies, "Well, then the pleasure is mine!"[150]

We shall not dwell longer, however, on the possible grounds that have motivated *Fædrelandet* in the aforementioned article to mention that piece in the *Flyvende Post*—that it has happened, that we see—and we shall now see what the latter paper has objected to in what has been stated in *Fædrelandet*.

(Conclusion to follow.)

[PSEUDONYMOUS]

A FEW WORDS ON THE CURRENT JOURNALISTIC POLEMIC,
WITH SPECIAL REFERENCE TO A PIECE IN *FLYVEPOSTEN*
TITLED "ON THE POLEMIC OF *FÆDRELANDET*"

(Concluded.)

After a few comments on the accusation by *Fædrelandet* about
lack of a love of truth[154] and a serious *quos ego* [you had better
watch out][155] in this connection, together with a nice, appropriate introduction in which the author uses, with new variations, his favorite theme, *Pereat*[156] *Kjøbenhavnsposten* [Let The
Copenhagen Post die], he decides to "dwell on the point first
mentioned by *Fædrelandet*."[157] Here he really shows himself in
his dialectical element. *Fædrelandet* says, namely: The author
in *Kjøbenhavnsposten* is accused of having conveyed to himself
some of the praise bestowed upon *Fædrelandet* and of having
shoved a good deal of the blame from himself onto this paper.[158] What is the reason for this accusation? One of two
things: *either* the fact that K.[159] mentions the press in general,
not *Kjøbenhavnsposten* in particular, *or* that K., against unjust
critics, recommends what *Fædrelandet* has once said: Not anxiously to pay attention to gossip.[160] "No!" says our author:
neither of the two is the reason; it must be sought in this, "that
the complaints about acrimony have been aimed almost solely
at *Kjøbenhavnsposten*."[161] Thus, *Fædrelandet* says: Is it because
K. mentions the press in general, thus also *Fædrelandet*, as the
object of the accusation of acrimony that it is said to shove
blame from itself on to *Fædrelandet*? —"No!" says our author—"on the contrary, it is because K. mentions the press in
general, thus also *Fædrelandet*, as the object of the aforementioned accusation, although the complaints about acrimony

have been aimed almost solely at *Kjøbenhavnsposten*" (we permit ourselves to supplement the elliptical sentence). The whole thing is to be regarded as dialectical sleight of hand. The author has wanted to explain the assertion that with every proposition the counterproposition is given, by showing that when he held the proposition in his right hand the counterproposition is inevitably found in the left and vice versa, but like a good Christian he has also wanted to observe the words of Scripture, that "the right hand must not know what the left is doing";[162] the right hand in writing has thus not known that the left contained the correct proposition, which was to be changed by a *coup de main* [sudden assault], and used what it had at hand. This one can call making reason prisoner of the obedience of time.

About the next point mentioned by *Fædrelandet*: "That *Kjøbenhavnsposten* has not blamed the past in general but only presented its lack of interest in common affairs and presented it as something that must of necessity follow from the course of events"[163]—our author comments that K., by describing that vanished time as "sentimental-idyllic," as "years of enfeeblement,"[164] has *eo ipso* [precisely thereby] denied it all vigor and ability, since an age can certainly lack receptiveness to a certain type of impression, but, if it is otherwise good for anything, it can no more "be sentimental-idyllic or enfeebled in one direction," than the individual person can. The other day I discussed this matter with one of my friends, who had terribly much to object to this reasoning. I shall write down some of his utterances, leaving it to the sensible reader to refute them himself. "What kind of assertion is this," he said, "that an age cannot be characterized by a kind of fundamental sentimentality and be totally enfeebled, even stunted, in a particular direction without immediately having to be declared dead and powerless in all respects! The author should just think of the one-armed sailor in the comedy,[165] who certainly must be regarded as a partial invalid and totally unfit to go aloft in a storm but who nonetheless 'plays an excellent game of ninepins' and empties his glass for the fatherland along with the best. And how he has developed and proved this his asser-

tion! What a 'gadding about in ideas'! What a 'soiree of contradictions'![166] What 'a genius of defeat' reveals itself in this
entire exposition! He says that every age has its own fundamental stamp, from which all its expressions of life must take
their color, which of course in turn determines that from the
particular expression of life the fundamental stamp can be inferred with certainty; yet it is undeniable that an idyllic joy
over Denmark's tranquillity and inner peace, a sentimental enthusiasm over the fusion of hearts and mutual love, which ar-
ticulated itself in the song of the lark as well as in the hymn of
the people, is surely a fairly universal expression of the life of
that time; thus he himself has proved that on the whole that
time was characterized as sentimental-idyllic. He says that the
political life, precisely because the fundamental character
stamps every expression of life, must stand in a necessary relation to the vigor of the age on the whole. Yet, it is certain
that in that period there was neither pith nor substance in political life—it evinced absolutely no expression of life—thus he
has himself proved that the age on the whole was enfeebled
and impotent.

"It is evident that the author has conceded much more than
was demanded. But even if the assertion were correct, that a
time cannot be enfeebled, even stunted, in a certain direction
without being so in everything, even if one would admit that
Kjøbenhavnsposten had characterized that time as impotent on
the whole, how is this then refuted by the account of its esthetic ability, 'its rich poetic abundance'?[167] From what did it
develop this rich abundance? From some particular distinguished individualities; but this strength in the individual—
can it not very well harmonize with the general enfeeblement,
yes, even bear witness to it? Does not the author know that
the lower the general level of the people's intelligence, the easier it is for the individual to rise above it—the more the spiritual element becomes widespread, the less noticed is the
excellence of the individuals! —And now this mixture of concepts, as if 'sentimental-idyllic' were one more expression for
'enfeeblement,' although both as concepts and in the accused
article in *Kjøbenhavnsposten* they are kept distinct! This petty

arguing about our time's 'lack of interest in esthetics and in the higher purposes of life,'[168] just as if the idea of the eternal could reveal itself only in that which directly turns to the eternal and could not just as well be drawn down to earth and develop itself in all art and science, for example, in politics! — No, my good friend! I must now as before endorse the opinion of *Fædrelandet* about the opposition in the *Flyvende Post*; on the other hand, I cannot agree with the aforementioned paper insofar as it seems to apply to itself remarks in the *Flyvende Post* 'about little dogs that always yap and in the moment of danger creep into hiding,'[169] for I always picture the *Flyvende Post* to myself in the image of Mrs. Bremenfelt,[170] who does the honors with *the large* poodle dog under her arm, which like Jemteland's king* yaps two words whenever it says one, while by turns she offers her guests beer, spirits, and coffee with syrup in it."—

So much for my friend. —After some half-ashamed words about the "shameless"[172] attack on Liunge, which we consider it a shame to repeat, but in which, by the way, the leading thought is that the editor of *Kjøbenhavnsposten* is not to be considered competent, because he does not succumb but understands how to "keep going,"[173] the author concludes his refutation of *Fædrelandet* with the witty comment that blindfolded and with a stick in his hand he would be able to smash one piece of Jylland-pottery foolishness after the other in the *Fædrelandet* article.[174] We are deeply indebted to the author for this *Sprikwort* [saying],** and since we suppose that he would undertake the operation in the capacity of "Christmas billy goat," in return[176] he should actually be remembered with a little Christmas present—only it is a pity that "Christopher" has already been given the horse with the whistle and "Peer" the fiddle.[177] If we were *Fædrelandet*, we would, however, reply with Jeronimus, "Enough, enough, Schoolmaster! I am well aware that I must admit defeat;[178] the parable about the

---

* See the poem *"Jemtelands Befolkning,"* by P. Møller.[171]
** See *Julestuen.*[175]

phoenix*[179] bird struck me particularly; I will therefore permit the holding of the Christmas party."**

Finally, our author adds as a kind of postscript some ingenious comments about the morals of *Fædrelandet* and "a certain Lafontaine-Kotzebue-like blubbering, snuffling, sermonizing tone in the polemic."[180] Here the author again shows the penetrating glance and the healthy philosophy of life over which we so often have had the opportunity of rejoicing. *Fædrelandet* is straightforward. It says with the Frenchman, *"J'appelle un chat un chat* [I call a cat a cat]"[181] and is probably even so free at times as to doubt its opponent's sincerity and to say straight out, "It is not true!" which of course must be doubly annoying when it really is not true. Our author, who feels oppressed by such modes of expression, fights against this straightforwardness and takes for granted the more politically correct proposition that in general one ought to call the cat a lion, since in addition (what especially should be noted), he is not a little offended on behalf of the whole party that *Fædrelandet* encroaches upon its rights and employs the same weapons and military arts that it has itself now used for so long and of which it indubitably is to be regarded as the first inventor.***

With just as much justice he wonders that *Fædrelandet* holds a eulogy over the editor of *Kjøbenhavnsposten*, whom, he says, he has never attacked, since he has only referred to him as "a fattened and well-fed sacrificial lamb,"[182] not a perfect nothing, and thus has not ascribed to him any bad quality but has let the matter stand at pronouncing him destitute of all good. But that makes no difference, says our author, "for Liunge could be a very truth-loving man and yet afford a counterpart

* *Scilicet* [That is to say]: who thus with blindfolded eyes can smash Jylland pottery.

** *Scilicet*: in the *Flyvende Post.*

*** One recalls among other things the perpetually echoing alarm and antiphonal songs [*Varsel- og Vexel-Sange*] about the *Kjøbenhavnsposten* editor's love of truth, his character and motives etc., in which respect the liberty has even been taken to draw conclusions about his private character as person and citizen from his public character as journalist—conclusions that could yield very suitable grounds for a court case.

to the foolish Gottlieb in the story"[183]—to this remark he consistently connects the proposition that morality and intelligence "stand in an essential relation to each other."[184] By the way, we maintain this last statement also with respect to the author and do so even if someone should dare to assert that he had no more love of truth than "a bumblebee."[185]

After reading an author who interests us, we usually form a picture of his personality according to the way his physiognomy develops from what is written, according to the way his person steps out of the words and walks up and down the printed page. In this manner we often see a Mephisto leap out of books and journals, but even more often some caricature on whom exaggerated arrogance, pedantic eccentricity, or other such qualities have placed a fool's cap scarcely inferior to Nebuchadnezzar's.[186] We would therefore have liked to have had the pleasure of sketching for the reader's eye a quick picture of our author as we have formed it also in this instance, if our observations had not already grown to a length that perhaps seems more dubious to the reader than it does to ourselves. We reserve this task for another occasion,[187] however, especially if the author through continued literary activity supplies us with further features for an outline of his own physiognomy.*

Before we leave this area, we cannot deny ourselves the pleasure of once again casting a glance at the battleground and rejoicing at the sight of these literary combatants whose "knightly heads itch for a laurel wreath"; we cannot take our eyes from this beautiful sight without shouting our congratulations to them and the Blücher watchword "*Vorwärts* [Forward],"**[188] as we exclaim with the poet:

For long one saw them shoot with bullets such as these,
Harsh curses at each other, aimed to cow;

* It follows of itself that an author's *literary* physiognomy has nothing to do with his bodily physiognomy, which is absolutely of no concern to us here.
** Of course everyone knows the story of the man who shouted to his calf, which was butting his neighbor's, "Keep at it, our calf !" but we are not partisan like that man.

> Of devils was there used a might flock,
> So this great battle did methodic go.
> They did the same as heroes did at Troy;
> Before the fight each other strongly cursed.[189]

But we hope that the conflict will continue for a while; and with this happy hope we conclude our comments and commit ourselves to the good graces of the well-disposed reader.

                                                      X.[190]

[ANONYMOUS]

THE *COLLEGIUM POLITICUM* [POLITICAL COLLEGE][192]
OF THE *FLYVENDE POST*
A TOUCHING COMEDY IN SIX SCENES

Characters

H., professor and Knight of *Guldkorset* [The Golden Cross],
Kjøge Huuskors [Kjøge Home Cross], etc.[193]

1234, a very serious man.[194]

x., a millionaire.[195]

K. (né B.), an opponent and in addition something of a genius.[196]

502, a patron of the Chinese.[197]

A sensible man from the provinces.[198]

An acquaintance of Professor H.

Several men from the country.

The Overskouian polemic, a ghost.[199]

Scene One

(A room with a table on which lie several numbers of the *Fly-
vende Post*, *Kjøbenhavnsposten*, *Fædrelandet*, pen, ink, paper.
Around it are chairs. Enter the members of the college [except
K.] one after another. They sit down at the table and Professor
H. sits at the head of the table.[200])

The professor: Welcome to all of you, good sirs! Where did
we leave off last time?[201]

x.: It was with the national debt. You will recall that Hage and
I could not agree; he says: There is a deficit of 300,000 rix-
dollars, an annual deficit that in his opinion would rise to
nearly a million. I, on the other hand, say that there is actually a surplus of 661,000 rix-dollars.[202]

The professor: That is right. Now I remember.[203] —And do
you know how he has come to commit such an error?

x.: Yes, he doesn't include the part-payment on the assets.

The professor: Quite correct; but do you know where the basic error that afflicts all his essays comes from; I mean the one-sidedness, the discontent, the desire to see the black side of everything that can be discerned in what he writes, the shaking of the head, if I may put it that way, that clearly guides the movements of his pen?

x.: No.

The professor: It arises from his not having come further than to the second part of logic, to the sphere of reflection.[204] He has remained standing there. It would have been better for him if he had remained in the sphere of immediacy, where so many thousands stand who find it agrees with them; for it is not good to be in the sphere of reflection if one does not work through it to the third, to the sphere of the concept, where all opposites are dissolved in unity and where abides *the heavenly quiet* in which Goethe breathed,[205] as you have certainly heard. As a transition,[206] as a bridge from the immediate to the speculative, the sphere of reflection is necessary and beneficial, but not as the place where one should pitch one's tent. An author who does this will be at the mercy of all winds;[207] he becomes aware only of the parts and not of the continuity of the subjects,[208] and because of this he becomes uncomfortable, and thus when he writes something he makes his readers uncomfortable also. So it has gone with the author in question concerning the national debt. One sees all too clearly how he has an eye only for the parts[209] in this, for he cannot tear himself away from the two ideas: it must be paid and economies must be made.

x.: Do not forget what you wanted to say, but I quite agree with the man about that—economies ought to be made.

The professor: Will you permit me to finish speaking? The whole thing takes on another complexion viewed from the speculative stage. —Thought—abstract thought—of course you know abstract thought?[210]

x.: Yes, I have heard tell of it.

The professor: For *thought*, gentlemen, the sole thing in the natural and intellectual world is to refind its definitions[211]—

one calls them by a foreign word, categories. "All it recognizes are only such things in which its own definitions are
to be found, and it recognizes them only insofar as its definitions are to be found therein; either there is nothing in the
subjects that falls outside these definitions, or, if there is
anything, it is certainly incomprehensible to thought, but
not because it surpasses thought; on the contrary, it is because it is infinitely deeply subordinate to it, because it is
incidental, because it is thus a something that with greater
justice can be called a nothing."[212] The national debt, gentlemen, is thus certainly not itself a category, but contains
nonetheless many categories,[213] as, for instance: quantity,
quality, means, purpose, etc. All these are definitions in
which thought refinds itself; but part-payment, economies,
etc. are not categories. In these, thought does not refind itself; on the contrary, they are deeply subordinate to
thought, because they are the *incidental*, a something that
with greater justice can be called a nothing. Now I hope,
gentlemen, that you have perceived *that* and *why* a state,
which is at the speculative stage [*Standpunkt*]—and the state
always is that; in any case it is a philosopher's duty to place
it there—can and ought to ignore part-payment on the debt;
and moreover I hope it has become clear to you how questionable it is to take the ideal to the law court of actuality.

x.: I have truly never thought of that before, but the professor
is perfectly right. Now that I know that author's stage
[*Standpunkt*], I can explain to myself his statement "that agriculture here in the land is in its childhood."[214] The first
time I heard it, I assure you that I became so angry that I
could not help saying to my brother-in-law, "Is it not disgraceful that he actually says of a land where, in addition to
the ordinary kinds of grain and leguminous plants, flax,
hemp, hops, red and white clover are cultivated—says this
of a land where, without having to search long, one can find
rapeseed for ten, twelve, yes, even sixteen dollars a barrel,
where timothy grass and turnips are no rarity, where there
is every probability that in five years we will come to culti-
vate mangel-wurzels, where the finest lowing cattle [*bø-*

gende Qvæg] walk under the refreshing beeches [*qvægende Bøge*] and give such good milk that from it is made the most excellent Swiss cheese imaginable (inferior only to that of Switzerland itself)—is it not disgraceful that he actually says of such a land, 'Agriculture is in its childhood'?"

The professor: I approve of your indignation at that time, but now when you know how it is with him—

x.: Now I forgive him from the bottom of my heart. Goodness! How hard it is for such a man, when he is otherwise said to be respectable, to have to be at that stage [*Standpunkt*].

The professor: You may well say that; I, too, am often very sorry for him, but—Sh! Here comes my secretary;[215] he is so fond of singing. He's a subtle fellow, to be sure. He can argue with his antipode and make him believe he is walking on his head.

Scene Two

The same. K. (comes in singing).[216]

K.:   Stay, my fine Count, for I want you to learn
        That I, though poor, my honor esteem—[217]

All: Welcome! Welcome!

S. K.[218] (without noticing them): Come here, you shall see I have a little something for you—[219]

The professor: For me?

K.: No, not for you, for the others I recently left. For I have just come from *Kjøbenhavnsposten*. I have been there to give them a piece of my mind.

All: What did you say?

K.: I said: penny ale—I said: moral stewed kale—I said: ditto buckwheat porridge—I said: parsley—I said: strong soup— I said: Niagara Falls—and then I said: into a gateway in a thunderstorm!—[220]

The professor (aside): *Abgeschmackt* [Tasteless].

1234: But didn't you get to the point of the matter[221] at all, for what you have told us is, of course, only what one calls witty phrases, which—

K.: Have I forgotten to tell you? Yes, of course, I got to the point of the matter. I said on that head: It does not matter to me what you do or do not call the point of the matter, any more than your calling something an irrelevant matter[222] proves that it does not concern the matter. The crux of the matter is that the matter be kept outside the matter, lest one become involved in contradictions, as you are, sir!—

The professor: Believe me, that hit them.

K.: Of course! They could not withstand life's dialectic.[223]

The professor: That I can imagine. (In a low voice to K.) Have you finished what you spoke about the other day?

K.: Here it is (gives the professor something written).

The professor (running through it): A new cloudburst [*Skybrud*] of witty phrases!

A man from the country (aside to his neighbor): What shipwreck [*Skibbrud*][224] is the professor talking about?

The neighbor (aside to him): He says there are a lot of shipwrecked witty phrases in the piece he is reading. That is metaphorical speech, cousin; by that he means that they are not good for anything.

The professor (laying the paper on the table): Your wealth of witty phrases, Mr. K., amazes me. I cannot understand how such a number can be contained in one person without his feeling greatly inconvenienced by them.

K.: I do suffer greatly from them as long as they are inside me. If I did not from time to time expel them through a course of sudorifics—as I metaphorically call my activity as a writer[225]—they would unquestionably attack the vital inner organs.

502 (annoyed, to his neighbor): It is a shame that the professor talks to him the whole time. We, too, are here in the room.

Neighbor (to 502): I'll soon disturb the dialogue and turn the professor's thoughts in another direction. (Aloud) By the way, Mr. Professor! You promised us you would explain the proposition in *Fædrelandet* "that the absolute monarchical forms of government are not as good as the constitutional."[226]

The professor: It is good you remind me about that. Since this proposition is a new piece of evidence concerning that author's stage [*Standpunkt*] in the sphere of reflection, it would not be amiss to discuss it in a little greater detail. What I have to say first is that the proposition is in itself extremely unclear and that the expression "not as good" is extremely ill-chosen. "An idea that little by little develops its content thereby certainly takes the latter further and further in its development, but it is a complete misunderstanding that each of these stages [*Stadier*] in the development should be better than each of the preceding. In the animal kingdom, nature has brought life's idea to a higher development than in the plant kingdom, but it does not follow from this that a fly is better than a rose. With the plant there is much good that is not to be found in the animal. In esthetics, one type of poetry is placed above the other because in the one there comes to development what was still only an embryo in the other, but only through a gross misunderstanding would one like to conclude from it that a higher type of poetry in this sense was better than another. Each of them includes the whole of poetry, just as every form of government includes all the elements of government, only at a different degree of development."[227]

A sensible man from the provinces: Perfectly correct, sir! Thus there can also be no question that one author is better than another but only that the one is at a higher level of development than the other. Likewise all comparison between individual poetic works of the same type ceases, and I therefore by no means share the opinion of the many who call your vaudevilles[228] better than the others our theater owns, for every vaudeville includes the whole of poetry and all the elements of vaudeville, only at a different degree of development.

1234: But Mr. Professor! Could you not have misunderstood the man in *Fædrelandet*? His words must unquestionably be understood relatively with regard to ourselves and the present time.

The professor: Yes, but then, of course, the question is an entirely different one. —And in any case it cannot be posed casually like that in the form of an indisputable proposition but must first be substantiated.

A man from the country (to his neighbor): I am really afraid to open my mouth in the presence of the professor if he wants everything one says substantiated. If I happened to say I was wearing a green dress coat, he would be able to demand that I prove it was green—and that I cannot do, curse it, for it is very possible that what is green in the sphere of immediacy is red in the sphere of the concept.

The professor (to the preceding speaker): You wish to say something?

A man from the country: No, not at all, Mr. Professor! (To his neighbor): He wanted to get me out on thin ice there, but shame on him who lets himself be tricked.

The professor (to x.): What are you pondering so deeply, my dear sir?

x.: I was just sitting and thinking about the amazing results that develop from your previous comment. Just as one cannot say of one type of poetry that it is better than another, so neither can one use this predicate when comparing people; indeed one cannot use it about any earthly thing. And as a consequence of this, much that supports that popular way of viewing things ought to be totally abolished, for example, examination grades [*Characterer*], for just because the one person's *specimina* [examination paper] is at a higher stage of development than another's, it by no means follows that it is better.

502 (gets up violently): No! —Now you must really permit me to say a few words too. I have sat so long and waited, but now that the conversation is about grades[229] I must certainly join in.

The professor: Would you explain yourself in more detail?

502: "When we follow the course of words, especially those that have had a long life, on their way through the classical and modern world, it is often very curious to observe their elastic nature and see how the concept expands from a narrow space out into the indefinite, but then again, according to time and opportunity, shrinks and becomes quite small.

"So it has gone with the word 'character,' which otherwise in its written form has remained whole and unabbreviated. That is, in the Greek language this word first designated the engraved or scratched, a stamp; next, through an enormous extension, the distinct individuality of each thing—and here we have the word in its classical sense. In the modern world, the word certainly did not entirely lose its wide application but nevertheless frequently had to put up with significant limitations. Thus, used of a person, it designated only moral distinctiveness in that this element was one-sidedly emphasized as that which gave the person his stamp. On further reflection, however, a loyal age found that a person's distinct individuality should rather be sought in the rank and title most graciously granted him from higher places; whereas others thought that it most clearly appeared from the greater or lesser virtuosity with which he could go through the ordeal of an examination. These last two points of view, however, are rather closely related, for both rank and examination grade of course designate external (often not completely reliable) marks; also, examinations lead, of course, to appointments, and appointments again to rank and titles. Our dear fatherland lies in the temperate zone of examinations and titles, and therefore we still meet many among us who regard the examination grade with orthodox respect and tender adoration, whereas among the well-intentioned the idea has gradually become prevalent that the examination grade is a mark necessary for greater and smaller societies, yet inadequate and slightly deceptive, a mark that neither the state nor the individual would do well to overlook, but which nevertheless must not be taken for more than it is, either. In short, it has something in its nature so vague and debatable that it would look comic if one were to subject it to a scrupulous and minute calculation as one does with the paths of the heavenly bodies."[230]

The professor (aside): If he hasn't spoken before, he is certainly taking his revenge now. (Aloud): *Was ist der langen*

Rede kurzer Sinn [In short, what does this long speech mean]?[231]

502 (continues): "It seems especially fitting for our liberal, practical time, striving toward a higher goal and holding every old blundering routine and pedagogical pedantry in contempt, to perceive within what limits the value and essence of the grades move, and it is therefore only by constant reference to human inconsistency that we are not surprised that the paper *Fædrelandet* for Saturday, March 14, has printed a survey by an arithmetical dunce, calculated with the pettiest pedantry, of the relations between the grades at the matriculation examination for the year 1835."[232]

The professor: You wanted to go in that direction? —*Per tot ambages* [By so many roundabout paths] . . ..[233]

A man from the country (to his neighbor): He is calling him Peer Tot [nincompoop]—

The professor: Gentlemen!

502: I have still not finished! Now comes the part about the Chinese.

The professor: Should we not keep that for the next session? (To 502) You must not take it amiss, but I have promised these good men (pointing to the men from the country) that I would read them the Tieckian short story "The Jellyfish,"[234] and they are already leaving tomorrow.

502 (sits down. Aside): He always wants to be the sole spokesman. I think I will leave the Society. (The professor reads the story. During the reading, x. writes down several sums, adds and multiplies them; 502 reads no. 75 of *Fædrelandet*; 1234 is listening seriously; K. is wrapped up in his own thoughts; several men from the country yawn).

Scene Three

An acquaintance of Professor H. (comes in breathlessly):
  Ihr Götter [Ye gods]! Idly you are sitting here
  In reading stories do you waste your time,
  While outside storms the enemy. For know
  That Overskou is loose and has attacked

With Titan's pride the elevated Pindus
And strives profane and brazen, without shame,
To smash the cross, which you have planted there,
With dramaturgic hammer.

The professor (rises): I beg your pardon?
    "Am I defied?" Well, well! Come out my sword!
    Fædreland, step back a little while!
    The muse is calling. I will come again,
    As soon as the barbarian is forced
    To bow before the cross that he has mocked.[235]
    (Goes away quickly with his acquaintance.)

Scene Four

A man from the country: I think the professor got angry.

1234: But what about, actually? I could not really understand the messenger. He spoke so loudly.

x.: I will tell you. The professor has translated from the French a piece called "The Golden Cross." Overskou has found something to criticize in it, but the professor says that there is nothing to criticize. He has already said this to Overskou once, but the latter still refuses to give in, and now he is furious. This has just been reported to the professor; he became angry about it and went away—and now in all likelihood he will go there and kill him.

Several men from the country: No! He is never going to do that, is he?

x.: I suppose so. Do you not know what Schiller says: *Der schrecklichste der Schrecken, das ist der Mensch in seiner Wuth* [The most terrible thing of all is man in his fury][236]—and "*wüthig* [furious]" he was.

A sensible man from the provinces: Gentlemen, may I now, while the professor is away, tell you my humble opinion of the secondary schools?

x.: Yes, of course you can. But it certainly comes somewhat unexpectedly.

A sensible man from the provinces: My opinion of the secondary schools is this. But before I tell you my opinion, I must first tell you the opinion of the others. By the others, I understand Ussing, Hage, and Gad.[237] But before I tell you the opinion of the others, I must first tell you my opinion of the others. Take Ussing now. He is a man who, as my brother-in-law says, deserves both claps and slaps. He has an extraordinarily popular way of speaking, has studied Holberg, and also owes several things to Heiberg's vaudevilles.[238]—*But*—

Scene Five

The professor (comes in gloomily).
All: What has happened?
The professor: He is dead.
All: Dead? You haven't killed him, have you?
The professor: No, he was already dead before I came—from a light cold.
Several men from the country (looking him straight in the eyes): Mr. Professor! Mr. Professor! It is not true! He has not died a natural death. Surely you have killed him. We can see it in your eyes.
The professor (shrugging his shoulders): Yes, now it is done.
Several men from the country: Fie, shame on you!
The professor: It is good it is done. Sooner or later it certainly had to happen. He has always kept himself in the region of imaginative representations [*Forestillinger*] and yet would never have reached up to that of the concept.
Several men from the country: But is that a reason for killing people?
The professor: It may not be a reason, but it is a cause.

Scene Six

The Overskouian polemic, a ghost[239] (reveals itself threateningly in the background. A chill of terror passes through them all, and involuntarily they shriek the following lines):
1234 (with trembling voice): The journalists seething with acrimony—
x. (likewise): —The part-payment on the assets—

502 (likewise): —Chinese handicrafts—
K. (likewise): —Into a gateway in a storm—
Several men from the country (are struck dumb).
The ghost (disappears).
The professor (with relief): Now he has gone!—
(The curtain slowly falls.)

Our Latest Journalistic Literature[240]

JOHANNES OSTERMANN

It was about four years ago that our journalistic literature first began to arouse interest and gain life among the people. This beginning occurred with the advent of Winther's well-known *Raketten* [The Rocket].[241] Winther thought himself personally injured and made use of the press in order to give vent to his anger and provide himself with a source of income in his helpless state. Since he had a certain virtuosity of expression and in a certainly coarse but quite amusing manner knew how to put forward his complaints, he not only acquired a considerable number of readers, especially among the lower classes, but also gave the people a taste for coming forward with their complaints and grievances through the press. It is still fresh in memory what a mass of gutter papers[242] flooded literature from that time onward. If we are to pass judgment on these as they actually were, we probably can do nothing but agree with the general opinion, since these papers often operated with untruths and probably more often with half-truths and almost always lacked decency of expression. It is another question whether there was not a healthy and permanent element in that literature. What this was we have already said: the desire to read and write was thereby awakened. About six years ago, the reading of papers was still very rare among the lower classes, and it was therefore very necessary that something absolutely exceptional occur that really accorded with popular taste in order to awaken the desire to read, and we can think of nothing more suitable to this end than that mockery of "the great," those continual assertions about the violation of rights in particular instances. Although this reading matter was not always the best, the bad in it seems to have been a necessary evil in order to promote a greater good.

Very essential, too, was the influence of this literature and

especially Winther's *Raketten* in arousing the desire to write.
There are many circumstances in the state under which the
individual can be personally violated without his therefore always being able or willing to use the risky legal process,[243] and
under such circumstances the press can often be of help to the
injured person. And even where one uses the law courts in
order to obtain one's rights, it is in many instances desirable
that the public be informed about the case in order that the
guilty can be given a warning example and the innocent person be put on the path to finding his lost rights. It is not so
very long ago that the people here silently assented to everything whenever they did not think it advisable to use the help
of the law courts, but the restraint that rested on the people in
this way became a useful cover for the dishonest official. But
then *Raketten* came, and the injured person saw in the press a
means of winning back his lost rights, and the wrongdoer began to fear the power lying in the general consciousness of the
people.

By means of that paper, one also finally learned to know
our press legislation in greater detail. Many among the public
wondered that one dared to take up arms so boldly even
against officials. But it soon became apparent that if one only
has truth on one's side, there need be no fear of the consequences of a bold use of the press, and it was not long, either,
before people began, with far greater life and freedom, to remove the veil from what previously had lain tightly wrapped
up and hidden from the world.

These were the essential and lasting consequences of the
gutter press, and certainly not too much is said when one asserts that these have had an unconscious influence on many,
perhaps on that paper's most ardent antagonists. We leave this
first development of a more lively journalistic literature in order to go on from there to point out some greater and more
essential elements lying in the background.

In the duchies, a more vigorous political life stirred somewhat earlier than with us. Here we recollect Lornsen's little
publication[244] and all that this provoked. This publication acquired historic significance by calling for what the king later

decided upon: the establishment of the Provincial Consultative Assemblies.[245] From this moment, everyone began to
take an interest in politics; in major and minor publications
opinions were expressed about the significance of the institution, its adequacy, its suitable form, etc., and several political subjects were expatiated upon with greater freedom
than was usual. Our best periodical, *Maanedsskrift for Litteratur*
[Monthly Review of Literature][246] supplied several outspoken
articles about related subjects. Whereas shortly before one had
feared sharp attacks only by *Raketten*, our leading critical journal now began—of course, absolutely honorably—to make
loud complaint. Who does not remember the outspoken article, which aroused so much attention, about the "monitorial
system of education"?[247] Here the more respectable part of our
writing public first began to speak its mind; here one first saw
what our press-freedom legislation gives us the right to say
and write. Those articles were a fruit of the spirit of the time,
and they had a retroactive effect on the same. However dissatisfied people were with those attacks by *Raketten*, it can never
be incorrect to say that the government on the whole, and especially particular members of it, were even more dissatisfied.
The edict concerning the authors punished for violation of the
press-freedom ordinance[248] shows the misgivings the government had about permitting those attacks. Thus it is quite un-
likely that it can have been so absolutely pleased with the
greater freedom that gradually spread among a better-class
public. Among the people, on the other hand, the political
consciousness had now awakened; they demanded a greater
publicity. Now if they received information and thought they
saw something questionable in it, they became all the more
curious to know more. If such information was denied, they
believed that there was more in it than met the eye. People
became more and more eager, indeed persistent, in their demands: "We have to pay taxes; therefore we should know
what they are used for" etc. What strengthened these views
among the people was also the idea that is the basis for the
institution of a provincial assembly, namely, that it would be
an advantage to the whole community if, as far as possible,

individuals living in the concrete situation could have the opportunity of expressing their opinions. The government itself
had given the word: Look with your own eyes and judge for
yourselves! And the people willingly responded to this appeal,
indeed, more willingly than many could wish. The government had been the constructive factor on so many points; no
wonder, then, that it reluctantly saw its own work torn down.
It had familiarized itself with many situations and in several
respects perceived these more clearly than did the people.
How natural if it insisted upon its experience! And when it had
granted greater freedom, how easy, then, to find presumption
in the demand for more than was given. The people, on the
other hand, readily complained about a futile half-measure
and demanded something whole as a condition for further
progress. The people thus had become braver and kept a
stricter eye on their superiors. This was, however, far from
creating such a tension that there could be anything to fear,
but the people's previous resignation and almost thoughtless
devotion had ceased. Here, then, we see an opposition between government and people that had arisen naturally, and
we ask readers to keep this in mind.

But as the people now became more and more convinced
that they ought to have an extension of their rights, should
have a better knowledge of the established order, and should
themselves participate more in many affairs, with this recognition there followed in our journalistic literature as the organ
of the people an ever greater boldness, a more severe judgment of the established order. *Kjøbenhavnsposten* [The Copenhagen Post], which earlier had for the greater part estheticized,[249] from now on attached itself to the Liberal party in
that it obtained well-written contributions from several talented staff members.[250] Some while after *Kjøbenhavnsposten*
had begun to attract the attention of the public, Professor
David announced the birth of *Fædrelandet* [The Fatherland],[251]
and people looked forward to its publication with close attention. It came. It was read widely, and people found several
exceptionally good contributions in it—and even if they found
something to criticize in some of the others, they were still on

the whole well satisfied. The external circumstance that came to attract even greater attention to this paper is sufficiently well known.[252] That this action did not exactly please the people, we know. We shall try to explain this as objectively as possible.

First, a couple of general comments. It is in the nature of things that every moderately liberal press freedom law is couched in rather indefinite and vague terms, even though the lawgiver at the moment of writing has assigned to the terminology a certain definite interpretation that is conditioned by the stage of development reached by the spirit of the time. But when the spirit of the time advances quickly and when the reading public therefore acquires a freer intellectual education, it is clear that what in an earlier period could, for example, make one feel dissatisfied with the established form of government—the same at a later time can be heard and read without any offense. In other lands, this understanding of the matter has most certainly had the result that freedom of the press cases have been submitted to a jury. The spirit of the time thus conditions the interpretation of the law, although of course without violating its spirit. That a liberal man in such a rapidly progressing time as ours is inclined to give the ordinance the widest interpretation follows of itself. If one adds to this that Professor David's predecessors had already—if I may use this expression—as good as tempted the law, then it was very natural that, instead of in everything slavishly having the letter of the law before his eyes, he first and foremost paid attention to what one was now in the habit of telling the public, and thus, even before he thought so himself, he perhaps stood on the boundary between the permissible and the impermissible.

So much for the editor. What appeared natural to him also occurred to the people: they were so accustomed to seeing daring and bold utterances that in a certain respect they had perhaps forgotten what bounds are set by our press-freedom legislation, and thus when the public saw *Fædrelandet* it did not expect to find in it anything deserving punishment. People spoke about "the right of petition" and "what use is it"[253] and found one or two things in it expressed quite boldly; but from the entire current manner of speaking, this could be seen as belonging to the order of the day. People no longer became as amazed as when the man in the street was scandalized by the article about the monitorial system of education.[254] Thus it did not occur to the public that those articles would be able to make the people feel dissatisfied with the established form of government, and far less to instigate rebellion. When one thinks of the people, one must view the David trial from this standpoint. The government looked at this case in another light. When *Fædrelandet* was published, the government had for a long time already, so it seems, looked with dissatisfaction and fear upon the growing liberty in the writing world, which in the eyes of those in power was far more serious in character than it was in the eyes of the people, and this seems to have provoked in the government the desire one way or another to set a limit to this, in its opinion, pernicious abuse. The people thought that the spirit of the time permitted the most lenient interpretation of the law, but this certainly would not easily occur to the government. Thus the action was brought. What we here again ask the readers to keep in mind is the naturally developing opposition, since the government did not easily go over to the people's view and vice versa.

At the same time as the David trial, a court case of lesser importance was begun, in which an author was convicted of having spread a rumor. Shortly afterward, the people submitted a petition[255] to the king concerning the retention of supreme power by the law courts in cases dealing with freedom of the press. The king replied. Meanwhile the David trial was decided by the law courts, and here and elsewhere the loudest expressions of joy were heard from the people. The government, on the other hand, thought it necessary to appeal the case to the highest court.

If in the preceding historical exposition we succeeded in clearly presenting the naturally progressing opposition between government and people, then we have now come to the standpoint from which we think we are able to give a survey of the case we here wish to illuminate. We admit that what has more particularly given us occasion to write down these lines is the general dissatisfaction that has expressed itself among the public, if not against the Liberal tendency on the whole, then against particular expressions of this to be found in our Liberal papers. In saying this, we no more wish to defend a certain political creed than we want to praise unconditionally each of its expressions; but it is a certain tendency, it is a certain prominent aspect of the life of the people, we shall here strive to present in its true light. The particular complaint has been about: (1) acrimony and an unseemly tone; (2) a certain lack of honesty and openness so dear to the Dane. We declare that we are so far from blindly being worshipers of every utterance bearing the sign of the Liberal party that we, on the contrary, are often compelled to admit what was true and well founded in those complaints. But it has nevertheless been unpleasant for us daily to hear these lamentations, daily to hear much good demolished, often only because the form of utterance was weak. If it were merely one particular fashionable clique that was in despair, then it would really not be worth wasting ink or paper on the clarification of this matter. We respect such as little as we do certain young Liberals who, with cigar in mouth, puff a whole state in the air on a single cloud of smoke. If this complaint came from some of that type of people whose Liberalism or non-Liberalism rests upon the size of the office the government gives them, then one could also keep silent. But these complaints come from many straightforward, honest, and truth-loving characters. If these people had put forward their complaints positively in some book or paper, then those attacked would probably have tried to defend themselves. But this has not happened. On the whole, it looks as if our Liberals had conquered the journalistic press, and this is in many respects irreparably damaging. If our Liberals had positively put forward opinions to fight against, the truth would gain infinitely by it. But it is a fact that among us there are many who would rather go about uttering petty complaints than frankly acknowledge their views to the world. We admit that the circumstance that our Conservatives avoid the light of day must arouse reasonable doubt concerning them. If the truth is stamped on their banner, they certainly have no grounds for hiding themselves; with far greater security, with far less danger of sacrificing temporal well-being and future fortune, they can engage in battle, and yet, how seldom does it happen? —If our Conservatives themselves believe in the tenets they profess, how, then, can they tolerate that another party influences the people in a direction that is the exact opposite of the one they themselves profess? But to the point. If one holds fast the above-mentioned relation between government and people and imagines what a Liberal journalistic literature, resulting from what we have discussed here, must become, then it is easy to see how the tension occurring between government and people must provoke a fairly active opposition that does not always sweeten the bitter pill. If it had been otherwise, then one would of course have expected a more unbounded confidence in the people. It is certainly well known that the Danish government, which on the whole has such friendly relations with the people, has sometimes of late evinced a certain uneasiness and on particular occasions has shown the people faithful in the days of danger something for which one had no other name than distrust. Although this actual or presumed distrust has in the particular instance given birth to sadness rather than acrimony among many, it is still easy to explain if that which wounded many in an opposition party took on a somewhat more serious and significant appearance. It will presumably be admitted, however, that the acrimony found here is nothing in comparison with the examples to be found in foreign periodicals. But, it is replied, should one, even if that distrust is something actual, repay it with acrimony? Could we not better say what we want to in a more calm and considerate manner? —We have no objection when that happens, but if at times it does not happen thus, then let us in all this considerateness still guard ourselves well against falling asleep and talking others to sleep. It is a truth we must never forget, that where an energetic and powerful character speaks, his words acquire a special form because the thought is special; and however unimportant it may seem to many to omit a word here and there, yet one ought to consider how essential this little word, as one calls it, is for the writer, how totally and entirely the thought that lies in it lies in the individuality of the writer and how precisely this word is for him a major issue. To force upon a writer a certain form is to put a muzzle on him. —But viewed from the aspect of reality, such acrimonies are still regarded as out of place and useless because they irritate the people and irritate the government. Irritate the people—truly it would not be good if the people's confidence in the government was so poor that a single word in a daily paper incited it to rebellion. Precisely the displeasure such utterances often encounter is proof of the opposite. Never forget that whatever good emerges emerges only through a struggle; never forget that the government can err as much as the people. The government has the power, and everyone who means honestly and well by his fatherland must wish that this power be respected and obeyed; but if it has, as is human, erred in something, then it is also reasonable that another voice be heard, and the greater the power the people have given others over its weal and woe, the more natural it is also that there be a strong opposition. This press opposition—so history shows—has always been in connection with a rather strong political development, and a government that on the whole is as moderate as the Danish has truly nothing to fear from a little acrimony in a daily paper. Remember, too, that such a word acquires power only by encountering a truth that lies in the consciousness of the people, and thus it is the people themselves or what has been at work among the people that is dangerous; but it is by no means the press that is so much to be feared; it has only an arousing, not a creative, power.

One feels the absence of a certain honesty and openness. We give this charge much attention. If something clearly false and untruthful has actually been reported, then let it receive its proper stamp. Be cautious, however, in pronouncing judgment. It is well enough known that just as a veil is still kept over many branches of state administration, so also many officials are able to commit much fraud and dishonesty, and the people cannot easily acquire the necessary proofs on which to base a legal charge. The inquisitorial form of process has been removed from our judicial procedure, and this should be regarded as a good; but thereby the accuser in many instances is prevented from producing evidence even where he is most obviously right. Nevertheless, if a man is absolutely convinced that in such a case he has the truth on his side, and he feels constrained to have this truth expressed, then it is entirely natural, at least very forgivable, if by means of the press he uses a sort of circuitous route in order to have his opinion expressed. The people will understand the cry; the attacked servant of the state will understand it, and that such a truth is said in print always has something deterrent about it. This is one of the instances in which one might well dare permit oneself to walk such a circuitous route, but—this we concede—there should be only the sparsest use of it. There is also another consideration that seems essential here. Not so long ago there was an animated dispute in our literature as to whether or not we had censorship. We shall not here embark upon a dispute about legal terminology. It seems undeniable, however, that it is a great advantage that we have the law courts instead of a board of censors as the highest instance in cases dealing with freedom of the press; but on the other hand we still have one basic inconvenience in common with the countries in which censorship in the strict sense of this word has been established, and that is that an author convicted of a breach of the Freedom of the Press Ordinance loses his right to acquaint the public with that for which he was convicted. Now it might easily happen that an author became guilty according to the positive law without therefore being guilty according to the moral law, and it would be a great consolation for him if the people's consciousness gave him a moral compensation for the loss he must suffer according to the law; but since this is not so with us at the moment, it does not really seem strange to me if an author guards himself with the greatest care against every expression that could entail responsibility under the law. Yet if he has something to say concerning an action of the government and he has the inner conviction that this truth must be said in a bolder and more forceful manner than the present press law permits, then it can easily happen that an author in such circumstances seeks to find a way out and thus leaves the straight path he most wished to tread. And with that, enough about this matter.

If we thus hold fast to the fact that the change that has taken place in our entire life has provoked this tendency in our journalistic literature as fruits of a particular seed, that some action by the government can give cause for complaints, that it is this that most often gives rise to the utterances of the publicist, that these utterances only gain weight by their encountering something resting in the people's general consciousness, that the state's progress and true welfare rest upon the people's own living interest in its affairs, and if one adds that our press law sets very narrow bounds for the journalist—then we hope that these utterances will not be judged too harshly and that what is true in substance will never be forgotten because of an error in form. Let us guard ourselves against a one-sided deification of this or that party, but let us also recognize the good wherever we find it.

On the whole we have here had in mind attacks on the government, since the so-called personal attacks seem to us less important. All the same, we do not deny that a couple of times we have found such a coarse passionateness and unembarrassed crudeness in these attacks that they deserve to be banned from all literature. Yet we will maintain that every attack is more or less a personal one insofar as that which is attacked originates from a person; and the converse: when one attacks a person, one can say that one attacks an action that originates from the person. If a person is the actual cause of a bad effect, is it surprising that the attack is made upon the person and not on the action?

Note: This essay was originally meant for a restricted group in the Student Association,[256] where it was read in a somewhat different form. Several have kindly thought that it might also be of some interest to a larger public, and it is chiefly this that has moved the author to let it be printed.

Letter from Johannes A. Ostermann to Hans Peter Barfod:[257]

Frederiksborg, May 28, 1867

Your letter, received this morning, I am honored to answer at once as far as my memory permits. With regard to the Kjerkegaard [*sic*][258] lecture, you are entirely on the right track. Some of us youngsters were at that time torn out of our poetic daydreams by the movements of the time and thrown into political life, for at that time, at least among the leading group in the Student Association, still only a few were gripped by the idea. But the alpha and omega of politics at that time was freedom of the press, which was exposed to persecution from the top and to constant grumbling from the public. Under these conditions, I read my lecture[259] to a large audience. It created quite a stir, and I was at once asked to give it to Johannes Hage, who printed it unaltered in *Fædrelandet*, except that the introduction, which was jesting in form, was given serious clothing.[260] Kjerkegaard, with whom in that period, or shortly before, I was frequently together (yes, almost daily), was as little interested in politics at that time as later, but his lively intellect seized every[261] subject going, and he exercised his brilliant dialectic and wit on it without worrying himself much about the reality of the matter. That my defense found sympathy drove him into the opposite camp, where as one indifferent he also most nearly belonged. He borrowed my lecture[262] after informing the student directorate that he would "do a reading," and the manuscript found by you can hardly, yes, I can readily say, cannot possibly be other than the lecture that shortly afterward—perhaps fourteen days after me—he read in the Student Association. There was a very large audience present. They expected us to debate the issue, but for one thing I had paid only superficial attention to the reading of the lecture, and for another, as an ardent politician, I felt little desire to engage with an opponent who I knew had only slight interest in the reality of the matter. The Kjerkegaard lecture, which, as far as I recollect, was rather heavy, bore the hallmark of his individual intellectual ability and was received with great applause. —*The lecture was read*, but it was not given as a talk, for, according to the convention of the time, it would have been an impertinence and impudence to offer this to a well-informed audience. If I remember rightly, it was not until a couple of years later that by agreement with Lehmann I gave such a talk.

Schønberg's lecture,[263] if my memory has not totally betrayed me, has nothing whatever to do with the matter *quaestionis* [in question]. He was a somewhat older man, about whom I think it was said that he was a law graduate with second class honors, and one was surprised to hear that he would "do a reading." What and who he was otherwise, I cannot say, but possibly P. T. Zartmann[264] (legation counselor) knew him or remembers who he is. But, as I have said, his lecture had nothing to do with my or Kjerkegaard's debate and was probably forgotten as soon as it was heard. Perhaps it was a story from the previous century??

I have thus just about answered your questions as far as I am able to do so. If I can serve you in any other way in the future or should you wish for any other information, I shall be very glad, to the best of my power, to let you have my recollections. Perhaps I may venture to ask you to give the bishop[265] my most respectful greetings.

Yours respectfully,
J. A. Ostermann

Mr. Secretary Barfod

A Comedy in the Open Air[266]

H. C. ANDERSEN

VAUDEVILLE IN ONE ACT
BASED ON THE OLD COMEDY:
AN ACTOR AGAINST HIS WILL[267]

Characters

Frank: Bailiff to a count
Dalby: Manager of a company of traveling players, disguised as:
  Farm hand
  Hairdresser
  Scenery painter
  Poet
  Prompter
  Wardrobe mistress

[Frank, bailiff to a count, opposes the count's plan to let a company of traveling players perform on the count's estate. When Dalby, manager of the players, hears of this, he takes revenge on Frank by making him an unwitting actor in an open-air comedy in which Dalby, disguised as various characters, confuses and teases Frank. When Dalby finally reveals the true identity of the characters, Frank is entirely won over by such splendid acting.] . . .

Scene Four

Frank and Dalby the Hairdresser
Dalby: Good morning, sir! Good morning!
Frank: Good morning! Have you anything good to tell me?
Dalby: Good? So, you still believe in something good in the world! It is only the centrifugal power of reason that, by holding these outward-striving forces together, creates a

relative peace, which, however, by no means could be called a permanent being. Do you understand it?[268]

Frank: You mean you are not satisfied with the world.

Dalby: The sublimate of joy in life, the battle-won confidence in the world, yielding a life-dividend, that is to say, the verified congruence of the heart's demands and announcements with life's achievements, which is not demonstrated *ex mathematica pura* [on the basis of pure mathematics] but is made more difficult *de profundis* [out of the depths], I have not appropriated, but there is something stable in the peace that philosophy gives me.[269]

Frank: You are very unhappy?

Dalby: I am a hairdresser! These four words give you the concept that, declined in the different cases of life,[270] tells you how unhappy I must be. Our art has foundered. Where is the teeming mass of full-bottomed wigs, graceful horseshoe toupees, magnificent canon curls? Vanished! Only on the stage are these mammoth bones, these Pompeian remains of beauty from a vanished past, still dug up.

Frank: You are a theater hairdresser?

Dalby: That's what I am! As an individual depressed by the world[271] but led by philosophy to what is necessary to the existence of my peace! I am a theater hairdresser!

Frank: Yes, there, of course, you have a great field before you.

Dalby: My future there is equal to the endless screw!

Melody, *La Tarantella*

In the negative being
Was my beginning as young hairdresser;
Hegel I read, and the teaching
Intensified my mood.
The stage now became my arena.
Behold my work, both great and small:
Hair for an Anne Boleyn,
Back curls for a Cinderella,
Black locks for a Spranze,
Padding for a Pompadour,
Bag-wig for Jean de France,[272]

> Magdelone's[273] great false plait,
> For a Laïs, a Brynhilde,
> One in hearts, one in spades,
> Blonde, brown, surly, gentle,
> Even for Mrs. de Potiphar!
> Everyone's hair I correctly set,
> Everything according to time and place;
> Moneylenders and courtesans,
> Dandies, heroes, even gods!
> Mayor, warriors, and peasant,
> Excellency and student.
> For the good, for the bad,
> That to me is all the same!
> *Viva, viva,* excellent!

Frank: But what has that to do with me? Tell me what you really will with me?

Dalby: What do I will? It is one thing to will, it is another to be able! Will is often a phenomenon in the most respectable form, as it appears in Hegel's great attempt to begin with nothing.[274]

Frank: May I have the honor of telling you that I am an entirely ordinary person. I do not understand these many intricacies; they only make me go astray. Won't you state your opinion quite simply?

Dalby: So it is the manifestation-form of the words that throws you into chaos?[275]

Frank: If you would just give it to me clearly and distinctly, for otherwise I cannot have the pleasure of talking with you.

Dalby: It was from the negative element, through which and by virtue of which all the movements occur,[276] I would go; it was from the great *Tohuwabohu*[277] of thought to light and clarity; but we two cannot converse. If only this summit of our meeting would transform itself into a vanishing element in existence![278] *Dixi* [I have spoken]!

(Exit.)

Af en

endnu Levendes Papirer.

Udgivet

mod hans Villie

af

S. Kjerkegaard.

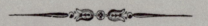

Kjøbenhavn.

Hos **C. A. Reitzel.** Trykt hos Bianco Luno.

1838.

From the

PAPERS OF ONE STILL LIVING.

———————

Published

Against His Will

by

S. Kjerkegaard.

———————

Copenhagen

Available at C. A. Reitzel's.   Printed by Bianco Luno.

———————

1838.

Draft page 1 of the Soap-Cellar drama

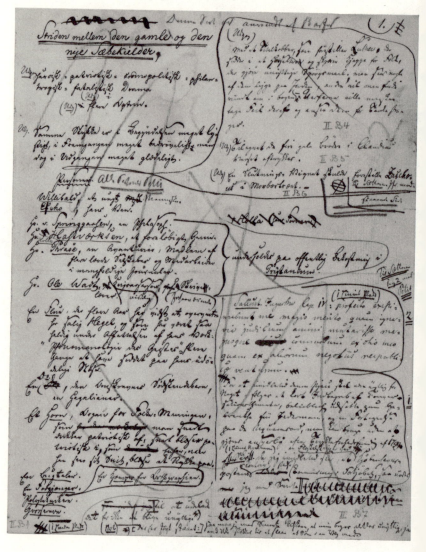

Draft page 2 of the Soap-Cellar drama

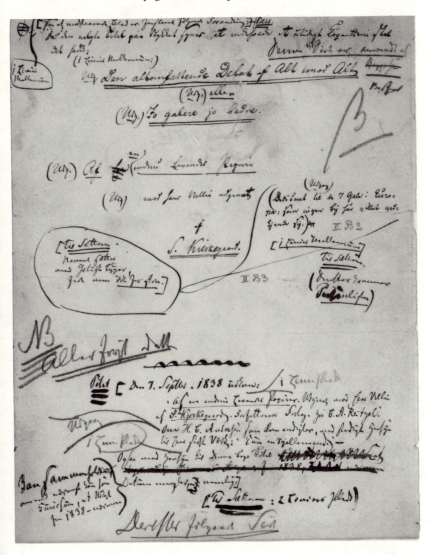

SELECTED ENTRIES FROM
KIERKEGAARD'S JOURNALS AND PAPERS
PERTAINING TO ARTICLES, ADDENDUM, AND
FROM THE PAPERS OF ONE STILL LIVING

A reply[279] provoked by the attempt of *Fædrelandet* [pp. 142-48] to refute the assertion made by me against *Kjøbenhavnsposten* [pp. 6-11].

—Pap. I B 5 *n.d.*, 1836

After this, *Kjøbenhavnsposten* ceased to reply[280] and consequently let me have the last word, but after a long time a new paper came out that called itself *Humoristiske Intelligentsblade*, edited and published by printer Jørgensen.[281] It is not yet known for certain who the author is, but it is, of course, some poet from the esthetic period of *Kjøbenhavnsposten*. The first two numbers came out simultaneously and were as good as solely directed against me and chiefly concerned themselves with the article against Hage [pp. 12-23]. Naturally, it would never occur to me to give a proper answer to these papers, because after such a long time my articles must surely be forgotten, and thus far he was both reporter and judge. I therefore merely wanted to draw out his comic side and expose his foolishness and intellectual poverty. After I had written the reply, it occurred to me, however, that it was not worth printing, because these *Intelligentsblade* had not aroused much sensation, and in the Student Association, for example—one of the few places where they were available for reading—they were regarded as so bad that not even admirers of *Kjøbenhavnsposten* ventured to praise them. No. 3 of these papers was directed against the entire *Flyvende Post*, and thus far it was not my business to reply but Heiberg's. Although it was undeniably the best of the three numbers, Heiberg declared that *they* must make a better reply if they wanted a reply from *him*.

The reply I had written went as follows:

Humoristiske Intelligentsblade, no. 1 and 2.

At Eastertime I let a barber shave my head,
The stubble that was left now rises up from fear,
And elevates my wig an inch above its place,
For who is called a sophist and shudders not thereat.[282]

Again a new opponent, again with due delay, again *Kjø-benhavnsposten* under guardianship—for the esteemed readers will surely agree with us when we see these papers in *such* an essential relationship to *Kjøbenhavnsposten* and they will be strengthened still more by the following observations. These papers have no or as good as no editor—likewise *Kjøbenhavnsposten*;[283] their spring observations match the morning ditto of *Kjøbenhavnsposten,* and their imagination, impregnated by fluids, water, and steam,[284] stands in an essential and necessary relationship to the *Post.* The esteemed readers will know that there has developed in this country not only a political, but also an esthetic, guild of dwarfs and that they are related to each other through Liunge. But since fluids in connected tubes always stand equally high,[285] from politicians we can infer esthetes. In other words, as the master is, so will the servants be; if the knight is a Don Quixote,[286] then we can know in advance what the poet and the humorist will be like. If, therefore, on a previous occasion[287] we met the honorable society in Auerbach's wine cellar, then we can be sure of meeting our humorist *there* also—and just listen to
the boisterous chorus:

I
B 6
181

> *Uns ist ganz kanibalisch wohl*
> *Als wie fünfhundert Säuen*
> [We feel so cannibally well
> Just like five hundred sows].[288]

See, this is the condition in which we must keep our humorist. Just as in the spring we see stampeding cows[289] mak-

ing short oblique gallops in the fields, with ingenious movements of their tails—a phenomenon that the experienced
farmer with deep irony explains as due to heat and gadflies—
so it is with our humorist: with springtime thoughts about
green fodder, *he* leaps round about. Now, to do the same to
him as we did on a previous occasion[290] to one of our politicians when he went berserk: fasten him on the horns of a dilemma—to tether him in this way, that we shall not do here,
and chiefly because there is no danger to the preserves of the
Flyvende Post. Since, however, this ingenious gadding about
would become somewhat monotonous, our humorist, thin
himself like those seven thin cows in Egypt,[291] has swallowed
seven fat ones without becoming thereby fatter—in other
words: our *humorist steals*. It is not only at Holberg's much-
frequented pawnshop[292] that he obtains things on credit; it is
not only from named and unnamed authors—no, it is even
from friends and from acquaintances.* But I would say to
him, "Watch your step, young man! Think what would happen if all owners distrained upon one's goods at the same time.
Remember, you are perhaps young; therefore do not in your
youth sink deeply in a debt that you will have a hard time
paying for the rest of your life.** Therefore, I will also promise
you that out of concern for you I shall not make any reply to
you, in order not to give you occasion and temptation again
to acquire so much on credit in your youth. You will misunderstand me. You will say it is an ill-timed meddling in others'
economic affairs, but I can assure you that even if you are
weak enough to misunderstand friendly advice I shall be
strong enough to do what I have once considered right."

  What in other respects will come out of the dispute, if it can
be called a dispute when the one party does not make a reply,
I do not know. But because a myth has grasped the genesis of
these papers so correctly, I shall, in the hope that with its pro-

I
B 6
182

---

  * This is why we are unable to use the measure our humorist proposed that
Mr. Hage should use on us: the cubic [p. 168]. We must use the surface measure: his writings always have length and breadth—but no depth.
  ** I hope the esteemed readers are aware that by nature *I* am in such fortunate circumstances that I can live on my *own* means.

phetic glance it has perhaps also seen correctly into the future, let it be reprinted here.

Nordens Mythologi, by Grundtvig,[293] p. 409: "For that reason the giants made themselves on *Steens-Vedd*[294] a warrior of clay and straw, fifty-four feet high and eighteen feet wide across the chest, and at long last found a horse's heart large enough for him. Yet it still could not help quaking when Thor appeared . . . . . Beside him (Hrungner) stood the clay warrior whom they called Narrifas, but he was so taken aback when he saw Thor that he staled."

*Note. Since our opponent so strongly suspects us of arrogance, and consequently the temerity to compare our situation to Thor's could possibly produce a harmful effect on him and other weak persons, I would point out that even if a Thor was needed to bring Narrifas to that necessity, there is certainly no need of any Thor to bring our humorist to it.—
—*Pap*. I B 6 *n.d.*, 1836-37

Addition to Pap. I B 5:

Something I would like to have added when I noted this down[295] but which I omitted, I must say, out of a ridiculous vanity—since I was afraid of being considered vain if I did so—is the success of both the lecture [pp. 35-52] and the articles [pp. 6-34], and I shall merely mention the fact that a paper was published (*Statsvennen*, no. 3 [pp. 149-51]) in which, in the conviction that the first article (that in no. 76 [pp. 6-11]) was by Heiberg, it was said "that he had written many witty things but never anything so witty, and that old Rahbek,[296] if he had lived, would have said that it was priceless." Next, that P. Møller,[297] also in the thought that it was by Heiberg, went after him in the street in order to thank him for it "because it was the best that had been since the *Flyvende Post*[298] had become political"—[he] did not catch up with him, however, and met E. Boesen,[299] who told him it was by me.—*Pap*. I B 7 *n.d.*, 1836-37

If Gjødwad[300] (licentiate I shall call him because he exercises so much license) is convicted, he could be called "former idol in the office of *Kjøbenhavnsposten*." —Incidentally, it will be easy for *Kjøbenhavnsposten* to get a new editor, since they engage random incarnations of Brahma—or Rosenhoff[301] could take over the paper also and become county barber with three shaving basins: *Kjøbenhavnsposten, Den Frisindede, Concordia.* —*JP* V 5312 (*Pap*. II A 728) April 15, 1838

Even if *Kjøbenhavnsposten* were published in imperial folio, this would not make it a *magna charta.*—*JP* V 5340 (*Pap*. II A 769) *n.d.*, 1838

But the Liberals have, as it says in the fairy tale,[302] a tongue and an empty head, like the tongue in a church bell.—*JP* IV 4088 (*Pap*. II A 774) *n.d.*, 1838

The story about clever Elsie[303] could be printed in its entirety—otherwise the caption could be used: What a clever Elsie we have!—*JP* IV 4089 (*Pap*. II A 775) *n.d.*, 1838

Every state, especially one that has so much of its own history as Denmark has, always . . . . .—*Pap*. II A 776 *n.d.*, 1838

Den Frisindede is related to *Kjøbenhavnsposten* the way Niels Klim's caraway kringles are related to him.[304]—*JP* V 5344 (*Pap*. II A 777) *n.d.*, 1838

Kjøbenhavnsposten is wind-warped (it twists with the wind).[305]—*JP* V 5346 (*Pap*. II A 779) *n.d.*, 1838

Precisely because politicians overlook continuity, they admit only two of the three marks of the validity of the public spirit,[306] *consensus* and *universalitas* (and even these in a rather trivial and arbitrary sense), but completely overlook the third—*antiquitas.*—*JP* IV 4090 (*Pap*. II A 783) *n.d.*, 1838

Presumably there is scarcely anyone among the gentlemen present who has not vividly experienced that in every intuition there is something, the ultimate and the best, that is so light, so ethereal, so evanescent, that it constantly disappears between the fumbling hands and, frolicking innocently, evades the searching eye—a truly inviolable *noli me tangere* [do not touch me (John 20:17)]. But just as most of you, gentlemen, have experienced how difficult it is to keep the mind free of every profane impression, you will no doubt concede that only within the true humanistic charmed circle—*procul o procul este profani* [away, away, O unhallowed ones]—I have ventured to express what every student feels and ought to feel, but which, proclaimed and trumpeted in the streets and lanes, is thereby betrayed, misunderstood, and mutilated. What better forum could I wish for, what more competent assembly, than the humanistic community: the Student Association, which, no doubt strict and incorruptible in its judgment, also possesses what to me is most important, that intellectual ear which with creative sympathy gives the words the inexpressible fullness they have in the speaker's breast but not upon his lips.—*JP* V 5115 (*Pap.* I B 1) *n.d.*, 1835

An esthetic thought-bridle on Knight Andersen's wild hunt through the shadowed valley of self-contradiction.[307]—*JP* V 5339 (*Pap.* II A 768) *n.d.*, 1838

My position is *armed neutrality*.[308]—*JP* V 5341 (*Pap.* II A 770) *n.d.*, 1838

> Sir Knight, so many from the ladder fell down,
> But open and broad is the *churchyard* [*Kirkegaard*] way.
>   eia! eia! eia!
>   eia! eia! eia![309]
>   —*JP* V 5342 (*Pap.* II A 771) *n.d.*, 1838

Take off your shoes, for the place where you are standing is holy.[310] . . . . . It does not help, of course, that many of them are—trouserless.—*JP* V 5343 (*Pap.* II A 772) *n.d.*, 1838

I shall advise them to answer soon *sub poena praeclusi et per-petui silentii.*[311]—*Pap.* II A 773 *n.d.,* 1838

There are many means of self-defense. It is well known that the musk ox exudes such a strong odor that no one can come near it.—*JP* V 5345 (*Pap.* II A 778) *n.d.,* 1838

One must be careful with my preface, for the same thing happens to it as happened to the treasure:

> but if you say one word
> it disappears again.
>
> Oehlenschlaeger's *"Skattegraveren"*[312]
> —*JP* V 5347 (*Pap.* II A 780) *n.d.,* 1838

But Andersen is not so dangerous, after all; from what I have experienced, his main strength is an auxiliary chorus of volunteer arrangers and invitation distributors, a few vagabond esthetes, who perpetually protest their honesty, and this much is certain, they can by no means be charged with any *reservatio mentalis* [mental reservation], for they have absolutely nothing *in mente* [in mind].—*JP* V 5348 (*Pap.* II A 781) *n.d.,* 1838

My witticisms, he says, are far-fetched; his are not—they are culls.[313]—*JP* V 5349 (*Pap.* II A 782) *n.d.,* 1838

However the conflict goes, I will still merely ask the god of war not to saddle me with

> One of those street girls
> Who at once dances attendance
> When a Josiah whistles.[314]
> —*Pap.* II A 784 *n.d.,* 1838

Come out here, Wolle-Petersen, or oi'll fetch 'ee and then the ribs'll start groaning.

See the place in Claudius;[315] the place is marked.— —*Pap.* II A 785 *n.d.*, 1838

Just a Moment, Mr. Andersen![316]

It is said of Till Eulenspiegel[317] that he was sent to town by his mistress to fetch four shillings'[318] worth of vinegar. He was away for nearly three years. Toward the end of the third year, he came charging in at the door, broke the flask to pieces, spilled the vinegar, and cried: The devil created haste. In almost the same way, Mr. Andersen, to my not inconsiderable fright, has come charging into the literary world with four shillings' worth of polemic, which he presumably has carefully collected in the two years that have passed since I had that unfortunate idea that is now being punished so hard.

But first a couple pieces of historical information that will be absolutely essential for the reading public, since at this moment I am unable to write about the poet Andersen, famous throughout Europe, who will soon start out on his triumphal tour, without touching upon my own insignificant personage. I take it for granted that the public has long since forgotten or rather perhaps has never known that in the year 1838 I published a little piece[319] in which, according to my abilities, I strove to capture the spotted and motley Andersenian poet-existence in all its bendings, twinings, turnings, twistings, grimacings. —In the summer of 1840,[320] a piece was performed at the Royal Theater called *En Comedie i det Grønne* [A Comedy in the Open Air].[321] I probably do not need to remind readers about this, for the piece was by Andersen. During that very same summer, however, rather important work prevented me from keeping up with the latest literary productions, and in my isolated existence [*Existents*] I would perhaps have remained ignorant of the existence [*Tilværelse*] of this piece had not a couple of acquaintances, perhaps out of interest in me, or more likely out of interest in the comic and in order to rejoice over my embarrassment, told me it existed, indeed, that Andersen—that is just the point—had put in the mouth of one of the characters whole long screeds from my little piece! This was too much. Everything went black. I could not, however, restrain the desire for further particulars about how Andersen had quoted me. I had hoped that the theater management would have bought the piece from Andersen—and, inconceivably, in truth, inconceivably, when this did not happen, the obvious never occurred to me at all at the time, that I could have bought it and given it to the theater management, that is, if it wanted it, in order if possible to gain some merit from the fine arts, in order if possible to provide proof that at least some people know how to value a poet.

But what happens—my desire was to be fulfilled in another way, and that precisely when I more and more began to give it up because I knew that Andersen's departure[322] approached at a rapid pace. I sank into a quiet sadness. I thought to myself: Now Andersen is going away, perhaps to Trebizond or to blazes to R . . . . . ;[323] who knows whether he will ever return, and yet we lack this little piece and in it perhaps a very large contribution to a sketch of his character. I had already thought that through the papers I would request him to publish it, and just as one often reads that a visiting family requests the theater management to perform a piece, so as a resident of this city I thought myself equally justified in requesting the departing Andersen to remedy and relieve a long-felt want by publishing this dramatic work. Yet it was perhaps good that I did not do it. The piece would probably have lost some of the surprise, some of the fragrance, that it keeps when one knows that no temporal or earthly consideration has called it into the world, except "poetry's own deep inner urge."[324] What even more caused me to wish that this piece would be published was that I hoped possibly to find in it a profounder explanation of one or two things that were not absolutely clear to me at the moment when I wrote them down.

But alas! alas! alas! How unfortunate we human beings are. Even in Andersen I sought it—in vain. Gone were my poetic dreams. My soul was gripped by a secret apprehension that there could have been another reason why the theater did not accept it and by a quiet fear that the reason for its coming out now could be other than the categorical imperative of genius.

III
B 1
107

I shall dwell especially on the last point. The poet Holst,[325] perhaps through external circumstances beyond the assailant's control, a few days before his departure became the object of an attack,[326] which just because of the unfavorable circumstances prevailing at the time aroused displeasure with the author. —The case with me is different. A few days before Andersen's departure, I became the object of an attack (that I was already attacked in the summer, I could not know with absolute certainty, because the pieces of information sounded extremely mysterious; consequently, I could not possibly reply and must therefore regard the entire Andersen machination as an empty gesture). He has probably already gone to order himself a pair of shoes with chamois leather soles[327] that will last the journey, and before one knows a word about it perhaps he has gone.

Yet back to the point. In this comedy, theater manager Dalby[328] appears in several roles, among others also as a hairdresser. I am dealing only with this performance. This character is meant to be a prating Hegelian. Now, if I were to say to Andersen that *I* have *never* passed myself off as a Hegelian and thus far it was *foolish* of Andersen to take sentences from my little piece and put them in the mouth of a Hegelian, then I would almost think myself crazy. For *either* I would have to associate with the word "Hegelian" the idea of a man who with seriousness and energy had grasped the world-view of this thought, had dedicated himself to it, found rest in it, and now with a certain genuine pride said of himself: I, too, have had the honor of serving under Hegel—and in this case it would be crazy of me to say it in a conversation with Andersen, because *he* probably would not be able to attach a sensible thought to it, just as I would at least hesitate to use such a significant predicate about myself, even if I were conscious that I had tried to make myself familiar with Hegel's philosophy. *Or* by a Hegelian I would understand a person who, superficially influenced by this thought, now deceived himself with a result he did not possess—and then it would be no less foolish to say this to Andersen, provided one agrees with me that the person who does not know what a Hegelian is in truth

III
B 1
108

does not know what a Hegelian is in his untruth, either, that is, can have no concrete idea on the subject.

On the other hand, in all possible conciliatory spirit, I shall inform Andersen of an advantage he possesses without perhaps really knowing that he possesses it or to what extent he possesses it. When, namely, one wants to put some nonsense in a character's mouth, for the creative writer (not entirely so for the reader) it can be achieved in two ways, either—by virtue of reason and with its superiority—one looks down into the foggy realm of nonsense, or one takes something one does not understand and silently draws the conclusion: When *I* do not understand it, it is nonsense (I say "silently," for it is not always advisable to hint this aloud), and thereupon copies or rather draws it, which, of course, *those* who have to copy anything they do not understand must always do. In this respect, I willingly grant Andersen the advantage over any poet now living, and I congratulate him on the vast scholarly common that stretches out before his gaze, and I merely wonder that he has wanted to select my poor small holding, *he*, poet Andersen, the monopolized negative owner of all philosophy and all higher scholarship, their master in the same sense "as tramps call themselves masters of palaces."[329]

But someone who has heard or read this comedy may say: Are the words Andersen puts in the mouth of this hairdresser actual quotations? I find this question the most natural one in the world, for it is only Andersen who—so enormously flattering for me—has remained convinced that the reading and play-going public not only have read my little piece but have *not forgotten* it in two years. And truly the flattery is sweet in my mouth, sweeter than honey, for I know nothing sweeter than when someone flatters *against* his will. —Yet my momentarily exiled intellect has returned again, and I indeed realize that there must be a misunderstanding here, and Andersen, perhaps believing with some displeasure that I have wanted to attach myself to his immortality with this little piece, has wanted to assure me of the impossibility of being forgotten at any moment. That the words are actually quotations can be difficult for me to prove to the reader, because, of

III
B 1
109

course, he does not have my piece at hand, but I can assure him that, for example, the lines "the sublimate of joy in life" etc.,[330] to be found on p. 3, col. 1,[331] are reprinted verbatim, and that the only indication that Andersen has wanted to make it his property, which to the finer observers of Andersen is not unfortunate, is that *he* writes mathematics without an *h*.

This must be enough for now.

III
B 1
110 Should Andersen wish to continue this dispute, then in order not to burden the papers with my insignificant scribblings, I would suggest to him that we publish a paper together, and in order to have nothing to reproach myself with through causing him expense, I will gladly defray the costs, and all the more since, of course, according to our administration of justice the loser is always sentenced to pay the legal costs. I ask but one thing of him, that as compensation for his having had two years for his first contribution he will at least let his reply come early enough before his departure for me to have a few hours for my counter-reply, and he can then have it before his departure—for the matter is not of the kind that I would care to write about when Andersen has left Copenhagen.[332]—*Pap*. III B 1 *n.d.*, 1840

EDITORIAL APPENDIX

ACKNOWLEDGMENTS

Preparation of manuscripts for *Kierkegaard's Writings* is supported by a genuinely enabling grant from the National Endowment for the Humanities. The grant includes gifts from the Dronning Margrethe og Prins Henrik Fond, the Danish Ministry of Cultural Affairs, the Augustinus Fond, the Carlsberg Fond, and the Lutheran Brotherhood Foundation.

The translator-editor is indebted to the late Gregor Malantschuk and to Grethe Kjær for their knowledgeable observations on crucial concepts and terminology. The translator acknowledges a special debt of gratitude to Grethe Kjær for her detailed criticism of the manuscript and gives special thanks to Minna Cannon, who helped with an earlier version of *From the Papers of One Still Living*, and to Teddy Petersen for permission to utilize his notes.

John Elrod, Per Lønning, Sophia Scopetéa, and General Editor Howard Hong, members of the International Advisory Board for *Kierkegaard's Writings*, have given valuable criticism of the manuscript on the whole and in detail. Catherine Gjerdingen has helpfully read the manuscript. Kathryn Hong, associate editor for *KW*, Kierkegaard Library, scrutinized the manuscript. She and assistant editor Regine Prenzel-Guthrie reviewed the page proofs and prepared the index.

Acknowledgment is made to Gyldendals Forlag for permission to absorb notes to *Søren Kierkegaards samlede Værker*.

Inclusion in the Supplement of entries from *Søren Kierkegaard's Journals and Papers* is by arrangement with Indiana University Press.

The book collection and facilities of the Department of Søren Kierkegaard Research, Copenhagen University, have been used in preparation of the translation. The book collection and the microfilm collection of the Kierkegaard Library, St. Olaf College, have been used in checking the Kierkegaard texts and in the preparation of the notes. The Royal Library, Copenhagen, has provided photographs of selected manuscript pages.

The original manuscript was typed by Dorothy Bolton. Word processing of the final manuscript was done by Kennedy Lemke and Francesca Lane Rasmus. The volume has been guided through the press by Cathie Brettschneider.

COLLATION OF THE ARTICLES
IN THE DANISH EDITIONS OF KIERKEGAARD'S
COLLECTED WORKS

Vol. XIII *Ed. 1* *Pg.*	*Vol. XIII* *Ed. 2* *Pg.*	*Vol. XIII* *Ed. 1* *Pg.*	*Vol. XIII* *Ed. 2* *Pg.*
5	11	23	28
6	11	24	29
7	12	25	30
8	13	26	31
9	14	27	32
10	14	28	33
11	15	29	34
12	16	30	35
13	17	31	35
14	18	32	36
15	19	33	37
16	21	34	38
17	22	35	39
18	23	36	41
19	24	37	42
20	25	38	43
21	26	39	44
22	27		

COLLATION OF
FROM THE PAPERS OF ONE STILL LIVING
IN THE DANISH EDITIONS OF KIERKEGAARD'S
COLLECTED WORKS

Vol. XIII Ed. 1 Pg.	*Vol. XIII* Ed. 2 Pg.	*Vol. 1* Ed. 3 Pg.	*Vol. XIII* Ed. 1 Pg.	*Vol. XIII* Ed. 2 Pg.	*Vol. 1* Ed. 3 Pg.
iii	v	13	70	75	36
iv	v	13	71	75	37
v	vii	14	72	77	38
vi	viii	14	73	78	39
vii	ix	15	74	79	40
50	x	17	75	80	41
51	xi	19	76	81	41
53	57	21	77	82	42
54	57	21	78	83	43
55	59	22	79	85	44
56	60	23	80	86	45
57	61	24	81	87	46
58	62	25	82	88	47
59	63	26	83	89	48
60	64	27	84	90	49
61	65	28	85	91	50
62	66	29	86	92	51
63	67	30	87	93	52
64	68	30	88	94	53
65	69	31	89	96	54
66	70	32	90	97	55
67	71	33	91	98	55
68	72	34	92	99	56
69	73	35			

NOTES

1. *"Ogsaa et Forsvar for Qvindens høie Anlæg,"* Kjøbenhavns flyvende Post, *Interimsblad,* 34, December 17, 1834, col. 4-6.

2. P.E. [Peter Engel Lind], *"Qvindens høiere Oprindelse forsvaret,"* Kjøbenhavns flyvende Post, Interimsblad, 33, December 4, 1834, col. 5-7. See Supplement, pp. 131-33.

3. See note 15 below.

4. See Genesis 3:1-6.

5. Beds were surrounded by hangings or curtains, hence these names for nocturnal discussions or unilateral lectures.

6. Socrates' nagging wife, about whom many stories were current in antiquity. See, for example, Diogenes Laertius, *Lives of Eminent Philosophers,* II, 36-37; *Diogenis Laertii De vitis philosophorum,* I-II (Leipzig: 1833; *ASKB* 1109), I, pp. 77-78; *Diogen Laërtses filosofiske Historier,* I-II, tr. Børge Riisbrigh (Copenhagen: 1812; *ASKB* 1110-11), I, pp. 72-73; *Lives of Eminent Philosophers,* I-II, tr. R. D. Hicks (Loeb, Cambridge: Harvard University Press, 1979-80), I, p. 167:

> When Xanthippe first scolded him and then drenched him with water, his rejoinder was, "Did I not say that Xanthippe's thunder would end in rain?" When Alcibiades declared that the scolding of Xanthippe was intolerable, "Nay, I have got used to it," said he, "as to the continued rattle of a windlass. And you do not mind the cackle of geese." "No," replied Alcibiades, "but they furnish me with eggs and goslings." "And Xanthippe," said Socrates, "is the mother of my children." When she tore his coat off his back in the market-place and his acquaintances advised him to hit back, "Yes, by Zeus," said he, "in order that while we are sparring each of you may join in with 'Go it, Socrates!' 'Well done, Xanthippe!' " He said he lived with a shrew, as horsemen are fond of spirited horses, "but just as, when they have mastered these, they can easily cope with the rest, so I in the society of Xanthippe shall learn to adapt myself to the rest of the world."

7. See I Corinthians 14:34.

8. In Paris, on November 10, 1793, a low actress-dancer represented the cult of reason at a festival starting in Notre Dame Cathedral. During the next few months, similar festivals were celebrated all over France. See Karl Friedrich Becker, *Verdenshistorie,* I-XII, tr. Jacob Riise (Copenhagen: 1822-29; *ASKB* 1972-83), XI, pp. 532-34. See also *JP* IV 4080; V 5638 (*Pap.* II A 219; IV A 74); *Pap.* VIII¹ A 419; X⁶ B 251, p. 415.

9. Adherents of the socialistic doctrine of the French count Claude Henri de Saint-Simon (1760-1825). See *Irony*, p. 328, *KW* II (*SV* XIII 392). *Kjøbenhavnsposten*, 290, December 9, 1830, p. 968, and 291, December 10, 1830, pp. 970-72, had already mentioned the Saint-Simonists in the year when the movement was at its strongest. Besides the demand for total equality and liberation for women, certain elements in the movement awaited a female Messiah and claimed that God was both masculine and feminine. By 1833, the movement had collapsed. See Teddy Petersen, *Kierkegaards polemiske debut* (Odense: Odense Universitetsforlag, 1977), pp. 26-28.

10. Probably a reference especially to Thomasine C. Gyllembourg-Ehrensvärd (1773-1856), mother of Johan Ludvig Heiberg and anonymous author of *Familien Polonius* (1827), *En Hverdags-Historie* (1828), and *Slægtskab og Djævelskab* (1830), all first published in *Kjøbenhavns flyvende Post*. Kierkegaard praises her authorship in *From the Papers* (see pp. 65-69) and was to write an enthusiastic review of her latest work, *To Tidsalder* (1845), in *Two Ages: The Age of Revolution and the Present Age, A Literary Review*, *KW* XIV (*SV* VIII 1-105). When *Kjøbenhavns flyvende Post* stopped at the end of 1830, she tried her hand as a dramatist, but one of her four plays (all four published by Heiberg, with his preface, as *Skuespil af Forfatteren til "En Hverdags-Historie"* [Copenhagen: 1834]), *Fregatskibet Svanen*, had bigamy as its central theme and for that reason was rejected by the Royal Theater. For Heiberg's correspondence (March 1832) with Jakob Peter Mynster about the play, see *Breve fra og til Johan Ludvig Heiberg* (Copenhagen: 1862), pp. 145-51.

11. Probably Hanna Irgens, *Orfanina, Digtninger* (Copenhagen: 1822), pp. 113-37. Poul Martin Møller reviewed this work negatively in *Dansk Litteratur-Tidende*, 33, 1824, pp. 513-22, esp. pp. 520-22; Poul Martin Møller, *Efterladte Papirer*, I-III (Copenhagen: 1839-43; *ASKB* 1574-75), II, pp. 28-33, esp. pp. 31-33.

12. *Christiane Rosens Oeconomisk Huusholdning-Bog*, I-II (Copenhagen: 1818).

13. A former cure for scurf involving the use of a cap smeared inside with pitch. When the pitch was dry, the cap was torn off to remove the scurf scabs. Permission to practice this cure was sometimes given to midwives and other lay medical helpers. See, for example, *Supplement-bind til "Bibliothek for Læger"* (1867), *Det kongelige Sundheds-kollegiums Aarsberetning for 1867*, ed. Frederik Wilhelm Theodor Bricka (Copenhagen: 1868), pp. 199-202.

14. Possibly Mariane Frederikke Stub (1790-1842), who in 1822-23 and 1826-30 exhibited several pictures of angels, cherubs, idealized women's heads, etc. at the Charlottenborg Gallery, Copenhagen. Her brother was the better-known artist Christian Gottlieb Kratzenstein Stub (1783-1816).

15. Almost certainly aimed at the series of introductory lectures on philosophy offered by J. L. Heiberg in the spring of 1833, when he took the unusual step of inviting women as well as men to attend. Because of insufficient interest (and only two women signed up), the lectures never took place. In his program *Om Philosophiens Betydning for den nuværende Tid* (Copenhagen: 1833;

ASKB 568), p. 53 (ed. tr.), Heiberg says that "in a series of lectures he will be able to present an *introduction to philosophy* intelligible to all *educated* people. Yes, this hope is indeed so living for him that he does not even assume that he need restrict himself to a lecture for *men* but ventures to think that educated *women* also, gracing the gathering with their presence, will be able to participate in the lecture's serious investigations. Although men usually have a sharper and more consistent reason, a greater capacity for dialectic, women usually have a surer, more infallible feeling for immediately grasping truth, for seeing, undisturbed by any finite considerations, the infinite in which these rest, the unity in which these have their being, and the author regards the one ability as being just as effective for knowledge as the other."

16. Heroic lovers of Danish legend. See Jacob Bernt Møinichen, *Nordiske Folks Overtroe, Guder, Fabler og Helte* (Copenhagen: 1800; *ASKB* 1947), pp. 199-202. See also Adam Gottlob Oehlenschläger, *Hagbarth og Signe* (1814), *Oehlenschlägers Tragødier*, I-X (Copenhagen: 1841-49; *ASKB* 1601-05 [I-IX]), II, pp. 1-104.

17. See Horace, *Odes*, II, 20, 10-11. *Q. Horatii Flacci opera* (Leipzig: 1828; *ASKB* 1248), p. 142; *Horace The Odes and Epodes*, tr. C. E. Bennett (Loeb, Cambridge: Harvard University Press, 1978), p. 165: "I am changing to a snowy swan above." In his article (see Supplement, p. 131), P. E. Lind had said that woman's "light clothing, gait, and manner of speech suggest an imprisoned soul on the point of spreading its wings to fly away." For a picture of women's balloon-sleeved dresses in 1835, see Jacob Davidsen, *Fra det gamle Kongens Kjøbenhavn*, I-II (Copenhagen: 1880-81), II, p. 215.

18. See Exodus 16:3.

19. "Snowdrop and winter fool [*Sommergæk og Vinternar*]" was the first line of one form of a verse sent anonymously to a friend before Easter. The letter (*Gækkebrev*, letter that fools or deceives) also contained a snowdrop and was clipped or pricked in various patterns. The receiver had to guess the name of the sender before Easter. The custom continues to the present day.

20. See the conclusion of Kierkegaard's newspaper articles "The Morning Observations in *Kjøbenhavnsposten* No. 43" (p. 11) and "On the Polemic of *Fædrelandet*" (p. 23), where he uses the pseudonym B. The pseudonyms A and B were to appear again with the papers of A and B in *Either/Or*, I-II, *KW* III-IV (*SV* I-II).

21. *"Kjøbenhavnspostens Morgenbetragtninger i Nr. 43,"* *Kjøbenhavns flyvende Post, Interimsblad*, 76, February 18, 1836, col. 1-6, was a reply to an article *"Trykkefrihedssagen V,"* *Kjøbenhavnsposten*, 43, February 12, 1836, pp. 169-72, which was anonymous but almost certainly written by Orla Lehmann. See Supplement, pp. 134-41. It also seems certain that Lehmann was author of the preceding four sections of the same article (see Petersen, *Debut*, pp. 158-59). Kierkegaard's title alludes to Lehmann's phrase "dawn of the life and freedom of the people." See Supplement, p. 135.

22. From Dick's song in Act I of *Ludlams Hule*, a musical by Adam Oehlenschläger (Copenhagen: 1814, printed December 1813), pp. 6-7. The mu-

sical, with music by Christoph Ernst Friedrich Weyse (1774-1842), had its premiere on January 30, 1816. The song tells of Peter Trimp, who borrowed a soup-kettle for his wedding feast from Mother Ludlam's cave. He forfeited his life through failure to return it by the promised date. Kierkegaard uses this verse to indicate that in regard to its various statements *Kjøbenhavnsposten* suffers from the same cheerful heedlessness as Peter Trimp. Also hidden in the use of this verse is a dig at Orla Lehmann, whose first name was Peter.

23. *Kjøbenhavnsposten*, 43, p. 169, col. 2: "It is this dawn of the life and freedom of the people in which we find ourselves at the moment." The above translation and all subsequent translations of quotations from various Danish publications are ed. tr. See Supplement, p. 135.

24. *Kjøbenhavnsposten*, 43, p. 169, col. 2: "this [public spirit] . . . is still in its early childhood." See Supplement, p. 135.

25. *Kjøbenhavnsposten*, 43, p. 170, col. 1: "a certain sentimental-idyllic mood had spread over the people, probably a natural consequence of the universal faintheartedness, but hardly at all matching the serious reforming spirit one otherwise regards as the salient feature of our time." See Supplement, p. 136.

26. *Kjøbenhavnsposten*, 43, p. 169, col. 1: "this accusation . . . has been almost entirely dropped." See Supplement, p. 134.

27. *Kjøbenhavnsposten*, 43, p. 171, col. 1: "But is, then, the press entirely guiltless? Has it not committed any error? —But, good Lord, who has made this assertion, and, we add, who thinks himself entitled to make such a claim? Here below where everything is imperfect, how could *this* alone be perfect?" See Supplement, p. 139.

28. *Politivennen*, 1046, January 16, 1836, pp. 33-36. *Politivennen* was a weekly domestic paper begun in 1798 by Klaus Henrik Seidelin (1761-1811). Its aim was to investigate the rights and wrongs of police matters, but it also attacked local social abuses and exposed faults in the establishment generally. *Politivennen* ran very successfully until Seidelin's death, but under Kristen Kristensen (1777-1849), who successfully restarted the paper in 1816, its tone and coverage improved. It became very widely read and respected, a favorite with the king, who intervened in many cases of hardship mentioned in its pages. During the 1830s, *Politivennen* declined through competition and political change. Kristensen gave up the paper (1842), and after several changes of editor and a change of name it finally joined the gutter press and perished in 1846 under horsedealer Michael Leonhard Nathanson (see *The Corsair Affair and Articles Related to the Writings*, pp. 287-88, note 79, *KW* XIII).

29. *Kjøbenhavnsposten*, 43, p. 169, col. 2: "quite natural, we could almost say necessary." See Supplement, p. 136.

30. *Kjøbenhavnsposten*, 43, pp. 170-71, col. 2-1: "We can well account for it, we said—No! It is impossible, impossible that any honest soul can seriously think of his time of degradation or this *misère générale* [general distress] without contrition and pain, impossible that anyone can look upon the seriousness and honesty with which everything now is striving forward without looking

with joy and gladness into the future that one day will harvest what the present sows." See Supplement, p. 138.

31. See note 25 above. Steen Steensen Blicher, in his patriotic essay, *"Danmarks nærværende Tilstand"* (1828), *Samlede Skrifter*, I-XXXIII (Copenhagen: 1920-34), XIII, p. 178, had praised the Danish form of government as "patriarchal" and the king as good father. C.G.N. David (see p. xx and note 51) attacked Blicher's idyllic description of the state of the country in a review in *Maanedsskrift for Litteratur*, I, 1829, pp. 11-19.

32. *Kjøbenhavnsposten*, 43, p. 170, col. 1, a description of patriotic songs and the like from the period under discussion. See Supplement, p. 137.

33. Possibly *Fædrelandet*.

34. See Miguel de Cervantes Saavedra, *Don Quixote af Mancha Levnet og Bedrifter*, I-IV, tr. Charlotta D. Biehl (Copenhagen: 1776-77; *ASKB* 1937-40), ch. XXXV, II, pp. 215-16; *Don Quixote*, tr. Samuel Putnam (New York: Modern Library, 1949), pp. 314-15. While dreaming that he is fighting a giant, Don Quixote attacks some wineskins with his sword.

35. *Kjøbenhavnsposten*, 43, p. 171, col. 2: "After rain, sunshine—this is the eternal order of nature. If reproaches rain down on the press—then it must put up its umbrella until the sun shines again, and if a thunderstorm is in the offing, then it goes into a gateway until the bad weather is over." See Supplement, p. 141.

36. *Kjøbenhavnsposten*, 25, January 25, 1836, p. 100, col. 2, has, for example, in its list of errors: "lying, read: flying." See *Kjøbenhavnsposten*, 23, January 23, 1836, p. 92, col. 2: "That we shall not enter into the lying *Post*'s polemic, which is as ignorant as it is low, needs no apology."

37. See p. xix and note 49.

38. *Kjøbenhavnsposten*, 43, p. 169, col. 1: "especially since the Ordinance of 1799." See Historical Introduction, p. x; Supplement, p. 134.

39. *Kjøbenhavnsposten*, 43, p. 170, col. 1: "On the whole, however, this barrel-organ music begins to go out of fashion, for the people's entire way of life has taken a far more dignified, more serious, and more positive direction." See Supplement, p. 137.

40. See p. 6 and note 26 above. *Kjøbenhavnsposten* is misquoted in both places.

41. See p. 7 and note 29 above.

42. *Kjøbenhavnsposten*, 43, p. 171, col. 1. See Supplement, p. 139.

43. *Kjøbenhavnsposten*, 43, p. 170, col. 2: "when one was so well satisfied with everything, when everyone took care of his own business and let the government take care of the rest." See Supplement, p. 138.

44. *Kjøbenhavnsposten*, 43, p. 170, col. 1: "We were like children who sing in the dark in order to banish or at least drown their anxiety." See Supplement, p. 136.

45. *Kjøbenhavnsposten*, 43, p. 170, col. 1: "The less satisfactory the state of the country, the more eager one became to impute to it falsely the lacking glory." See Supplement, p. 136.

46. *Kjøbenhavnsposten*, 43, p. 169, col. 1: "While domestic cares thus weighed down the people's courage . . . the exhausted people now sought consolation." See Supplement, p. 134.

47. *Kjøbenhavnsposten*, 43, p. 170, col. 2: "when one went on picnics or to comedies, rejoiced over every forget-me-not one found in Danavang." "Danavang" is a poetic name for Denmark; cf. "Albion" or "Columbia." See Supplement, p. 138.

48. See Genesis 19:26.

49. In that year Oehlenschläger had published a volume of poems, *Digte* (Copenhagen: 1803).

50. See p. xix and note 49.

51. *Kjøbenhavnsposten*, 43, p. 170, col. 2. See Supplement, p. 138.

52. *Kjøbenhavnsposten*, 43, p. 169, col. 1: "It was acrimony we were talking about last time." See note 26 above; Supplement, p. 134.

53. *Kjøbenhavnsposten*, 43, p. 171, col. 2. See Supplement, p. 140.

54. *Kjøbenhavnsposten*, 43, p. 170, col. 2: "and those whose ear was accustomed to perpetual hymns find it both unesthetic and tone-deaf to speak of making the national finances public and of the abolition of villeinage." See Supplement, p. 137.

55. See note 35 above.

56. I.e., Grete, in J. H. Wessel's play *Kierlighed uden Strømper*, *Johan Herman Wessel's samtlige Skrivter*, I-II (Copenhagen: 1787), I, p. 89 (ed. tr.):

Mads: Madam, there stands a thief.
Grete: There stands a hero, traitor [*Forræder*].
Mads: I say now as before, Madam, there
stands a tailor [*Skrædder*].

57. Breath [*Aandedrag*], a possible play on "reforming spirit" [*Reformations Aand*].

58. See Genesis 3:1-19.

59. See Exodus 4.

60. Daniel O'Connell (1775-1847), the Irish "Liberator," famous Catholic orator and politician active in Ireland in the period 1805-45.

61. See p. xix and note 49. Although Liunge was formally editor in this period, Giødwad and Lehmann constituted the real power behind the throne. Liunge was one of J. L. Heiberg's pet aversions.

62. Johann Wolfgang v. Goethe, *Faust*, 2313-2336, *Goethe's Werke. Vollständige Ausgabe letzter Hand*, I-LX (Stuttgart, Tübingen: 1828-33; *ASKB* 1641-68 [I-LV]), XII, pp. 117-18; *Faust*, tr. Bayard Taylor (New York: Random House, 1950), p. 83. In Auerbach's cellar, Mephistopheles makes the drinkers believe that they are walking through a vineyard. When they grasp the grapes in order to cut them, they discover that instead of grapes they are really holding one another by the nose.

63. Mimed movements.

64. *Kjøbenhavnsposten*, 43, p. 171, col. 1: "then one must rejoice over the more forceful style our press is beginning to use." See Supplement, p. 139.

65. *Kjøbenhavnsposten*, 43, p. 170, col. 2: "It was a jolly time, when privateering went with a vengeance, when one could get a hundred-dollar bill for a specie [2 rix-dollars] and a royal bond for a score of dollars." See Supplement, p. 138.

66. See Supplement, p. 134.

67. See p. 8 and note 35.

68. See note 30 above.

69. An old schoolmaster in Nordrup near Ringsted, Sjælland. In several articles, *Kjøbenhavnsposten* denounced the circumstances surrounding his forced retirement as unjust and opened a subscription fund for him. See *Kjøbenhavnsposten*, 304, December 10, 1835, pp. 1213-15; 7, January 7, 1836, pp. 25, 27; 9, January 9, 1836, p. 36; 30, January 30, 1836, p. 120.

70. See note 20 above.

71. *Kjøbenhavns flyvende Post, Interimsblad*, 82, March 12, 1836, col. 1-8, and 83, March 15, 1836, col. 1-4, a reply to *"Om Flyvepostens Polemik,"* by editor Johannes Hage, *Fædrelandet*, 77, March 4, 1836, col. 633-47. See Supplement, p. 142. Barfod (*Eft. Pap.*, I, p. 101, ed. tr.) gives J. L. Heiberg's reply to Kierkegaard's request for extra copies:

Enclosed six extra copies of the *Flyvende Post*, no. 82 & 83. I suppose you know already from Mr. Langhoff that the delay is not my fault.

Once more, my thanks for your essay. It has pleased me even more on the fresh reading.

March 16, 1836.

Respectfully,
J. L. Heiberg

See also *Letters*, Letter 6, *KW* XXV.

72. Mozart, *Figaros Givtermaal eller Den gale Dag*, tr. Niels Thoroup Bruun (Copenhagen: 1817), I, 2, p. 12. Kierkegaard makes three unimportant deviations from the text. Cf. *The Marriage of Figaro*, tr. Edward J. Dent (New York: Riverrun, 1983), p. 52.

73. See Supplement, p. 148.

74. *Fædrelandet*, 77, col. 633-42 (see Supplement, p. 142 and note 50) contains a factual polemic against an article on the budget, *"Om Budgetten,"* *Kjøbenhavns flyvende Post, Interimsblad*, 65, December 11, 1835, col. 1-8, 66, December 15, 1835, col. 1-5. This article, *"Fra en Mand paa Landet,"* is pseudonymous: x. See also *"Et Par Bemærkninger angaaende Ugebladet 'Fædrelandet' "* (anonymous), 71-73, January 27, 30, February 3, 1836.

75. Three articles, *"Nogle Bemærkninger om de saakaldte 'liberale' Journalister i Danmark,"* by 1234 (possibly P. V. Jacobsen, a member of J. L. Heiberg's circle), *Kjøbenhavns flyvende Post, Interimsblad*, 75, February 16, 1836, col. 1-6; 78, February 22, 1836, col. 1-5; 79, February 26, 1836, col. 1-5. *Fædrelandet*,

77, col. 644-46 (see Supplement, pp. 145-47), refutes these articles, although not without some approval.

76. See note 130 below.

77. *Dagen*, a conservative newspaper begun in 1803 by Klaus Henrik Seidelin, founder of *Politivennen* (see p. 7 and note 28). Originally published four times weekly, in 1811 it became a daily paper and also acquired the right to print foreign political news, of which for a long time it was the most important source. It reached the peak of its importance and popularity in the period 1822-35 under the editorship of Frederik Thaarup (1766-1845). After this, it began to decline because of editorial problems and competition from the rival *Berlingske Tidende*. In the years 1835-40, *Dagen* went through several different editors, beginning 1836-38 with Thomas Overskou (1798-1873) and ending (1841) with Lars Jakob Fribert (1808-1863). The paper collapsed in 1843. In 1836, Johan Carl Ernst Berling (1812-1871) took over a paper that had been in the family since 1749. It was the official organ of the Danish government and a descendant of Joachim Wielandt's *Extraordinaire Relationer* of 1721. There were several changes in title, format, and number of issues. In 1808, it was known as the *Danske Statstidende*. Berling's name first appeared in the title in 1833. Jørgen Johan Albrecht Schønberg (1782-1841) edited the paper from 1834 to 1838 and was followed by Mendel Levin Nathanson (1780-1868) from 1838 to 1858. By 1841, the *Berlingske Tidende* was a regular daily paper. Containing foreign as well as domestic news, Berling's paper was the father of the modern Danish newspaper.

78. *Kjøbenhavns flyvende Post*. See p. xvi and note 35.

79. *Kjøbenhavnsposten*, 23; see p. 8 and note 36 above.

80. See Deuteronomy 25:5-10.

81. In his article in *Fædrelandet*, 77, Johannes Hage had defended *Kjøbenhavnsposten*. See Supplement, pp. 142-43.

82. *Fædrelandet*, 77, col. 644: "Anyone knowing the editor of *Kjøbenhavnsposten* will be unable to deny him zeal in gathering materials, industry in working them up, a high degree of discretion and deep respect for truth without petty, egotistic motivation." See Supplement, p. 144.

83. *Fædrelandet*, 77, col. 633. See Supplement, p. 142. The italics are Kierkegaard's.

84. See Supplement, p. 142.

85. *Fædrelandet*, 77, col. 633: "Only rarely does it contain factual information." See Supplement, p. 142.

86. *Fædrelandet*, 77, col. 642: "But not rarely it also uses other weapons in seeking to amuse its readers with witticisms without caring whether or not the truth suffers on that account." See Supplement, p. 142.

87. *Fædrelandet*, 77, col. 643, the phrase used to describe Orla Lehmann's article, *Kjøbenhavnsposten*, 43. See Supplement, p. 142.

88. Moonlight [*Maaneskins-Belysning*], a dig at Lehmann's use of "dawn" (see p. 6 and note 23 above) and a pun on the figurative and literal meanings of *Belysning* [light].

89. "The unclearly expressed is also the unclearly thought," from Esaias Tegner, *"Epilog vid Magister-promotionen i Lund 1820," Samlade Skrifter,* I-VII (Stockholm: 1847-51), III, p. 160: *"Det dunkelt sagda är det dunkelt tänkta."*

90. *Fædrelandet,* 77, col. 643. See Supplement, p. 143.

91. *Fædrelandet,* 77, has "by a K."; this attribution designates Orla Lehmann, who put no name to his article in *Kjøbenhavnsposten,* 43 (see note 21 above). There are five other unimportant deviations in spelling and punctuation from the piece as published in *Fædrelandet.* See Supplement, p. 143.

92. *Kjøbenhavnsposten,* 43, p. 171, col. 2: "What is to be done about this? — What Hage recommends: not bother too apprehensively about the tiresome *qu'en dira-t-on* [what will people say about it] but trustfully follow the path dictated by honor and conscience." See Supplement, pp. 140-41.

93. *Kjøbenhavns flyvende Post,* 76; see p. 6.

94. *"Trykkefrihedssagen IV,"* in which Orla Lehmann defends *Fædrelandet, Kjøbenhavnsposten,* 38, February 7, 1836, pp. 149-52.

95. *Fædrelandet,* 77, col. 643: "But this censure does not touch the author in *Kjøbenhavnsposten.* He has not blamed the past in general; he has presented only its lack of interest in common affairs and presented it as something that must of necessity follow from the course of events." There are also minor deviations in punctuation and spelling from the text in *Fædrelandet.* See Supplement, p. 143.

96. *Fædrelandet,* 77, col. 643: "And now with regard to that looking back at the vanished past—it is natural enough that one dwells on it, but this must not, however, weaken the vigor with which we are going to meet the future." See Supplement, p. 143.

97. *Kjøbenhavns flyvende Post,* 76, col. 4. See p. 9.

98. *Fædrelandet,* 77, col. 643: "in a nostalgic dwelling on past events or in a misplaced patriotism." See Supplement, p. 143.

99. *Kjøbenhavnsposten,* 43, p. 169, col. 2. There are minor deviations from the text. See Supplement, p. 135.

100. The Danish flag. Cf. Union Jack, Stars and Stripes.

101. Codan or Kodan, an old Roman name for the Baltic Sea. "Old Denmark," "Sjælland's beech groves," "Codan's billows," etc. appear in patriotic songs of the period, such as, for example, those by Bernhard Severin Ingemann (1789-1862): *"Dannevang, med grønne Bred"* and *"Vift stolt paa Codans Bølge."*

102. *Kjøbenhavnsposten,* 43, p. 170, col. 2. See Supplement, p. 137.

103. *Kjøbenhavns flyvende Post,* 76, col. 1-6. See pp. 6-11.

104. See Supplement, p. 136; cf. p. 7.

105. *Kjøbenhavnsposten,* 43, p. 169, col. 2: "through the—if we dare to express ourselves thus—vegetative vigor dwelling in every people." See Supplement, p. 135.

106. *Fædrelandet,* 77, col. 643. See Supplement, p. 144; cf. p. 10.

107. See p. 10; Supplement, p. 141.

108. *Fædrelandet,* 77, col. 644. See Supplement, p. 144.

109. See p. 10.

110. See note 82 above.

111. Dionysius I (c. 432-367 B.C.), tyrant of Syracuse, was reputed to have had a prison cell constructed so that unseen he could hear everything the prisoners said; hence the name "Dionysius-ear." Cf. *JP* V 5352 (*Pap.* II A 275).

112. See note 82 above.

113. Virgil's description of the hero of the *Aeneid*, who is shown praying before decisive or difficult events. See, for example, IV, 393; VIII, 67-70; *Virgils Aeneide*, tr. Johan Schønheyder (Copenhagen: 1812), I, p. 167; II, p. 363; *Virgil*, I-II, tr. H. Rushton Fairclough (Loeb, Cambridge: Harvard University Press, 1978), I, p. 423; II, p. 65. In antiquity, prayer was made with hands raised palm upward.

114. See p. 10.

115. See p. 7 and note 28 above.

116. *Fædrelandet*, 77, col. 644: "this paper has existed for a number of years while various other similar papers have gone under in the course of a short time." See Supplement, p. 144.

117. In physics, the passive object impelled by two unequal forces cannot choose its path but is carried along in the direction corresponding to that of the combined thrust.

118. A type of hand-made black earthenware pottery produced solely in Jylland, chiefly in the west. The typical pot was cauldron-shaped, with two small handles and three stumpy legs. A good-sized pot could hold about forty liters.

119. *Fædrelandet*, 77, col. 646: "That the Liberal papers in their fight against the Conservative ones take refuge in assigning ignoble motives to their opponents is an accusation we certainly read in no. 78, but we find it more applicable to the opposite party. For how often are not the Liberals charged with acting out of vanity, ambition, lust for revenge? . . . How precisely the author of the aforesaid number makes himself guilty of attributing ignoble motives to the Liberals is shown by the quotation given above." See Supplement, p. 147.

120. August Heinrich Julius Lafontaine (1758-1831), German author of tear-ridden, sentimental sagas of family life. Of the Danish translations, Kierkegaard mentions *Skjebnens Veie* (Copenhagen: 1826-27) in *JP* V 5060 (*Pap.* I C 17). See also p. 75. August Friedrich Ferdinand von Kotzebue (1761-1819), German dramatist who wrote a number of light, sentimental plays that were translated into Danish, for example, *De Sandsesløse* (Copenhagen: 1810).

121. See Supplement, p. 142; note 86 above.

122. See pp. 10-11; Supplement, p. 144.

123. *Fædrelandet*, 77, col. 644: "wit and dialectical skill when these are not matched by a love of truth but serve only to glorify one's own little self." See Supplement, p. 144.

124. See Supplement, pp. 144-45.

125. An old hospital foundation in Copenhagen for the poor and aged,

from 1666 situated between Farvegade, Løngangstræde, and Vestervold. It had its own church, in which Nicolai Frederik Severin Grundtvig (1783-1872) was pastor from 1839 to 1872. See *Pap.* XI³ B 182, pp. 300-01.

126. A character in Ludwig Tieck, *Der gestiefelte Kater, ein Kindermärchen in drei Akten.* *Ludwig Tieck's sämmtliche Werke,* I-II (Paris: 1837; *ASKB* 1848-49), I, pp. 466-90.

127. See note 123 above.

128. "Invitation" designates a lead in cards whereby one's partner is invited to play in a particular manner. Like "color [*Couleur*]," "best color [*bedste Couleur*]," "trumps [*Trumf*]," and "blank suit [*Renonce*]," "invitation [*Invite*]" is a technical term from card-playing, especially *L'Hombre,* in Kierkegaard's day.

129. "Standing [*staaende*]" is a play on the introductory line in Lehmann's article, *Kjøbenhavnsposten,* 43. See Supplement, p. 134: "It was acrimony we were talking about last time [*Det var ved Bitterheden, vi sidst bleve staaende*]." Cf. also p. 10.

130. *Fædrelandet,* 77, col. 643, 644, corrects Kierkegaard's use of a common gender instead of neuter and of a personal pronoun instead of a reflexive: "a terrible hurry [*en (et) forskrækkelig(t) Hastværk*]" and "might prefer [*ønske dem (sig)*]." See Supplement, p. 144. Kierkegaard probably rejects the second as an error because in spoken Danish *dem* was often used instead of *sig.* See Christian Molbech, *Danske Ordbog,* I-II (Copenhagen: 1833; *ASKB* 1032), II, p. 303, *Sig.* Both "errors" are normal usage in Jylland dialect.

131. *"Til Hr. Orla Lehmann," Kjøbenhavns flyvende Post, Interimsblad,* 87, April 10, 1836, col. 1-8. A reply to Orla Lehmann, *"Svar til Flyvepostens Hr. B.," Kjøbenhavnsposten,* 96, March 31, 1836, pp. 383-85. See Supplement, pp. 152-59.

132. J. L. Heiberg, *Kjøge Huuskors* (Copenhagen: 1831), 13, p. 22 (Blase's song).

133. See note 21 above. The article *"Trykkefrihedssagen I-IV"* appeared in *Kjøbenhavnsposten,* 15, January 15, 1836, pp. 57-58; 16, January 16, 1836, pp. 61-62; 19, January 19, 1836, pp. 73-75; 38, February 7, 1836, pp. 149-52.

134. Orla Lehmann names Hage in *Kjøbenhavnsposten,* 96, 384-85, col. 2-1: "the opinions Mr. Hage puts forward as the train of thought of the attacked article . . . an attack that surely others besides Hage have found 'shameless'." See Supplement, pp. 156-57.

135. *Kjøbenhavnsposten,* 90, March 27, 1836, p. 360, col. 2, contains in an editorial comment a general rejection of current attacks on the editor: "We believe that the honorable subscribers will be none the less grateful to us for not filling the columns of this paper with replies to the incessant and unwearied attacks on *Kjøbenhavnsposten* and its editor by the *Flyvende Post* and *Dagen,* not to mention our many paltry little lampoonists."

136. An indoor game in which one player sits on a chair in the middle of a circle of players while another, using the formula "What are you wondering?" asks the others what they want to know about the sitter. The questioner then repeats the whispered questions to the sitter, who tries to guess the author of

each question. The first correct guess places a new victim on the chair. This game is referred to also in *Philosophical Fragments, or A Fragment of Philosophy*, p. 52, *KW* VII (*SV* IV 219); *The Sickness unto Death*, p. 5, *KW* XIX (*SV* XI 117); *JP* V 5100, p. 37 (*Pap.* I A 75, p. 57).

137. *Kjøbenhavnsposten*, 96, p. 383, col. 2: "I would have made some rejoinders even earlier if I had not known that a reply would come elsewhere. But since the writer in question [Mr. B.] has not been pleased with that reply, there may still be time for this." See Supplement, p. 153.

138. *Kjøbenhavnsposten*, 96, p. 385, col. 2: "On the other hand, I must apologize to my honorable opponent that my reply comes somewhat late, but earlier I had something better to do." See Supplement, pp. 158-59.

139. *Kjøbenhavnsposten*, 96, p. 383, col. 2. See Supplement, p. 153.

140. *Kjøbenhavnsposten*, 96, p. 383, col. 2: "Neither would I in this respect let myself be disturbed by the B. put under the article, for although it is probably to indicate that this comes from another hand than the rest, which is also amply demonstrated by its robust and energetic language, yet I regard such a mark as an entirely permissible means of indicating a certain shading of opinion in the common main direction." See Supplement, p. 153.

141. *Kjøbenhavnsposten*, 90, March 27, 1836, p. 360: "When, for information about an issue or a particular fact, it is necessary to speak, we shall certainly not keep silent, but to embark upon a polemic that either hangs itself up on particular expressions in an article or with impudent vulgarity moves into the domain of personality would be a breach of the respect we owe our readers and ourselves."

142. See note 135 above.

143. See Supplement, p. 158.

144. See note 141 above.

145. *Kjøbenhavnsposten*, 96, p. 385: "I therefore do not need any excuse for ignoring all irrelevant matters." See Supplement, p. 158.

146. *Kjøbenhavnsposten*, 96, pp. 384-85: "Thus, to the best of my judgment, the first charge is groundless. Indeed, Mr. B. himself seems to have given it up in reality, since in a way he acknowledges the opinions Mr. Hage puts forward as the train of thought of the attacked article and complains only that he has not also reproduced the style that prevailed in *Kjøbenhavnsposten*. Now, this is indeed a strange requirement for a summary consisting of a couple of lines from which one usually seeks no more than a faithful account of the leading idea; but if the entire complaint collapses into a mere dissatisfaction with the form, perhaps even merely with a few somewhat strong words, then this is a matter of taste about which everyone must be permitted to have his own opinion." See Supplement, p. 156.

147. See note 146 above.

148. *Kjøbenhavnsposten*, 96, p. 385, col. 2. See Supplement, p. 158.

149. See note 134 above.

150. *Kjøbenhavnsposten*, 96, p. 385, col. 1: "the entire direction of our time,

for this tends to democratize everything, wealth, science, yes, even character."
See Supplement, p. 157.

151. Lehmann's summary is to be found in *Kjøbenhavnsposten*, 96, p. 384, col. 1. See Supplement, pp. 154-55.

152. *Kjøbenhavnsposten*, 96, p. 384, col. 1: "in the last three decades of the previous century, Denmark found herself in a lively and very promising development, which revealed itself in important reforms in our legislation, in a fruitful industrial and commercial activity, and in a vigorously budding life in the people; approximately at the beginning of this century . . .." See Supplement, p. 154.

153. *Kjøbenhavnsposten*, 96, p. 384, col. 2. See Supplement, pp. 155-56.

154. See note 152 above.

155. *Kjøbenhavnsposten*, 96, p. 385, col. 1. See Supplement, p. 156.

156. See pp. 12-23.

157. *Kjøbenhavnsposten*, 96, p. 384, col. 2. Kierkegaard has no introductory quotation marks, and *Kjøbenhavnsposten* has: "can even develop a certain virtuosity." See Supplement, p. 156.

158. Irony on Kierkegaard's part if he knows that Lehmann is the author of the five-part article.

159. See note 158 above.

160. *Kjøbenhavnsposten*, 43, p. 169, col. 1. See Supplement, p. 134.

161. See note 152 above.

162. *Kjøbenhavnsposten*, 96, p. 384, col. 2: "the period from 1807 to 1827, which was primarily intended." See Supplement, p. 156.

163. See note 158 above.

164. *Fædrelandet*, 77, col. 643: "a number of years ago Europe's general as well as Denmark's particular fate had weakened the public spirit." See Supplement, pp. 142-43.

165. See note 146 above.

166. *Kjøbenhavnsposten*, 96, p. 385, col. 1: "when he first substitutes *our reformers* for the *reforming endeavor* of our time, and then identifies these with *the publisher and staff of Kjøbenhavnsposten*." See Supplement, p. 157.

167. *Kjøbenhavnsposten*, 96, p. 385, col. 1: "When he pronounces our reformers destitute of vigor and manliness, one can readily agree with him in that—naturally with exceptions, which he probably will recognize of course—because one thinks that a more serious and more vigorous spirit is beginning to awaken among the people." See Supplement, p. 157.

168. *Kjøbenhavnsposten*, 96, p. 385, col. 1-2: "Thus the second complaint might also be due to a misunderstanding, since Mr. B. is certainly right that our political life and its reforming tendency have not yet displayed any great vigor but is wrong in objecting this against an article that has asserted the selfsame thing." See Supplement, p. 158.

169. The mismanaged, unsuccessful crusade of peasants led by Peter the Hermit and Walter the Penniless in 1096. The successful First Crusade, in

which Godfrey of Bouillon (c. 1060-1100) was a leading figure, took place immediately afterward in 1096-99.

170. *Kjøbenhavnsposten*, 96, p. 385, col. 2: "but I am, of course, far from being sure that I have seen the point, since the kernel is certainly hidden inside a very thick shell." See Supplement, p. 158.

171. See *Kjøbenhavnsposten*, 96, p. 385, col. 2: "When I put my name to these lines, I hope Mr. B. will regard it as a little courtesy toward him." See Supplement, p. 159.

172. The source has not been located. See *Repetition*, p. 150, *KW* VI (*SV* III 190).

173. See note 140 above.

174. Cf. p. 14.

175. *Kjøbenhavnsposten*, 96, p. 385, col. 2. See Supplement, p. 158. Kierkegaard's quotation contains five minor deviations in punctuation and spelling.

176. To demonstrate the element and process of will in a situation (motive, deliberation, decision, action), late Scholasticism used the example of a donkey halfway between two identical bundles of hay, "Buridan's donkey," after a fourteenth-century French Scholastic.

177. Ludvig Holberg, *Mester Gert Westphaler eller den meget talende Barbeer*, 8, *Den Danske Skue-Plads*, I-VII (Copenhagen: 1788; *ASKB* 1566-67), I, no pagination; cf. *Master Gert Westphaler or The Talkative Barber, Seven One-Act Plays by Holberg*, tr. Henry Alexander (Princeton: Princeton University Press for the American-Scandinavian Foundation, 1950), p. 30.

178. See note 171 above and *Kjøbenhavnsposten*, 96, p. 385, col. 2: "since I see that it pleases him to know with whom he has to do, but I must also ask him not to let it prevent him from preserving his own anonymity, since it is totally immaterial to me what my opponent is called." See Supplement, p. 159.

179. Here Kierkegaard signs his own name for the first time in his authorship.

180. *JP* V 5116 (*Pap.* I B 2). See Historical Introduction, note 40. Johannes A. Ostermann gave a paper under the title *"Vor nyeste Journalliteratur"*; see Supplement, pp. 189-99. Kierkegaard's paper is not mentioned in the *Rapportbog*.

181. *Pap.* I B 1 is presumably the draft of an introduction to the paper. See Supplement, pp. 215-16.

182. See Luke 2:7.

183. See Mark 4:31-32; Luke 13:19.

184. Probably the Liberals' hopes of a free constitution.

185. The mount of the transfiguration; see Matthew 17:1-8; Mark 9:2. Kierkegaard rather means Mount Nebo. See Deuteronomy 34:1-4; cf. Numbers 14:20-25.

186. According to a letter from Johannes Ostermann to Hans Peter Barfod (May 28, 1867), Kierkegaard borrowed the manuscript of Ostermann's talk. See Supplement, pp. 200-01.

187. See note 180 above.

188. See Supplement, p. 189 and note 241.

189. See p. 7 and note 28 above.

190. On the Public Assistance Administrator devil [*Fattigbestyrer-Djævelen*], see *Raketten*, 1831, pp. 178-79; 1832, pp. 20-21, 47-48. See also Matthias Winther, *Skrivelse til Hr. Major, Ridder og Fattigdirektør Mangor om en Fattigbestyrerdjævel, med et Par Ord om, hvorledes en Fattigbestyrer ikke bør være* (Copenhagen: 1831). *Forpostfægtning* [Outpost skirmishing] refers to Matthias Winther, *Forpostfægtning med Oberst Christian Høegh-Guldberg og Stabskirurg Tønder, med et Par Livsbilleder* (Copenhagen: 1831). Cf. *Raketten*, 1831, pp. 12-14, 31-32; 1832, pp. 99, 146, 257-59, 670; 1833, p. 56 and elsewhere. Winther had a personal grievance against all three men. Hannibal Sehested (1606-1666) was a Danish statesman who at one point in his career was found guilty of defrauding the state of funds due to it. See *Raketten*, 1832, pp. 145-47, 189-91, 654-56, 665, 822-23; 1833, pp. 60-62, 107-08, 184-86.

191. This paper ran from 1834 to 1837 and, being more in the style of *Politivennen*, was a better quality paper than its fellows. No. 1-88 were edited by H. J. Hald; 89-108 by Johan Christian Lange; 109-73 by F. Hergetius, with Hald helping with the publication throughout.

192. See Historical Introduction, note 49.

193. The July Revolution of 1830. See note 195 below.

194. See p. 120 and note 63.

195. On July 25, 1830, Charles X of France, who had assumed a kind of provisional dictatorship, promulgated the five ordinances of St. Cloud, which suspended liberty of the press, dissolved the chamber of deputies, changed the election system, called a new chamber, and appointed some ultra-Royalists to the Council of State. Under the leadership of Louis Adolphe Thiers, the "fourth estate" made a collective revolt against what was generally regarded as illegal power. Insurrection broke out on July 27. On July 29, Charles X, after Paris was out of hand, accepted the insurgents' condition that the five ordinances be withdrawn, but it was too late. The Duke of Orleans declared his acceptance of the office of Lieutenant-General of the Realm, and on August 2, 1830, Charles X abdicated. On August 9, 1830, Louis Philippe, Duke of Orleans, became "Citizen King," a constitutional monarch.

196. Karl Ludwig Börne (1786-1837), famous German journalist and author.

197. Address of thanks, drawn up by J. P. Mynster and handed to the king by the Provincial Consultative Assemblies on October 4, 1835. See *Fædrelandet*, II, 58, October 23, 1835, col. 305-07, especially col. 307; J. P. Mynster, *Meddelelser om mit Levnet* (Copenhagen: 1854), pp. 249-54.

198. The king's order of May 28, 1831, concerning preparations to be made for the introduction of the Provincial Consultative Assemblies. See *Kjøbenhavnsposten*, 37, February 12, 1831.

199. Founded in 1832 to commemorate the order of May 28, 1831. *Kjøbenhavnsposten*, 109, May 31, 1832.

200. *Ueber das Verfassungswerk in Schleswig-Holstein.* See Historical Introduction, p. xi.

201. See Supplement, p. 191.

202. Polish Revolution. Influenced by the July Revolution in France, Polish students tried to capture the Russian regent, Grand Duke Constantine, on November 29, 1830. They failed, but the insurrection spread. After months of struggle and the intervention of Russia, Poland was declared a Russian province on February 26, 1832.

203. In fact from *Kjøbenhavnsposten*, 281, November 28, 1830.

204. Drawn up at a meeting in Kiel, November 22, 1830, and printed in *Kjøbenhavnsposten*, 293, December 13, 1830.

205. See note 198 above; Supplement, p. 191.

206. The stick Nille uses on her husband Jeppe in Holberg's *Jeppe paa Bjerget*, IV, 1, *Danske Skue-Plads*, I, no pagination; *Jeppe of the Hill or The Transformed Peasant* (IV, 2), *Comedies by Holberg*, tr. Oscar James Campbell Jr. and Frederic Schenck (New York: American-Scandinavian Foundation, 1914), p. 340. The reference is to J. L. Heiberg, whose paper, *Kjøbenhavns flyvende Post*, did not appear in 1829.

207. *Kjøbenhavnsposten*, 121, July 31, 1829; *Extra-Blad*, August 2 (see also following issues); 159-61, October 6-9, 1829.

208. On the smallpox service, see *Kjøbenhavnsposten*, 126, August 10; 131, August 18, 1829. On Mohammed II, see *Kjøbenhavnsposten*, 115, July 21; 116, July 23; 118, July 27, 1829. On the Emperor Alexander, see *Kjøbenhavnsposten*, 2, January 5; 3, January 6; 5, January 9; 7, January 13; 167, October 20, 1829. On Turkish jurisprudence, see *Kjøbenhavnsposten*, 112, July 16; 114, July 20, 1829. On Migueliana, see *Kjøbenhavnsposten*, 120, July 30; 121, July 31; 123, August 4; 124, August 6; 125, August 7, 1829; Johan Christian Riise, *Historisk-geographisk Archiv*, I-LXXV (Copenhagen: 1820-38).

209. In *Kjøbenhavnsposten* there was a special section under the heading *Conversations- og Nyheds-Post* (from 1832 called *Nyheds-Post*).

210. From *Kjøbenhavnsposten*, 212, September 9, 1830; cf. note in no. 212, col. 1.

211. The July Revolution and its offshoots.

212. See note 198 above.

213. Eilert Peter Tscherning (1767-1832), military officer and industrialist, father of Anton Frederik Tscherning (1795-1874), military officer and politician. The "T." articles began in *Kjøbenhavnsposten*, 58, March 9, 1831. In *Kjøbenhavnsposten*, 21, January 25; 24, January 28; 25, January 29, 1831, Tscherning had translated an article from Italian, *"Discussionen."*

214. See *"Blandede Betragtninger," Kjøbenhavnsposten*, 121, May 25 (in 121 the heading is "*Smiger* [flattery]"); 125, May 30; "*gode Hjerter* [good hearts]," 70, March 23; "*ondskabsfuld* [malicious]," 98, April 26; "*Egoisme* [egotism]," 107, May 7; "*Statsoekonomie* [national economy]," 69, March 22; "*Aristokrater og Demokrater* [aristocrats and democrats]," 72, March 25, 1831.

215. In *Kjøbenhavnsposten*, 95, April 22, 1831, there is a piece (signed "I."),

"En Stemme on Forordningen af 14de April 1831," on duty-free imports and reduced ship tax. Kierkegaard mistakenly thought the article was by T.

216. In 1831 appeared Christian Georg Nathan David's *Om de preussiske Provindsial-stænders Væsen* (mentioned in advance in *Kjøbenhavnsposten*, 37, February 12, and reviewed in 44, February 21) and A. F. Tscherning's *De preussiske Provindsialstændernes Historie i korte Træk* (reviewed in *Kjøbenhavnsposten*, 58, March 9). Both appeared in German in the same year under the title *Ueber das Wesen und die Geschichte der Preussischen Provinzialstände. Zwei Abhandlungen von C.G.N. David und A. F. Tscherning. Aus dem Dänischen übersetzt. Mit einem vorworte herausgegeben von N. Falck.* Both works are critical of the electoral principles used for the Provincial Consultative Assemblies, for example, that eligibility be dependent on the ownership of property. Also in 1831 appeared E. P. Tscherning's *Sammenlignet Oversigt over Communal- og Municipal- Indretninger, Justitsvæsenet, Geistligheden, Skolevæsenet, det Militaire, Søemagten, Postvæsenet og Regjeringen. Efter Rumpfs almindelige Oversigt over det Preussiske Statsværtskab* (reviewed in *Kjøbenhavnsposten*, 65, March 17).

217. See *Maanedsskrift for Litteratur*, V, 1831, pp. 147–48.

218. The Ordinance was announced in *Kjøbenhavnsposten*, 130, June 4.

219. Already in *Kjøbenhavnsposten*, 48, February 25, 1831, and several following issues, mention is made of *Cholera morbus*.

220. See *Kjøbenhavnsposten*, 218, September 15, 1831, and several following issues.

221. The popular Danish name for a team of three experts advising in political or economic affairs. See *Kjøbenhavnsposten*, 68, March 21, and 71, March 24, 1832.

222. See *Kjøbenhavnsposten*, 77, March 31; 85, April 10; 90, April 17; 91, April 19; 94, April 26, 1832.

223. See *Kjøbenhavnsposten*, 109, May 31; 111, June 5, 1832; note 199 above.

224. See *Kjøbenhavnsposten*, 83, April 27, 1833.

225. On *Hamburger Korrespondent*, see *Kjøbenhavnsposten*, 11, January 15; 12, January 17; 16, January 22; 17, January 24, 1833; on *Kieler Korrespondent*, see 13, January 18; 67, April 4, 1833; on *Zeitung*, see 48, March 8, 1833; on *Eremit*, see 18, January 25; 19, January 26; 43, March 1; 49, March 9; 78, April 20, 1833; on Latin, see 108–09, June 4, 6; 123, June 25; 127, July 1; 130, July 5; 134, July 11; 135, July 12, 1833, and several following issues.

226. A. F. Tscherning (see note 213 above) went into unofficial exile (1833-38 in Paris) because of articles in *Kjøbenhavnsposten* at the beginning of the 1830s, in which he sharply criticized the military. See *Kjøbenhavnsposten*, 119, June 20; 120, June 21, 1833.

227. See *Kjøbenhavnsposten*, 77, April 19; 98, May 20; 111, June 8, 1833, and several following issues. On the king's sickness, see *Kjøbenhavnsposten*, 132, July 8; 133, July 9, 1833, and several following issues.

228. See *Kjøbenhavnsposten*, 27, February 7; 32, February 14; 35, February 18, 1834, and several following issues.

229. Tage Algreen-Ussing (1797-1872), politician and lawyer. See *Kjøbenhavnsposten*, 60, March 25, 1834, and several following issues.

230. See *Kjøbenhavnsposten*, 74, April 12; 83, April 26; 85, April 29, 1834, and several following issues; *Pap.* I B 2, p. 170 fn.

231. See *Kjøbenhavnsposten*, 106, May 28; 107, May 29, 1834.

232. See *Kjøbenhavnsposten*, 103, May 24, 1834, and several following issues. See *Pap.* I B 2, p. 170 fn.

233. See *Kjøbenhavnsposten*, 137, July 10; 138, July 11, 1834.

234. See *Kjøbenhavnsposten*, 142, July 17; 144, July 19, 1834, and several following issues. See *Pap.* I B 2, p. 170 fn.

235. The first issue of *Fædrelandet*, edited by C.G.N. David, came out on September 14, 1834. See Historical Introduction, note 51.

236. See *Kjøbenhavnsposten*, 179, September 6, 1834, and several following issues.

237. By patent of May 8, 1835. See *Kjøbenhavnsposten*, 112, May 11, 1835. The meeting took place on October 1, 1835.

238. See Historical Introduction, note 51. See also *Kjøbenhavnsposten*, 253, December 16; 254, December 17; 263, December 30, 1834; 117, May 18; 120, May 21; 295, December 2, 1835, and several other issues.

239. The usual abbreviated version of the king's message to the Chancellery, February 26, 1835, regarding the petition of February 21. See Historical Introduction, p. xii; *Kjøbenhavnsposten*, 51-52, February 28, March 1, 1835.

240. Resolution of September 22, 1835. See *Fædrelandet*, 56, October 9, 1835.

241. The petition delivered to the king on February 20, 1835, as a response to the king's note to the Chancellery, December 14, 1834. See Supplement, p. 194 and note 255.

242. Correspondence on this subject is to be found in the English *Morning Chronicle* for March 1835 (dated February 20), also in the *Times*, February 21.

243. For attorney Haagen's contribution for the defense, see *Fædrelandet*, 20-21, February 1, 1835; 24, March 1, 1835.

244. The German philosopher Johann Gottlieb Fichte (1762-1814).

245. Maximilien François Marie Isidore de Robespierre (1758-1794), Jacobin and president of the Committee of Public Safety during the French reign of terror.

246. Daniel François Esprit Auber (1782-1871), French composer. During the previous ten years, numerous operas by Auber had been presented in Copenhagen. See Historical Introduction, note 11.

247. See, for example, J. L. Heiberg's esthetic theories of 1827-28, *Prosaiske Skrifter*, I-XI (Copenhagen: 1861-62), III, pp. 169-284.

248. The source has not been located.

249. Cervantes, *Don Quixote*, I, p. 47. The section, "There is always something Don Quixotic . . . remain windmills," is crossed out in Kierkegaard's ms.

250. See note 237 above. The first meeting of the Provincial Consultative Assemblies in Denmark proper was held in Roskilde.

251. See Supplement, p. 195.

252. See p. 10 and note 52.

253. See Supplement, p. 196.

254. See Supplement, pp. 196-97. Kierkegaard erroneously puts "color" instead of "form" and moves the word "precisely."

255. As was, for example, tightrope virtuoso Roat when he made his fatal performance at Rosenborg Palace on June 12, 1827. See *Kjøbenhavnsposten*, 48, June 16, 1827.

256. Most articles in the papers of the time were either anonymous or pseudonymous.

257. See Supplement, pp. 196-97.

258. See note 251 above.

259. Johannes Hage was editor of *Fædrelandet* 51-143, September 4, 1835 through June 24, 1837, after C.G.N. David retired from the paper. See Historical Introduction, notes 4 and 51.

260. A journal published by a society and edited 1831-36 by Joakim Frederik Schouw (1789-1852), botanist, politician, author.

FROM THE PAPERS OF ONE STILL LIVING

Title Page. Several reasons can be alleged as to why Kierkegaard chose this title: to refer to a projected suicide; to note that he was still alive despite his frail constitution and his belief he would die young; to refer to the deaths in his family and the death of his friend Poul M. Møller. It is quite likely that the title is a play on a literary fashion of letters and papers "from one deceased" set by the much-traveled Hermann Pückler-Muskau in the period 1830-35. That both Kierkegaard and Hans Christian Andersen definitely had contact with the Pückler-Muskau literature is shown by a Kierkegaard allusion in the journals, *JP* V 5071 (*Pap.* I A 41, 1835), and by Andersen's references to Pückler-Muskau, *Briefe eines Verstorbenen* (Letters from One Deceased), in *Kun en Spillemand*, I-III (Copenhagen: 1837; *ASKB* 1503), notably in I, p. 69; *Only a Fiddler*, I-III, tr. anonymous (London: 1845), I, p. 66; *The Life of Denmark. O.T. and Only a Fiddler*, tr. Mary Howitt (London: 1845), I, pp. 45-46. It is interesting to note that as late as 1847 Kierkegaard contemplated using *Af en Afdøds Papirer* [From the Papers of One Deceased] as a subtitle for *The Crisis and a Crisis in the Life of an Actress*, together with *Christian Discourses, KW* XVII (*Pap.* VIII² B 90:1).

Published Against His Will. This phrase may indicate Kierkegaard's reluctance to publish, possibly because the essay was not the positive review Andersen thought he could expect (see Hans Christian Andersen, *Mit Livs Eventyr* [Copenhagen: 1855]), p. 198; *The True Story of My Life* [New York: American-Scandinavian Foundation, 1926], p. 125). See also p. 202 and note

267. The idea of following the last will and testament of a deceased person also presents itself—with the thought that where a person "still living" is concerned, one may be acting against his will. The preface humorously describes Kierkegaard's battle with his other self over publication.

In the original edition (1838), the publisher's name is given as S. Kjerkegaard (see Supplement, p. 206), which indicates that the spelling of the family name was not yet fixed. There are no manuscripts of the essay.

1. *Forord bryder ingen Trætte.* This Danish proverb has developed out of different sayings and means here that a word given in advance—an agreement—prevents a quarrel later. As in *Prefaces* [*Forord*], *KW* IX (*SV* V 71), Kierkegaard indulges in wordplay with this proverb: *Forord* [preface] and *Forord* [word in advance], *bryde* [break] and *afbryde* [interrupt, break continuity].

2. From a verse sung by the city night-watchmen:

> Vor Klokk' er slagen Tolv.
> Med Tung' og Mund
> Af Hjærtens Grund
> Befal dig Gud i Vold
> [Our clock has now struck twelve.
> With tongue and mouth
> From deepest heart
> Commend yourself to God]!

The quotation is based on a poetic paraphrase of Psalm 51 by Thomas Hansen Kingo, *Psalmer og aandelige Sange af Thomas Kingo,* ed. Peter Andreas Fenger (Copenhagen: 1827; *ASKB* 203), 231, st. 15, p. 520. The same verse is alluded to in *JP* V 5324 (*Pap.* II A 228). Other watchmen's songs are mentioned in *JP* V 5064, 5323 (*Pap.* I A 39; II A 753); *Christian Discourses, KW* XVII (*SV* X 168). See also Michael Viggo Fausbøll, *Instruction for Natte-Vægterne i Kiøbenhavn* (Copenhagen: 1784), esp. p. 21.

3. See p. 106 and note 8.

4. Literally, "magnetically diverging." Kierkegaard is here thinking of physics, of the fact that two like poles repel each other. The analogy was possibly prompted by Hans Christian Ørsted's discovery of electromagnetism (findings published 1820). There are other scientific allusions in Kierkegaard's essay, for example, to "specific gravity," pp. 65, 67.

5. Cf. Aristotle, *Magna Moralia,* 1211 a, *The Complete Works of Aristotle,* I-II, ed. Jonathan Barnes (rev. Oxford tr.; Princeton: Princeton University Press, 1984), II, p. 1917: "When we wish to describe a very great friend, we say 'my soul and his are one'."

6. See I Samuel 16:14-23. See also *JP* V 5336 (*Pap.* II A 760), where Kierkegaard speaks of his good mood pursued by Saul's evil spirit.

7. On the author's private personality as his inner sanctum, see *Two Ages,* p. 99, *KW* XIV (*SV* VIII 92).

8. That which influences or is influenced by something else through a mysterious affinity.

9. An expression from dogmatics: the interaction of the two natures of Christ.

10. An old German song, *"Die schwarzbraune Hexe."* See Ludwig Achim v. Arnim and Clemens Brentano, *Des Knaben Wunderhorn,* I-III (Heidelberg: 1819; *ASKB* 1494-96), I, p. 34; *JP* V 5215 (*Pap.* II A 51).

11. See Genesis 32:29-31.

12. See II Peter 3:8.

13. I.e., that readers will be without prejudice.

14. Johannes Ewald, *"Fiskerne,"* *Samtlige Skrifter,* I-VIII (Copenhagen: 1850-54; *ASKB* 1537-44), V, p. 136.

15. The source of this quotation has not been located.

16. A frequent transitional verse in Homer's *Odyssey.*

17. See John 19:22.

18. This form of title occurs again in 1841 in Kierkegaard's dissertation, *Om Begrebet Ironi med stadigt Hensyn til Socrates* [*The Concept of Irony, with Continual Reference to Socrates, KW* II (*SV* XIII 93-393)]. In *Kun en Spillemand,* Hans Christian Andersen's third novel, the hero, Christian, is a failed genius who dies disappointed and in poverty because the circumstances of his life have thwarted him. Fortune has not given him the patron he needed in order to develop his artistic talent and to achieve recognition in the world. The genius in the story is thus presented as a passive victim of fate, a view rejected by Kierkegaard. Andersen's novel was translated into English by Mary Howitt in 1845 and by an anonymous translator in the same year.

19. An expression used by Kierkegaard to indicate German speculative philosophy. See, for example, *JP* II 1580; III 3265 (*Pap.* II A 488, 706).

20. A reference to Hegel, who, in order to avoid starting his philosophy at an arbitrary point, tried to get behind all intellectual assumptions and arrive at what he claimed was a basic presuppositionless foundation concept. He saw this in the concept of being (*Sein*)—being, stripped of all intellectual definitions or conceptual distinguishing marks, hence pure and abstract and therefore also describable as "nothing (*Nichts*)." Thus Kierkegaard also speaks in the essay (pp. 62, 64) of "beginning from nothing." See also, for example, *JP* III 3306 (*Pap.* VI A 145); *Concluding Unscientific Postscript to* Philosophical Fragments, *KW* XII (*SV* VII 91, 93-94).

21. See Genesis 3:19.

22. See note 20 above.

23. Another reference to Hegel, in whose philosophy negation or the negative is important as the contradicting force ever present in the positivity of existence as the latter struggles toward perfection. See note 35 below.

24. Kierkegaard uses this phrase again; see *JP* II 1541; V 5824 (*Pap.* I A 340; VI A 79). The quotation marks here may indicate literary borrowing; see, for example, Jens Baggesen, *Asenutidens Abracadabra, Danske Værker,* I-XII (Copenhagen: 1827-32; *ASKB* 1509-20), VII, pp. 187, 200.

25. A Byzantine Christian saint who lived on the top of a pillar near Antioch in the fifth century (Stylites: pillar-dweller). Emanuel Hirsch believes that Kierkegaard is thinking of the German theologian and Hegel follower Carl Daub (1765-1836), who was notorious for his complicated, obscure style. Kierkegaard might, however, be thinking of Johann Gottlieb Fichte, who is also so described, or Johann Georg Hamann. See *JP* II 1188, 1541 (*Pap.* I A 252, 340).

26. Here Kierkegaard touches upon a key theme in his authorship, the relationship between ideality and actuality, and the failure of speculative philosophy to take the individual's existence into proper consideration.

27. Georg Wilhelm Friedrich Hegel, *Wissenschaft der Logik* (1812-16).

28. Johann Wolfgang v. Goethe, *Faust*, Part I, 1976-77 (Mephistopheles and the student). See *Goethe's Werke. Vollständige Ausgabe letzter Hand*, I-LX (Stuttgart, Tübingen: 1828-33; *ASKB* 1641-68 [I-LV]), XII, p. 97; *Faust*, tr. Bayard Taylor (New York: Modern Library, 1950), p. 67.

29. Earlier a name for a creature with frog legs and salamander tail. It was believed that its development was the opposite of a frog's and that finally it became a fish. It turned out to be a large tadpole. See Bernard de la Cepède, *Naturgeschichte der Amphibien*, I-II (Weimar: 1800), II, p. 391, and pl. XXXI. Kierkegaard mentions it again in *The Concept of Anxiety*, p. 76, *KW* VIII (*SV* IV 344-45).

30. Jean Paul (pseudonym of Johann Paul Friedrich Richter), *Flegeljahre*, I, 14, *Sämmtliche Werke*, I-LX (Berlin: 1826-28; *ASKB* 1777-99), XXVI, p. 113.

31. The source of this saying has not been located.

32. Ernst Theodor Amadeus Hoffmann, *Klein Zaches genannt Zinnober*, *E.T.A. Hoffmann's ausgewählte Schriften*, I-X (Berlin: 1827-28; *ASKB* 1712-16).

33. See Genesis 30:32-39.

34. Cf. "national facial types," *Either/Or*, I, p. 260, *KW* III (*SV* I 232-33); *JP* II 1967 (*Pap.* I A 337); *Pap.* I C 86.

35. The relation of opposition or contradiction that reveals itself in a concept after a first immediate or unreflective definition. In Hegel this relation is the propelling agent that sets going a dialectic by which the concept is further developed in the ascending process of thesis, antithesis, synthesis.

36. A popular slogan in France in the period after the July Revolution in 1830, used especially of Louis Philippe's nervous attempt to maintain a political power balance between crown and people. Frequently denoting a middle course in politics, it is used here to indicate an equality of mediocrity. For Kierkegaard's criticism of the "middle way," see *JP* I 850 (*Pap.* I A 141).

37. A man from an area of the east coast of Jylland, Mols, where the people were supposedly thick-witted and foolish. There are many tales of their exploits. In the story alluded to by Kierkegaard, *"Det tørstige Træ,"* several Molbos hang in a chain from a tree in the attempt to drag down its branches to the stream beneath so it can drink. See *Postscript*, *KW* XII (*SV* VII 327); Mi-

chael Viggo Fausbøll, *Beretning om de vidtbekjendte Molboers vise Gjerninger og tappre Bedrifter* (Copenhagen: 1827), 7, pp. 13-14.

38. The cycle of short stories by Thomasine Gyllembourg-Ehrensvärd, the mother of Johan Ludvig Heiberg. *En Hverdags-Historie* was first published, pseudonymously, in 1828. Kierkegaard was to review her larger work *To Tidsalder*; see *Two Ages*, esp. pp. 11-23, *KW* XIV (*SV* VIII 11-22).

39. A German nonsense verse from the Romantic period. Somewhat like "The Twelve Days of Christmas," it develops through an adding to and a repetition of the theme. It begins: "Here is the key of the garden, / In it three young girls are waiting, / The first is called Sip, the second Sip-Sipperlip, the third Sipsipperlip-Sipperlonika."

40. The Romans so described those who achieved high office in the state when none in their family had held such before.

41. See Baggesen, *Asenutidens Abracadabra, Værker*, VII, p. 139.

42. Catholicity means universality, but there is also wordplay on "catholic" and the traditional statement that "outside the Church there is no salvation." Cf. traditional Catholic teaching dating from Cyprian: "the true Catholic faith outside which none can be saved."

43. I.e., avoid ill-omened and disturbing words. A Roman admonition to those who had brought a sacrifice to the temple.

44. The beginning of Psalm 130: "Out of the depths I cry unto thee, O Lord." See the Latin Vulgate Bible, Psalmus 129 (130).

45. This incredibly lengthy sentence, together with other pieces of *From the Papers*, was parodied by Andersen in the character of Dalby in *En Comedie i det Grønne* [A Comedy in the Open Air] (Copenhagen: 1840), subtitled "Vaudeville in One Act, After the Old Comedy: 'Actor against His Will.' " Apart from deliberate alterations, such as "made more difficult *de profundis*" for "illustrated *de profundis*," Andersen possibly also makes fun of Kierkegaard's tendency to quote inaccurately. Compare, for example, Andersen's "the heart's demands and announcements" with Kierkegaard's "youth's demands and announcements." For the relevant section of the play and an unpublished reply to it, see Supplement, pp. 202-04, 218-22 (*Pap.* III B 1).

46. Gyllembourg, *Nye Fortællinger af Forfatteren til "En Hverdags-Historie,"* I-III, ed. J. L. Heiberg (Copenhagen: 1835-36), I, p. 198.

47. See *Two Ages,* p. 13, *KW* XIV (*SV* VIII 12); *JP* I 28; V 5234 (*Pap*. I A 334; II A 611).

48. Benoni, son of my sorrow; Benjamin, son of my right hand, i.e., of blessing, happiness. See Genesis 35:18.

49. See Deuteronomy 32:48-52; Joshua 1:1-3. Cf. *JP* I 859 (*Pap*. II A 165): "It is always the Moses in our life (our whole, full, poetic life-power) who does not enter the Promised Land; it is only the Joshua in our life who enters; as Moses is related to Joshua, so the poetic morning-dream of our life is related to its actuality."

50. The refrain in stanzas 44 and 46 of *"Turneringen."* See *Udvalgte danske Viser fra Middelalderen*, ed. Werner Hans Abrahamson, Rasmus Nyerup, and

Knud Lyne Rahbek, I-VI (Copenhagen: 1812-14; *ASKB* 1477-81), I, pp. 10-11.

51. The source has not been located.

52. Like Sigfred in *"Berner Rise og Orm Ungersvend," Udvalgte danske Viser,* I, pp. 64-72.

53. Palmer, an old artist in Gyllembourg, *Extremerne, Nye Fortællinger,* II, p. 20.

54. Gyllembourg, *To Noveller,* ed. J. L. Heiberg (Copenhagen: 1837), pp. 1-244.

55. A saying that occurs in the New Testament after a parable or a teaching by Jesus. See, for example, Matthew 11:15, 13:43; Mark 4:23; Luke 8:8, 14:35.

56. Probably the background tones of I John 5:4, faith as the victory that overcomes the world, and Kierkegaard's experience of an "indescribable joy" (*JP* V 5324; *Pap.* II A 228). Cf. also *JP* III 3364 (*Pap.* II A 201): the religious assurance that has conquered the world.

57. An expression found in Georg Christoph Lichtenberg, *Ideen, Maximen und Einfälle,* I-II (Leipzig: 1831; *ASKB* 1773-74), I, p. 122. See also *JP* V 5245, 6079, 6099 (*Pap.* II A 124; VIII¹ A 440, 655).

58. The minotaur was a mythical monster said to live in the Labyrinth on Crete; it demanded a yearly tribute of young girls and boys. See *JP* V 5100, p. 36 (*Pap.* I A 75, p. 55).

59. Carl Bernhard, *Noveller,* I-IV (Copenhagen: 1836-38; *ASKB U* 18 [III]).

60. Ibid., II, pp. 135-364; see *JP* II 1626 (*Pap.* I A 208).

61. Motto on the volume I title page of Steen Steensen Blicher, *Samlede Digte,* I-II (Copenhagen: 1835-36; *ASKB U* 23), and slightly altered in *Forsang* to *Jyllandsrejsen,* II, p. 5.

62. Literally, born of the earth itself, a term used by the Greeks to designate tribes accepted as being native, nonimmigrant.

63. See II Timothy 4:7.

64. The French naturalist Georges C. L. Cuvier (1769-1832), who in his work *Recherches sur les ossements fossiles,* I-V (Paris: 1821-24), I, p. iii, aimed to prove that one could reconstruct an animal species from a single bone. See also *Either/Or,* I, p. 314, *KW* III (*SV* I 287).

65. H. C. Andersen had previously published among other things: *Fodreise* (Copenhagen: 1829); *Kjærlighed paa Nicolai-Taarn* (1829); *Digte* (1830); *Phantasier og Skizzer* (1831); *Skyggebilleder af en Rejse til Harzen* (1831); *Bruden fra Lammermoor* (1832); *Ravnen* (1832); *Aarets tolv Maaneder* (1833); *Samlede Digte* (1833); *Agnete og Havmanden* (1834); *Improvisatoren* (1835); *Eventyr* (1835); *O. T.* (1836); *Skilles og Mødes* (1836).

66. With this endorsement, the censor gave permission for a book to be published. Denmark gained full freedom of the press in 1851.

67. I.e., a chromatic scale. Proceeding by semitones, and therefore including sharps as well as flats, such a scale is associated more with lament or elegy than is an ordinary diatonic scale.

68. See Hegel, *Vorlesungen über die Aesthetik, Georg Wilhelm Friedrich Hegel's Werke. Vollständige Ausgabe*, I-XVIII, ed. Philipp Marheineke, et al. (Berlin: 1832-45; *ASKB* 549-65), X³, pp. 220-581; *Sämtliche Werke. Jubiläumsausgabe* [*J.A.*], I-XXVI, ed. Hermann Glockner (Stuttgart: Frommann, 1927-40), XIV, pp. 220-581; *The Philosophy of Fine Art*, I-IV (tr. of *V.A.*, 1 ed., 1835-38; Kierkegaard had this ed.), tr. F.P.B. Osmaston (London: Bell, 1920), IV. In Hegel's interpretation of the three stages of poetry, epic is the spontaneous expression of Spirit, things described naively as they are; lyric is the epic's negation by reflecting Spirit, the expression of artistic subjective feeling in collision with the world; and drama is the higher synthesis or union of epic and lyric, of the objective and the subjective. In Kierkegaard, despite an apparent initial hesitation (see *JP* II 1179; I 126; *Pap.* I C 58, A 212), the epic appears as the second, negative and reflective, stage, thus following J. L. Heiberg's order of lyric, epic, drama.

69. Aimed at the growing tendency in the Romantic period to write autobiographies or autobiographical novels, of which Andersen's are examples.

70. The title of Goethe's autobiography, published originally in three parts (1811-14), *Werke*, XXV-XXVI. On the relation between an author's life and his writing, see *Two Ages*, pp. 98-99 and note 72, *KW* XIV (*SV* VIII 91-92). Here it is clear that Kierkegaard thinks that private experience must not be used directly in writing, but only as an instance of universal human experience. Personal particulars must therefore be removed so that while private experience can be utilized artistically as common human experience, a barrier is placed between the reader and the private life of the author.

71. Baggesen, *Asenutidens Abracadabra*, also uses this wordplay; see *Værker*, VII, pp. 186-87, 194-95.

72. It was said that those who entered the Pythagorean School had to pledge themselves to silence for a certain period.

73. Cf. *JP* V 5761 (*Pap.* VI B 222); *Fragments*, p. 5, *KW* VII (*SV* IV 175-76); *Postscript*, *KW* XII (*SV* VII 52).

74. On the process of turf to peat, see Niels Nicolai Lund, *Underretning om Tørvemosers Opmaaling Undersøgelse, Beregning osv.* (Copenhagen: 1809), p. 20. In 1831, Westphalian "peat-makers" were called in to teach the peasants improved methods (*Tidsskrift for Landøkonomi*, 1831, p. 135).

75. Horace, *Epistles*, I, 5, 29; *Q. Horatii Flacci opera* (Leipzig: 1828; *ASKB* 1248), p. 561; *Horace Satires, Epistles and Ars Poetica*, tr. H. Rushton Fairclough (Loeb, Cambridge: Harvard University Press, 1978), pp. 282-83.

76. Peter Wilhelm Lund, *"Om de Brasilianske Myrers Levemaade," Danske Ugeskrift*, II, 1833, p. 27.

77. In IV, 11 (1826), there is a treatise by Hans Christian Lyngbye, pastor at Søborg and Gilleleje 1827-37. In 1818, he had received the silver medal of the Danish Royal Society for his piece of research on the whale and whaling in the Faroe Islands.

78. Louis Adolphe Thiers, *Consulatets og Keiserdømmets Historie*, I-XVII, tr. Jacob Johannes Carl Magnus (Copenhagen: 1845-60; *ASKB* 2016-23 [I-VII]),

XIV, p. 647, relates that the cold deprived the French soldiers in Russia of both sight and hearing. Kierkegaard is probably thinking of a description of the North African deserts in *Danske Ugeskrift*, IV, 1834, pp. 153-64, esp. pp. 154-55, from which he made an excerpt (*JP* IV 3797; *Pap*. I A 131). Mention is made in it of a lack of something by which to measure what one sees in the desert.

79. Cf. *Irony*, p. 78, *KW* II (*SV* XIII 170); Genesis 1:3-15. The source of the entire quotation has not been located.

80. The editors of all three editions of Kierkegaard's *Samlede Værker* think that *vice versa* [the reverse] is used inaccurately here to mean "with variations."

81. An allusion taken from the penultimate verse of Adam Gottlob Oehlenschläger, *"Morgen-Vandring," Langelands-Rejse i Sommeren 1804, Poetiske Skrifter*, I-II (Copenhagen: 1805; *ASKB* 1597-98), I, p. 364. The verse is quoted somewhat imprecisely in *JP* II 1689 (*Pap*. II A 101).

82. See note 122 below.

83. The German poet Heinrich Heine (1797-1856). On Heine's offense at Christianity, see *JP* II 1622-24, 1730 (*Pap*. II A 142-43, 729; III B 16). Cf. *Stages on Life's Way*, p. 452, *KW* XI (*SV* VI 421); *Sickness unto Death*, p. 130, *KW* XIX (*SV* XI 239).

84. See pp. 64-69.

85. I.e., production. Here Kierkegaard criticizes Andersen for producing works that fail to portray authentically the characters intended.

86. Like many others of his time, Andersen passed through a period of enthusiasm for Walter Scott. See, for example, *Gjenfærdet ved Palnatokes Grav* (Copenhagen: 1822); *Bruden fra Lammermoor* (1832); *Festen paa Kenilworth* (1836).

87. See Matthew 13:24-30.

88. August Heinrich Julius Lafontaine (1758-1831). See p. 21 and note 120; *Postscript*, *KW* XII (*SV* VII 381).

89. The impression that Andersen is a character in a poem or novel.

90. Mentioned also in *Fragments*, p. 42, *KW* VII (*SV* IV 210). In both places, Kierkegaard has apparently confused center-of-gravity dolls [*Tyngdepunktsdukker* or *Hyldemarvsdukker* (elder-tree pith dolls)] with divers [*Dykkere*]. The Cartesian devil or diver is a hollow doll that rises or sinks in a water-filled container according to the pressure on the membrane top. The center-of-gravity doll or tumbler doll, weighted at the feet or head, when pushed down, inevitably returns to its original position as soon as one lets it go.

91. A grammatical analogy. See p. 74. Kierkegaard uses this analogy elsewhere; see, for example, *Fragments*, p. 100, *KW* XI (*SV* IV 112); *Postscript*, *KW* XII (*SV* VII 305, 541).

92. Cf. Cicero, *De oratore*, II, 11, 44; *M. Tulli Ciceronis opera omnia*, I-IV and index (Halle: 1756-57; *ASKB* 1224-29), I, p. 422; *Cicero De oratore*, I-III, tr. H. Rackham (Loeb, Cambridge: Harvard University Press, 1982), I, pp. 230-31.

93. A military expression.

94. I.e., impersonality.

95. See Romans 8:38-39.

96. See pp. 79-84.

97. Carl Daub (1765-1836), professor of theology at Heidelberg. He abandoned the ideas of Schelling and tried to use the dialectical method of Hegel in the service of Protestant theology. See also *Fragments*, p. 80, *KW* VII (*SV* IV 243) on Daub as a "prophet in reverse." This refers to Carl Daub, *"Die Form der christlichen Dogmen- und Kirchen-Historie," Zeitschrift für spekulative Theologie*, ed. Bruno Bauer, I-III (Berlin: 1836-38; *ASKB* 354-57), I, 1836, p. 1 (ed. tr.): "The act of looking backward is, just like that of looking into the future, an act of divination; and if the prophet is well called an historian of the future, the historian is just as well called, or even better so, a prophet of the past, of the historical." Kierkegaard repeats this thought of Daub, putting it together with the thought that life is "lived forward." Life can be interpreted only after it has been experienced, but the past informs one's understanding and grasp of the future. See note 25 above; *JP* I 1030, 1025; III 3553 (*Pap.* IV A 164; II A 725, 558). See also *JP* I 619 (*Pap.* II A 624).

98. See Daniel 5, esp. v. 25.

99. In Andersen's novel *O. T.* (1836), the hero Otto Thostrup had these letters tattooed on his shoulder when he was a poor child in the Odense Reformatory [*Tugthus*]. He lets the reminder of his origins spoil his life, does not face up to the task "lying behind" him, does not come to terms with the past and thereby become free of its negative burden for the future.

100. An old German saying. Cf., for example, Goethe, *"Sprichwörtlich," Werke*, II, p. 259. The reference to Grabbe has not been located. See *Either/ Or*, I, p. 144, *KW* III (*SV* I 122), a reference to Christian Dietrich Grabbe, *Don Juan und Faust, Eine Tragödie* (Frankfurt: 1829; *ASKB* 1670). The editors of the first edition of *SV* think that Kierkegaard's note should perhaps belong to line 20 rather than to line 18.

101. A reference to Aristotle's Lyceum, where he taught while walking (*peripatetikos*, given to walking about [*peri*, about + *patos*, path]).

102. See Ludvig Holberg, *Erasmus Montanus eller Rasmus Berg*, III, 2, *Den Danske Skue-Plads*, I-VII (Copenhagen: 1788; *ASKB* 1566-67), V, no pagination; III, 3, *Comedies by Holberg*, tr. Oscar James Campbell, Jr., and Frederic Schenck (New York: American-Scandinavian Foundation, 1935), p. 145. The play here involves a conflict between Erasmus, who knows the world is round, and the villagers, who think it is flat.

103. See Ecclesiastes 1:2.

104. A proper vantage point is given by a life-view. Kierkegaard touches upon this theme again in *Either/Or* when he contrasts the esthete with the ethicist, who, having the correct vantage point, has his mood "beneath him." See *Either/Or*, II, pp. 228-30, *KW* IV (*SV* II 205-07).

105. Danish: *ellers*; Andersen's text reads *eller* [or].

106. Danish: *herlige*; Andersen's text reads *hellige* [holy].

107. Danish: *Skue*; Andersen's text reads *Beskuelse* [contemplation]. The punctuation also is a little different.

108. Like Minerva, who was said to have been born in full armor from the head of Jupiter. See *JP* V 5270 (*Pap.* II A 189).

109. Cf. Matthew 6:28-29.

110. The source (if any) has not been located.

111. Danish: *mangekantede*. See *Postscript, KW* XII (*SV* VII 106), where Johannes Climacus rejects the wrong kind of subjectivity in a person: "the accidental, the angular [*kantede*], the selfish, the eccentric, etc."

112. The tendency to be didactic and moralizing.

113. Cf. *JP* V 5249 (*Pap.* II A 634).

114. See II Timothy 4:7; cf. p. 69.

115. See *Two Ages*, p. 55, *KW* XIV (*SV* VIII 52), where Kierkegaard alters the words of Pliny and *omnia ad conscientiam, nil ad ostentationem* becomes *omnia ad ostentationem, nil ad conscientiam*. See Pliny the Younger, *Letters*, I, 22, 5; *Plinii, C., Epistolae et Panegyricus* (Halle: 1789; *ASKB A I* 182); *Pliny Letters and Panegyricus*, I-II, tr. Betty Radice (Loeb, Cambridge: Harvard University Press, 1949), pp. 68-69.

116. See *JP* IV 4396 (*Pap.* I A 322).

117. The first six chapters depict the hero's childhood. See, for example, *Kun en Spillemand*, I, pp. 15, 18 (ed. tr.): "But for childhood imagination a wealth lay in it." "Childhood imagination needs only to scratch in the ground with a stick in order to create a castle with halls and corridors."

118. If the wrong clef is printed at the beginning of a tenor's part or, in the case of the C clef, the sign is printed in the wrong place at the beginning of his part, he would find himself directed to sing soprano.

119. See, for example, *Kun en Spillemand*, I, p. 50 (ed. tr.): "A stranger suddenly transported to this mild air and to this luxuriance would imagine himself to be in a more southern land; Svendborg Sound would certainly remind him of the Danube."

120. From epic to lyric.

121. *Kun en Spillemand*, I, p. 156, describes how encouraged the hero feels when a prostitute calls him a genius who will certainly get on in the world (ed. tr.): "He thus had the same assurance as every other true genius who puts his fate in the hands of a wealthy man or woman; and these as often as not have the intelligence to judge—much as she had!"

122. See p. 73. Kierkegaard compares the genius to fire that is only incited by the wind or storm of adversity. Elsewhere he likens geniuses to thunderstorms; see *JP* II 1290, 1298 (*Pap.* II A 535; X¹ A 590); *The Moment*, 6, in The Moment *and Late Writings, KW* XXIII (*SV* XIV 219). For Andersen, genius is a fragile egg needing warmth; see p. 81, *Kun en Spillemand*, I, p. 161. Kierkegaard also uses the simile of an unquenchable fire concerning the one who sincerely trusts in God; see *Upbuilding Discourses in Various Spirits, KW* XV (*SV* VIII 195).

123. See a review of *Improvisatoren* and *O. T.* in *Maanedsskrift for Litteratur*, XVIII, 1837, pp. 66-70, presumably by Frederik Christian Olsen.

124. See pp. 74-76.

125. *Kun en Spillemand*, I, p. 146, a reference to the remark about the governess's poem about Møen. I, p. 141 (ed. tr.): "He was also a poet, had in his time written in *Aftenposten* and *Poulsens Nytaarsgave*, but under a pseudonym."

126. The metaphorical allusion is to a box, the contents of which appear only after pressing a concealed spring. Kierkegaard uses the same thought in *Christian Discourses*, *KW* XVII (*SV* X 116); *The Moment*, 7, in Moment, *KW* XXIII (*SV* XIV 246).

127. See Genesis 2:21-22.

128. Steffen-Karreet, proprietress of a Copenhagen brothel visited by sailors.

129. *Kun en Spillemand*, I, pp. 110-16; II, p. 125.

130. Ibid., II, pp. 80, 108-22.

131. For example, ibid., II, pp. 17, 96, 98, 118, 130; III, pp. 77, 106.

132. Bishop Nicolai Edinger Balle (1744-1816), *Lærebog i den Evangelisk-christelige Religion, indrettet til Brug i de danske Skoler* (Copenhagen: 1824; *ASKB* 183), a catechism used everywhere in Danish primary schools from its first printing in 1791 to its revision in 1854. See Hans Lassen Martensen, *Af Mit Levnet*, I-III (Copenhagen: 1882-83), III, pp. 25, 33-37.

133. *Evangelisk-christelig Psalmebog til Brug ved Kirke- og Huusandagter* (Copenhagen: 1798).

134. In the 1830s, the Grundtvigian party attacked the Evangelical-Christian hymnal for its rationalism. See, for example, *Nordisk Kirke-Tidende*, 1833, col. 90-93, 100-03, 122-25.

135. Name of an Austrian fortress in Moravia (now in modern Czechoslovakia). See note 137 below.

136. The "Leads of Venice" (*Piombi*), famous Venetian prison under the lead roof of the Doge's palace, a prison notorious for its oppressive heat. See note 137 below.

137. A well-known book by the Italian poet Silvio Pellico (1788-1854). Pellico was imprisoned in the Spiegelberg fortress for ten years on a charge of conspiracy and mentions the famous Venetian Piombi prison in chapter XXIII of his book. Andersen refers to the book in *Kun en Spillemand*, III, p. 15.

138. See Historical Introduction, p. xi, on Provincial Consultative Assemblies.

139. A figure, usually a cross, written by physicians above their prescriptions. Different meanings are ascribed to it. See *"Recept,"* *Salmonsens Konversations Leksikon*, I-XXVI (Copenhagen: 1915-30), XIX, pp. 982-93. See also *Letters*, Letter 96, *KW* XXV; *JP* III 2865 (*Pap.* X[1] 221).

140. Jacob Jacobsen Dampe (1790-1867), Danish scholar and politician. After a fine academic record at the University of Copenhagen followed by a

career in teaching, Dr. Dampe, because of his keen interest in politics, began to agitate and lay concrete plans for reform of the Danish constitution. He was imprisoned for high treason from 1820 to 1848 but in his last years received a state pension as the first martyr for the cause of political Liberalism.

141. Danish: *hellenistisk* [Hellenistic]; Andersen's text reads *hellenisk* [Hellenic].

142. The name given to a group of writers who in the 1830s expressed their political resistance to the reactionism following the collapse of the July Revolution. The group was created after the edict of the Federal Diet, December 10, 1835, suppressed the writings of Heinrich Heine, Karl Gützkow, Ludolf Wienbarg, Theodor Mundt, Heinrich Laube, and Ludwig Börne. The group was mildly Saint-Simonistic (see p. 4 and note 9) and affirmed the essential relation between literature and contemporary social problems. It had considerable influence on German literature of the time. Kierkegaard mentions the group in *Irony*, p. 275, *KW* II (*SV* XIII 347). Danish: *for det unge* [for the young]; Andersen's text reads *af det unge* [of the young].

143. *Kun en Spillemand*, III, pp. 57-77.

144. See Ephesians 6:4.

145. Possibly an allusion to the arbitration of Pope Alexander VI in the boundary dispute between Spain and Portugal. The Pope drew a hypothetical line from pole to pole through a point one hundred leagues west of the westernmost point of the Azores. The territory west of this line was to belong to Spain, and the territory east of this line to Portugal. See *Postscript, KW* XII (*SV* VII 48).

146. The quoted passages contain variations in the forms of some Danish words and unimportant deviations in punctuation.

147. See I Kings 3:16-28.

148. Danish: *rivende* [rapid]; Andersen's text reads *rindende* [running].

149. Danish: *Tryllesang* [incantation]; Andersen's text reads *Trøstesang* [song of consolation].

150. *Kun en Spillemand*, I, pp. 73-74, 95. Kierkegaard mentions the Venusberg legend in *Either/Or* I, p. 90, *KW* III (*SV* I 71); *Works of Love, KW* XVI (*SV* IX 155); *Pap*. II A 180; *JP* IV 4439 (*Pap*. VIII¹ A 17).

151. *Kun en Spillemand*, I, p. 37. Ole Bornemann Bull (1810-1880), world-famous Norwegian violinist. Amphion was a gifted mythological lyre-player. Jubal was the father of music; see Genesis 4:21.

152. A theme Kierkegaard mentions again in his writings. See, for example, *Either/Or*, I, p. 154, *KW* III (*SV* I 131); *Stages*, pp. 250-52, *KW* XI (*SV* VI 236-37); *JP* V 5430, 5664, 5669 (*Pap*. IV A 114; II A 805; IV A 107, p. 43).

153. While playing hide and seek, Christian conceals himself in the bell chamber of the church tower. He collapses from the sound when the bells begin to ring at sundown and suffers the first of many attacks of "convulsions" that weaken him bodily but make him more sensitive spiritually. See *Kun en Spillemand*, I, pp. 55-59.

154. Ibid., I, pp. 62, 65; cf. I, p. 59. Danish: *ulyksalige* [disastrous]; Andersen's text reads *ulykkelige* [unfortunate].

155. Ibid., I, pp. 62-63 (ed. tr.): "As the nerves became more irritated, so the ear became more open to the language of music. The unfortunate convulsions returned more often and left a strange vibration in the eyelashes, a pain in the eyes themselves, while all objects appeared in motley, ever-shifting colors."

156. A Danish rix-dollar, worth about $5 (1973 money).

157. See Ecclesiastes 1:2; cf. p. 80.

158. See *Kun en Spillemand*, II, pp. 29, 31.

159. See ibid., II, pp. 68-71.

160. See ibid., II, p. 83; Genesis 37:5-11.

161. See *Kun en Spillemand*, II, pp. 105-07.

162. See ibid., I, p. 61. See also p. 97. Naomi does not use these words about the hero of the book.

163. In *Kun en Spillemand*, III, only a few pages here and there in chapter IV (pp. 23, 82-83) and the conclusion (ch. IX) deal with the hero; the rest of part III is about Naomi's adventures abroad. Andersen divided the second edition of *Kun en Spillemand* (Copenhagen: 1854) into only two parts.

164. Danish: *seet* [seen]; Andersen's text reads *seet ude* [seen abroad].

165. See *Kun en Spillemand*, III, pp. 83, 116.

166. Danish: *de Hellige*. See *JP* III 3318 (*Pap.* X³ A 437) and note 962.

167. See title page and note. Since, like Pückler-Muskau, Andersen had traveled, Kierkegaard contrasts Andersen's success as a traveler with his failure as an author when depicting the psychological development and fate of his characters.

168. See *Kun en Spillemand*, III, p. 65.

169. See note 150 above.

170. See *Kun en Spillemand*, I, pp. 129-30.

171. Suppressed Church, therefore the Church concealed or hidden.

172. Invisible ink. See *Sickness unto Death*, p. 124, *KW* XIX (*SV* XI 233). Such ink usually needs heat, chemicals, or water to reveal the hidden message. It seems that in Kierkegaard's time the writing became visible in watermark form and thus needed to be held up to the light. See *JP* I 618 (*Pap.* II A 620). Through this wordplay on "sympathetic," Kierkegaard urges Andersen to look for the positive and even friendly message hidden in the complicated language of a somewhat lengthy review.

THE BATTLE BETWEEN THE OLD AND THE NEW SOAP-CELLARS

Title Page. Although the editors of Kierkegaard's *Papirer* suggest 1838 as the date of this drama, it has also been placed in 1838-39 and between July 1839 and spring 1840. The play could well have been planned for spring 1840. For a full discussion of dating and the play generally, see Niels Thulstrup, *Kier-*

kegaards Forhold til Hegel (Copenhagen: Gyldendal, 1967), pp. 156-71; *Kierkegaard's Relation to Hegel*, tr. George L. Stengren (Princeton: Princeton University Press, 1980), pp. 180-200. On Graabrødretorvet, near the University of Copenhagen, there was fierce competition between rival soap-dealers. A. Møller's soap-cellar had a sign: "Here is the genuine old soap-cellar where the genuine old soap-cellar people live." His rival's sign proclaimed: "Here is the new soap-cellar; the old soap-cellar people moved in on May 1, 1808." Møller retaliated with a newspaper advertisement. Kierkegaard's allusions in 1836 (*JP* V 5156; *Pap.* I A 220) suggest further developments in soap-cellar rivalry. The rivalry became somewhat proverbial, and Kierkegaard may have used the soap-cellars for his title to indicate two rival student clubs: the old *Studenterforening* and *Den akademiske Læseforening*, popularly known as *Akademikum*, founded in April 1839.

1. *Pap.* II B 4. The translation of the first draft pages follows the order indicated by the manuscript.

2. *Pap.* II B 5. See *JP* IV 4406 (*Pap.* II A 279). Matthias Claudius, *ASMUS omnia sua SECUM portans, oder Sämmtliche Werke des Wandsbecker Bothen, Werke,* I-IV (1-8) (Hamburg: 1838; *ASKB* 1631-32), II (4), pp. 112-15. An etching of the four brothers faces p. 114; the verse is on p. 115:

> Ach, Herr! lass dein' lieb' Engelein
> Am letzen End' die Seele mein
>   In Abrahams Schooss tragen,
> Den Leib in sein'm Schlaf-Kämmerlein,
> Gar sanft ohn' ein'ge Quaal und Pein,
>   Ruhn bis am jüngsten Tage
> [O Lord, let your dear little angels
> At my end bear my soul
>   To Abraham's bosom;
> Let my body rest in its little bedroom,
> Softly, without any agony and pain,
>   Until judgment day].

3. *Pap.* II B 6. See Luke 19:1-10; *JP* V 5228 (*Pap.* II A 600).

4. *Pap.* II B 3. See Wessel, *Kierlighed uden Strømper,* refrain from the final song in the play, *Johan Herman Wessels samtlige Skrivter,* I-II (Copenhagen: 1787), I, pp. 119-20.

5. *Pap.* II B 3. See p. 53. It is impossible to use this part of the title as a means of dating the play precisely. Kierkegaard may have contemplated using the pseudonym if *From the Papers* had already been published.

6. *Pap.* II B 2.

7. Willibald may be the young Søren Kierkegaard, Echo Kierkegaard's "other self" (see pp. 55-58) or Henrik Hertz. The party and projected suicide on pp. 107-08 have been viewed as based on a Heiberg party of June 4, 1836, and on *JP* V 5141 (*Pap.* I A 161). See, e.g., Thulstrup, pp. 189-200;

Frithiof Brandt, *Den unge Søren Kierkegaard* (Copenhagen: 1929), pp. 419-46. That Henrik Hertz is Echo is argued from Hertz's diary entries of 1836, his friendship with Kierkegaard, and the characterization of the latter as the Translator in his novel *Stemninger og Tilstande* (Copenhagen: 1839). The "other self" theory is supported by references to Kierkegaard's journals, for example, *JP* V 5186, 5320, 5390 (*Pap*. I A 333; II A 742, 444). Although Kierkegaard did use material from his life in his authorship, direct identifications are very dubious. *JP* entries 5141 and 5186, for example, are regarded by some as part of a "Faustian Letters" project (see *JP* V, p. 481 and note 245; *Either/ Or*, I, p. 662, note 1, *KW* III), and although, like many an author, Kierkegaard identified himself closely with his literary models, some ideas were already in the literary atmosphere. Both Jens Baggesen and Hans Christian Andersen, for example, make use of the double or "other self" motif. See, for example, Jens Baggesen, *Gjengangeren og han selv* (1806-07), *Danske Værker*, I-XII (Copenhagen: 1827-32; *ASKB* 1509-20), V, pp. 397-488; cf. VI, p. 130; cf. *JP* V 5125 (*Pap*. I C 78); Hans Christian Andersen, *Fodreise fra Holmens Canal til Østpynten af Amager* (1828-29), *Samlede Skrifter*, I-XV (Copenhagen: 1877), VI, pp. 187-88, 245-47. Thus one probably should not view Willibald as more than a parody of a young Faustian doubter flying into the arms of Hegelianism. His name may well have been inspired by the Willibald in Joseph v. Eichendorf's story *Viel Lärmen um Nichts* (Berlin: 1833; *ASKB* 1850). Cf. *Pap*. I C 86; Carl Roos, *Kierkegaard og Goethe* (Copenhagen: 1955), pp. 144-46; Emanuel Hirsch, *Kierkegaard-Studien*, I-II (Gütersloh: 1933), I, p. 304. See also Thulstrup, pp. 189-92. A main character is also named Willibald in Christoph Martin Wieland, *Euthanasia, C. M. Wielands sämmtliche Werke*, I-XXXIX, Suppl. I-VI (Leipzig: 1794-1811; 1797-98), XXXVII.

8. See note 7 above.

9. *Springgaas* (jumping jack). In Kierkegaard's time, this was the name of a jumping toy made by twining a string a couple of times around the backbone of a goose. A small stick or pin pushed between the fastened string and bone was turned until the string became extremely taut. One end of the stick was then daubed with pitch in order to glue it temporarily to the bone. The resulting arrangement would spring in the air unexpectedly and in unexpected directions. H. C. Andersen has such a toy in his story *"Springfyrene," Nye Eventyr, Første Bind. Tredie Samling* (Copenhagen: 1845), pp. 27-32; "The Jumping Competition," *The Complete Fairy Tales and Stories*, tr. Erik Christian Haugaard (New York: Doubleday, 1974), pp. 195-96. Mr. von Jumping-Jack, as the caricature of a philosophizing esthete, may be based on Johan Ludvig Heiberg, although he talks like Hans Lassen Martensen. See notes 11 and 48 below; Thulstrup, *Kierkegaards Forhold til Hegel*, pp. 162, 188-89. See also Henning Fenger, *Kierkegaard-Myter og Kierkegaard-Kilder* (Odense: Odense Universitetsforlag, 1976), p. 116; *Kierkegaard, The Myths and Their Origins*, tr. George C. Schoolfield (New Haven: Yale University Press, 1980), pp. 141-42. The name may have been suggested by Professor Springgaas, a

character mentioned in Steen Steensen Blicher, *Fjorten Dage i Jylland, Samlede Noveller,* I-V (Copenhagen: 1833-36; *ASKB* 1521-23), V, p. 100.

10. Mr. Holla Hastværksen (Mr. Holla Hurrison). In the manuscript, Kierkegaard is inconsistent in the spelling of Holla. It seems likely that Orla Lehmann is the model for Mr. Hurrison. If so, the variation in spelling and the fact that "Holla" is added as an afterthought in the list of characters may indicate that Kierkegaard decided to search for a name resembling "Orla" in sound and spelling. Kierkegaard also has a marginal note "Holla (his first name)" crossed out in the ms.

11. Mr. Phrase. As one who has studied Hegel but has now gone further (see pp. 116, 119), this character may be a figure poking fun at Hans Lassen Martensen (1808-1884). Martensen became a lecturer in moral philosophy in the University of Copenhagen theology faculty in 1838, later professor of theology and, after Jakob Peter Mynster, bishop of Sjælland, in 1854. On Martensen's attitude to Hegel, see *JP* V 5200 (*Pap.* II A 7) and Martensen's autobiography, *Af mit Levnet,* I-III (Copenhagen: 1882-83), esp. I and II.

12. A public building in a Greek city in which foreign embassies, distinguished citizens, and others were entertained officially. Socrates suggested at his trial that he be rewarded with free meals in the prytaneum. See *Irony,* p. 195, *KW* II (*SV* XIII 276).

13. Ole Wadt may well be modeled on Jens Finsteen Gi(j)ødwad (1811-1891). See Historical Introduction, notes 48-51.

14. Of the remaining characters, not all are on Kierkegaard's list, whereas some that are do not appear in the play. Those appearing in the play but not on the list are the physician, the police agent, two of the three revivalists, the president, and some philologists. Those who are on the list but not in the play are the fly's nephew, the ventriloquist, the fighter for orthography, and the wholesalers. Possibly identifiable are the revivalists (see note 39 below) and the president, who may be intended to be Chairman Parmo Carl Ploug if the prytaneum is the *Akademikum* (see title page note above). The horn may possibly be an allusion to the "bellowing" "Ale-Norse" Grundtvig (see, for example, *JP* V 6097, 5740 [*Pap.* VIII¹ A 487; V A 58]; see also pp. 120, 121, and notes 64, 66) or even to Heiberg's *Flyvende Post,* with its front page picture of a winged messenger blowing a horn. The "Fighter for Orthography" could point to Johannes Hage of *Fædrelandet* (see p. 23 and note 130). "Polytechnic Students" refers to the Polytechnic, Denmark's first technical college, started in Copenhagen under royal ordinance by Hans Christian Ørsted in 1829.

15. *Die Phänomenologie des Geistes* by Georg Wilhelm Friedrich Hegel had appeared in 1807.

16. Added as a marginal note by Kierkegaard.

17. *C. Sallustii Crispi, Opera quae supersunt* . . . , I-II, ed. F. Kritzius (Leipzig: 1828-34; *ASKB* 1269-70), II, pp. 22-23; *Sallust,* tr. J. C. Rolfe (Loeb, New York: Putnam, 1921), pp. 136-37. Kierkegaard also had *Opera omnia,*

ed. Guil. Lange (Halle: 1833; *ASKB* 1271) and *Opera* (ed. stereot., Leipzig: 1829; *ASKB* 1272).

18. See Historical Introduction, p. x; *JP* V 5228 (*Pap.* II A 600).

19. Possibly a dig at Orla Lehmann.

20. From September 1, 1837, Kierkegaard had lived in a room at Løvstræde 7, the end of which opened across another street into Graabrødretorvet.

21. Wolfgang Amadeus Mozart, *Don Juan*, I, 1, tr. Laurids Kruse (Copenhagen: 1807), p. 3; cf. *Don Giovanni*, tr. Ellen H. Bleiler (New York: Dover, 1964), p. 85. See also Johan Ludvig Heiberg, *Skuespil*, I-VII (Copenhagen: 1833-41; *ASKB* 1553-59), IV, p. 259 (Hummer's song).

22. See Augustin Eugène Scribe, *Bruden*, I, 2, tr. J. L. Heiberg, *Det Kongelige Theaters Repertoire*, 35 (1831), pp. 1-2 (Madame Charlotte's song).

23. See Adelbert v. Chamisso, *Peter Schlemihl's wundersame Geschichte* (Nürnberg: 1835; *ASKB* 1630), p. 328; *The Wonderful History of Peter Schlemihl* (Emmaus, Pa.: Story Classics, 1956), p. 10. See also *JP* V 5160 (*Pap.* I C 102, p. 276); *Either/Or*, II, p. 10, *KW* IV (*SV* II 10).

24. Tithonos, the husband of Aurora (Dawn), was immortal, yet without possessing eternal youth. He became a grasshopper and faded away until only his voice remained. See *Irony*, p. 272, *KW* II (*SV* XIII 344); *JP* II 1189 (*Pap.* I A 302).

25. Cf. *JP* V 5186, p. 87 (*Pap.* I A 333, p. 149).

26. See note 7 above.

27. See Suetonius, "Caligula," 30, *The Lives of the Caesars*; *Caji Suetonii Tranquilli Tolv første Romerske Keiseres Levnetsbeskrivelse*, I-II, tr. Jacob Baden (Copenhagen: 1802-03; *ASKB* 1281), I, p. 312; *Suetonius*, I-II, tr. J. C. Rolfe (Loeb, New York: Macmillan, 1914), I, p. 453: "Angered at the rabble for applauding a faction which he opposed, he cried: 'I wish the Roman people had but a single neck . . . .' "

28. See Gottfried A. Bürger, "Lenore," *Bürgers Gedichte* (Gotha, New York: 1828), p. 52.

29. Brandt, in *Den unge Søren Kierkegaard*, p. 435, maintains that the "compassionate devil" is the young Kierkegaard's "demon of wit" that took control of him at times. See, however, note 7 above.

30. See note 24 above.

31. See p. 55.

32. In Kierkegaard's time, Kjøbmagergade was divided into Great and Little. The latter is now Frederiksborggade.

33. Cf. *JP* V 5092, p. 23 (*Pap.* I A 72, p. 51).

34. As Kierkegaard did. See Carl Weltzer, *Peter og Søren Kierkegaard*, I-II (Copenhagen: 1936), I, p. 162.

35. Κοινωνικὸν ζῶον ὁ ἄνθρωπος [Man is a social animal]. Cf. Aristotle, *Politics*, 1278 b; *Aristoteles graece*, I-II, ed. Immanuel Bekker (Berlin: 1831; *ASKB* 1074-75), p. 1278; *The Complete Works of Aristotle*, I-II, ed. Jonathan Barnes (rev. Oxford tr.; Princeton: Princeton University Press, 1984), II, p. 2029: "man is by nature a political animal."

36. See Augustin Eugène Scribe and Casimir Delavigne, *Muurmesteren*, tr. Thomas Overskou, I, 1, *Repertoire*, 17 (1829), p. 1; cf. III, 13, p. 18. Kierkegaard's version deviates slightly from the original text.

37. The idea of rotation occurs again in "Rotation of Crops," *Either/Or*, I, pp. 281-300, *KW* III (*SV* I 253-72).

38. Soil consisting of clay and carbonate of lime, formerly popular as a fertilizer until it was discovered that too frequent use actually impoverishes the land.

39. Cf. Acts 5:41. It has been suggested that the three revivalists represent Kierkegaard's brother Peter Christian (1805-1888), Jacob Christian Lindberg (1797-1857), and Andreas Gottlob Rudelbach (1792-1862). All three at that time were staunch Grundtvigians. In favor of this interpretation is the fact that Lindberg held religious meetings in his home without permission from the Church authorities, who tried to stop him.

40. Cf. *Postscript*, *KW* XII (*SV* VII 445). In the manuscript, this note comes before marginal note II B 14.

41. See Adam Gottlob Oehlenschläger, *Palnatoke*, V, 2 (Copenhagen: 1809), pp. 175-76. Palnatoke's lines are somewhat freely recalled. Cf. *The Moment*, 1, in Moment, *KW* XXIII (*SV* XIV 108).

42. See note 39 above.

43. *L'Hombre*, a Spanish card game, usually with three players. The triangular arrangement is a play on the Hegelian scheme of thesis, antithesis, synthesis.

44. Steel pens were used in Denmark from 1830. See *Postscript*, *KW* XII (*SV* VII 266).

45. "The longer leg" suggests the stick or pin of a jumping jack.

46. Mr. Phrase's argument is the exact opposite of Kierkegaard's in later journal entries, where he recommends the intensive and condemns the extensive. See, for example, *JP* II 2102, 2103 (*Pap.* X⁵ A 26; XI¹ A 500).

47. Kierkegaard's humorous polemic (see also pp. 117-19) against a current idea in philosophy that truth can be achieved only by beginning with doubt. In Kierkegaard's view, doubt cannot be conquered by knowledge, since reflection is an infinite process unless broken off by an act of the will. Against misuse of the Cartesian *de omnibus dubitandum est*, Kierkegaard was to write his *Johannes Climacus*, *KW* VII (*Pap.* IV B 1-17, 1842-43).

48. The speech from "doubt is the specific character" to *"de gustibus non est disputandum"* is drawn with alterations from Martensen's review (1836) of J. L. Heiberg's *Indlednings Foredrag til det . . . logiske Cursus* (Copenhagen: 1835), *Maanedsskrift for Litteratur*, XVI, 1836, pp. 518-19.

49. Cf. note 47 above.

50. This old Latin saying was first found in its published Danish form, *"Om Smag og Behag kan man ikke disputere,"* in J. L. Heiberg's comedy *Guldkorset*, I, 4, *Repertoire*, 95 (1836), p. 3.

51. Danish: *kantede*, literally, "with sides," "with edges."

52. To the question "What is life?" in the elementary first-year philosophy

course, philosophy professor Frederik Christian Sibbern's (1785-1872) lengthy answer began with *"Livet er en af en indre Kilde kommende Virksomhed . . .* [Life is an activity coming from an inner source]." His definition was used in several shorter and longer forms, and a detailed version can be found in his *Menneskets Aandelige Natur og Væsen. Et Udkast til en Psychologie,* I-II (Copenhagen: 1819-28), I, pp. 14-18; cf. F. C. Sibbern, *Psychologie, indledet ved almindelig Biologie, i sammentrængt Fremstilling* (Copenhagen: 1856), p. 15.

53. Attributed to Archimedes: Give me a place to stand and I will move the world. See Plutarch, "Marcellus," 14, *Lives; Plutark's Levnetsbeskrivelser,* I-IV, tr. Stephan Tetens (Copenhagen: 1800-11; *ASKB* 1197-1200), III, p. 272; *Plutarch's Lives,* I-XI, tr. Bernadotte Perrin (Loeb, Cambridge: Harvard University Press, 1968-84), V, p. 473: ". . . Archimedes, who was a kinsman and friend of King Hiero, wrote to him that with any given force it was possible to move any given weight; and emboldened, as we are told, by the strength of his demonstration, he declared that, if there were another world, and he could go to it, he could move this." See also, for example, *Either/Or,* I, p. 295, *KW* III (*SV* I 266); *Repetition,* p. 186, *KW* VI (*SV* III 221); *JP* III 3426; V 5099, 5468 (*Pap.* IX A 115; I A 68; III A 73).

54. The Danish editors suggest that "that we [*at vi*]" in the manuscript probably should read "to know [*at vide*]." It is more likely, however, that Willibald, for the first time completely cut off from Echo, has not yet become accustomed to freedom from his "double."

55. Doubt. See *JP* V 5092, pp. 20-21 (*Pap.* I A 72, p. 47).

56. In Greek mythology, the Hyperboreans were a happy, virtuous people living in everlasting bliss in an inaccessible springlike land. This land lay beyond lofty mountains whose caverns were supposed to send forth the piercing blasts of the north wind. Later the term was applied to the inhabitants of northern lands.

57. *Store Bededag* (Great Day of Prayer, the fourth Friday after Easter), dating from 1686, the special general day of penance and prayer in the Danish Church.

58. See note 47 above.

59. Originally, in ancient Troy, a wooden statue of Pallas Athene on which the safety of the city was believed to depend. The word is now used to describe anything affording protection and security.

60. In Greek mythology, one of the three Gorgons, whose look turned people to stone. She was slain by Perseus.

61. A possible thrust at David Friedrich Strauss (1808-1874) and his mythological interpretation of the life of Jesus, *Das Leben Jesu,* I-II (Tübingen: 1835-36); *The Life of Jesus Critically Examined,* tr. George Eliot (tr. of 4 ed., 1892; Philadelphia: Fortress, 1972).

62. The Scottish engineer John Loudon Macadam (1756-1836) had invented his road-making process in 1819.

63. See Kierkegaard's paper given to the Student Association, p. 39 (*Pap.* I

B 2, p. 162). On May 28, 1835, at a celebration commemorating "The Ordinance of May 28, 1831" (introducing Provincial Consultative Assemblies to the king), people were exhorted to "celebrate the day so beautifully called by the poet: 'Denmark's May and Denmark's Morning.' " See *Kjøbenhavnsposten*, 127-30, May 27-June 2, 1835, esp. 130. "The solemn break of day" etc. are typical of Orla Lehmann. See p. 135: the " 'dawn of the life and freedom of the people' "; cf. p. 6.

64. A year marking a special jubilee or occasion of importance. This was a favorite expression of Grundtvig's. See, in connection with the final coming of the Kingdom of Christ, *Den Danske Salmebog*, 277, v. 11: *"Vidunderligst af alt pa jord"*; cf. 60, *"Blomstre som en Rosengaard."* See *Either/Or*, I, p. 413, *KW* III (*SV* I 380); *Pap.* VI B 11, p. 87. Peter Christian Kierkegaard used it in a poem written in February 1838; see Weltzer, *Peter og Søren Kierkegaard*, I, p. 119.

65. See I Corinthians 5:7. On the Jesuits, see *JP* II 1770; V 5181, p. 81 (*Pap.* I A 196, 328, p. 141).

66. Kierkegaard is thinking of Grundtvig's *Skolen for Livet og Academiet i Soer* (Copenhagen: 1838), in which Grundtvig strongly recommends the kind of high school that prepares students for life and provides education for all classes.

67. On the last day of school examinations, Danish gymnasium graduates in student caps drive in a horse-drawn cart to the equestrian statue of King Christian V in Kongens Nytorv, Copenhagen. There they go hand-in-hand around the statue. In Kierkegaard's time, it was common to drive around the statue. See also *Kun en Spillemand*, I-III (Copenhagen: 1837; *ASKB* 1503), II, p. 25; *Only a Fiddler*, I-III, tr. Mary Howitt (London: 1845), I, p. 127.

68. The sign of Capricorn, December 22-January 20. One supposed attribute of a person born under the sign of Capricorn is that of having strange ideas about duty, love, social position, etc.; such persons are for this reason frequently regarded as eccentric.

69. In the Hegelian system, thought or philosophy is viewed as the highest stage.

70. Danish: *slet* and German: *schlecht*, literally, "bad." Hegel translators use "spurious" (Miller) and "wrong" (Wallace). See, for example, G.W.F. Hegel, *Encyclopädie der philosophischen Wissenschaften im Grundrisse*, I, *Die Logik*, 94 and *Zusatz*, *Georg Wilhelm Friedrich Hegel's Werke. Vollständige Ausgabe*, I-XVIII, ed. Philipp Marheineke et al. (Berlin: 1832-45; *ASKB* 549-65), VI, pp. 184-85; *Sämtliche Werke. Jubiläumsausgabe* [*J.A.*], I-XXVI, ed. Hermann Glockner (Stuttgart: Frommann, 1927-40), VIII, pp. 222-23; *Hegel's Logic* (tr. of *L.*, 3 ed., 1830; Kierkegaard had this ed.), tr. William Wallace (Oxford: Oxford University Press, 1975), pp. 137-38:

This **Infinity** is the wrong or negative infinity: it is only a negation of a finite: but the finite rises again the same as ever, and is never got rid of and absorbed. In other words, this infinite only expresses the *ought-to-be* elimination of the finite. The progression to infinity never gets further than a statement of the contradiction involved in the finite, viz. that it is somewhat as well as somewhat else. It sets up with endless iteration the alternation between these two terms, each of which calls up the other.

If we let somewhat and another, the elements of determinate Being, fall asunder, the result is that some becomes other, and this other is itself a somewhat, which then as such changes likewise, and so on *ad infinitum*. This result seems to superficial reflection something very grand, the grandest possible. But such a progression to infinity is not the real infinite. That consists in being at home with itself in its other, or, if enunciated as a process, in coming to itself in its other. Much depends on rightly apprehending the notion of infinity, and not stopping short at the wrong infinity of endless progression. When time and space, for example, are spoken of as infinite, it is in the first place the infinite progression on which our thoughts fasten. We say, Now, This time, and then we keep continually going forwards and backwards beyond this limit. The case is the same with space, the infinity of which has formed the theme of barren declamation to astronomers with a talent for edification. In the attempt to contemplate such an infinite, our thought, we are commonly informed, must sink exhausted. It is true indeed that we must abandon the unending contemplation, not however because the occupation is too sublime, but because it is too tedious. It is tedious to expatiate in the contemplation of this infinite progression, because the same thing is constantly recurring. We lay down a limit: then we pass it: next we have a limit once more, and so on for ever. All this is but superficial alternation, which never leaves the region of the finite behind. To suppose that by stepping out and away into that infinity we release ourselves from the finite, is in truth but to seek the release which comes by flight. But the man who flees is not yet free: in fleeing he is still conditioned by that from which he flees. If it be also said that the infinite is unattainable, the statement is true, but only because to the idea of infinity has been attached the circumstance of being simply and solely negative. With such empty and other-world stuff philosophy has nothing to do.

See also, for example, *Postscript*, *KW* XII (*SV* VII 91-95, 292-93); *JP* II 1577, 1579 (*Pap*. II A 381, 487).

71. By the spring of 1840, the *Akademikum* was one year old. See title page note above.

72. The speculative concept. The idea that nature can grasp it may have been prompted by Schelling.

73. See title page note above.

74. Efterslægten [Posterity], a famous civic secondary school founded in 1797 and inspired by the same principles as Borgerdydskolen. It was at the peak of its fame in the first half of the nineteenth century. See *Letters*, Letter 1, p. 38, *KW* XXV.

SUPPLEMENT

1. See Historical Introduction, pp. xv-xvi. See also p. 229, note 2.
2. Jean Paul (pseudonym of Johann Paul Friedrich Richter) (1763-1825). On

the poet and the philosopher, see, for example, *Vorschule der Aesthetik*, I-II (Vienna: 1815; *ASKB* 1381-83), II, p. 244; *Jean Paul's sämmtliche Werke*, I-LX (Berlin: 1826-28; *ASKB* 1777-99), XLIII, p. 118.

3. A basic proposition in Plato's philosophy; see, for example, *Meno*, 81 d; *Platonis quae exstant opera*, I-XI, ed. Friedrich Ast (Leipzig: 1819-32; *ASKB* 1144-54), IX, pp. 224-25; *The Collected Dialogues of Plato*, ed. Edith Hamilton and Huntington Cairns (Princeton: Princeton University Press, 1963), p. 364.

4. The artistic representation of the soul as a butterfly.

5. See Genesis 4:8-16.

6. In Islam, Adam is the first of the prophets. Satan fell through refusal to worship him at God's command.

7. Possibly the church father Basil the Great (c. 330-379).

8. George Sand. See Historical Introduction, note 29.

9. Usually ascribed to Marcus Fabius Quintillianus, *Institutio oratorio*, 8, 6, 23; *M. Fabii Quintiliani de institutione oratoria libri duodecim*, I-IV, ed. Georg L. Spalding (Leipzig: 1829; *ASKB* 1267-68 [I-II]), III, p. 314. Here, however, we should think of a Latinization of the original Greek word "metonymy."

10. Jean Paul's anonymous first work (1783) was *Grönländische Processe oder satirische Skizzen*. The reference here is to the section *"Ueber Weiber und Stutzer."* See *Werke*, V, pp. 89-115.

11. Daniel Chodowiecky (1726-1801), German painter and engraver who illustrated the works of the German poet Matthias Claudius (1740-1815). The engraving in question is presumably that of a group of ducks being lectured to or presided over by a drake. The ducks are sleeping, walking about, etc. See Matthias Claudius, *ASMUS omnia sua SECUM portans, oder Sämmtliche Werke des Wandsbecker Bothen, Werke*, I-IV (1-8) (Hamburg: 1838; *ASKB* 1631-32), I (3), engraving facing p. 107.

12. *Uden mad og drikke duer helten ikke* [The hero is powerless without food and drink]. See T. Vogel-Jørgensen, *Bevingede Ord* (Copenhagen: 1975), pp. 995-96.

13. See Ephesians 4:28. Paul, however, is speaking to any thieves in the Christian community, not to women.

14. *Kjøbenhavnsposten*, 43, February 12, 1836. The four previous articles on the freedom of the press issue appeared in *Kjøbenhavnsposten* (Andreas Peter Liunge, ed. and pub.), 15, January 15; 16, January 16; 19, January 19; and 38, February 7, 1836.

15. Article IV in *Kjøbenhavnsposten*, 38, February 7, 1836.

16. See "Press Freedom Affair, I," *Kjøbenhavnsposten*, 15, January 15, 1836, esp. col. 1. The enactment proposed was an appendix to the Ordinance of September 27, 1799. See Teddy Petersen, *Kierkegaards polemiske debut* (Odense: Odense Universitetsforlag, 1977), pp. 103-04. The proposed enactment stipulated that an author who expressed himself improperly concerning the constitution, its laws, or government action, although without clear liability under paragraphs 2, 3, and 7 of the Ordinance of 1799, would be subject to a fine. The three paragraphs of the Ordinance of 1799 included the follow-

ing: (2) prohibition against censure, mockery, or seeking to spread hate and discontent with the constitution or the king's government in general or a particular action; (3) prohibition against censure or mockery of the monarchical form of government in general; (7) prohibition against making acrimonious remarks about the government or expressing one's comments about its measures in improper and unseemly language. See *Kjøbenhavnsposten*, 15, January 15, 1836, col. 1.

17. See note 16 above.

18. Denmark found itself on Napoleon's side in the war against England and other countries, and defeat was sealed at the Peace of Kiel, January 14, 1814. On January 5, 1813, national bankruptcy was declared, and the following years produced very bad harvests.

19. The period 1814-30 in France.

20. At the Vienna Congress of September 1814-June 1815, the leading rulers and statesmen of Europe agreed to preserve "throne" and "altar," i.e., to uphold the position of both monarchy and Church.

21. November 20, 1815 (the first was in 1814), a confirmation of the Vienna Conclusion.

22. The Vienna Conclusion (June 1815) ratified the Peace of Kiel.

23. At a meeting in Carlsbad, August 1819, German ministers agreed to subdue the national commotion through censorship, supervision of the universities, etc.

24. A congress in Verona (1822), where representatives of the "Holy Alliance" met to discuss how the political stability of Europe could be secured.

25. Reference to a favorite theme of romantic poetry, for example in Oehlenschläger and Grundtvig.

26. See p. 17 and notes 100, 101.

27. Mendel Levin Nathanson (1780-1868), one of the leading economists of the time, in several journals defended the monarchy's economic policy, for example, in *Danmarks Handel, Skibsfart, Penge- og Finansvæsen*, 1832.

28. See Historical Introduction, p. viii.

29. See Historical Introduction, pp. xi-xii.

30. Probably an anonymous review in *Maanedsskrift for Litteratur*, XIII, 1835, pp. 164-76.

31. See p. 7 and note 31. Published October 1, 1828, in Randers. The full title was *Om Danmarks nærværende Tilstand kortelig fremstillet i Anledning af Deres kongelige Højheders, Prinds Frederik Carl Christians og Prinsesse Wilhelmine Maries, Formæling, den første November, 1828*. It was Steen Steensen Blicher's intention "chiefly to know *what we have*, since in that—especially with regard to other nations—we shall find sufficient reason for the love we bear to King and Fatherland." He thought that his publication's "faithful picture of Denmark's present condition explains naturally the love that the people bear to King, National Constitution, and Fatherland." *Samlede Skrifter*, I-XXXIII (Copenhagen: 1920-34), XIII, pp. 171, 187-88.

32. Poul Martin Møller's poem from his voyage to China (November 1819-July 1821), *"Glæde over Danmark,"* first printed in Rahbek's *Tilskuerne* (1823).

33. Johan Gerhard Frederik Garbrecht (1799-1857), wholesaler, who praised the king to the point of exaggeration in various pieces, mostly in poems, for example, *"Den eiegode Landsfader," "Danmarks elskede Konge," "Frederik den Sjette"* (1811). Only one volume of *Skjold* was published (Copenhagen: 1830).

34. A name given to *Fyens Stifts Adresse-Avis og Advertissementstidende*, published by Søren Hempel.

35. *Aarhus Stiftstidende.*

36. *Ribe Stifts Adresse-Avis.*

37. See p. 10 and note 54.

38. See Matthew 6:31-34.

39. See p. 113 and note 43.

40. Frederik VI ruled with the help of numerous adjutants who functioned as royal government officials.

41. With the government's approval, citizens (also some of the Kierkegaard family) equipped private ships to capture English merchant ships, inasmuch as the English had taken away the Danish fleet in 1807. See Jacob Gabriel Davidsen, *Kjøbenhavnerliv i ældre og nyere Tid* (Copenhagen: 1889), pp. 84-93.

42. See p. 11 and note 65.

43. See p. 9 and note 47.

44. Niels Thoroup Bruun (1778-1823) provided numerous translations for the Royal Theater.

45. Horace, *Ars poetica*, 388; *Q. Horatii Flacci opera* (Leipzig: 1828; *ASKB* 1248), p. 697; *Horace Satires, Epistles and Ars Poetica*, tr. H. Rushton Fairclough (Loeb, Cambridge: Harvard University Press, 1978), pp. 482-83.

46. See p. 15 and note 92.

47. *Fædrelandet*, 77, March 4, 1836. Kierkegaard's own copy (*Pap.* I B 3), marked with his underlinings etc., is in the Royal Library, Copenhagen. On Hage, see Historical Introduction, notes 4 and 51.

48. J. L. Heiberg's *Kjøbenhavns flyvende Post.*

49. See Historical Introduction, pp. xi-xii.

50. The full newspaper article is not given because up to p. 642, col. 2, of *Fædrelandet*, 77, Hage deals with several problems that touch only indirectly upon the Kierkegaard polemic. That Kierkegaard is uninterested in the first part of the article is clear from the markings in his copy (see Historical Introduction, pp. xxi-xxii). On Kierkegaard's markings, see Petersen, *Debut*, pp. 73-78 and 166. On the first part of Hage's article, see Marcus Rubin, *Frederik VI's Tid* (Copenhagen: 1895), pp. 371-474.

51. One of the sources is Kierkegaard's article; see pp. 6-11.

52. The Danish *Glosserne* can figuratively mean "sneers" as well as "words," "glossary," "vocabulary." The word is marked with a question mark in Kierkegaard's copy of the paper.

53. See Supplement, pp. 134-41.

54. See p. 15 and note 91.

55. See p. 9.

56. See p. 10.

57. See pp. 10-11.

58. These articles are signed "1234" (Peder Vilhelm Jacobsen, who belonged to the Heiberg circle).

59. *Kjøbenhavns flyvende Post, Interimsblad*, 75, February 16, 1836.

60. Ibid.

61. *Fædrelandet*, 72, January 29, 1836, col. 552.

62. Algreen-Ussing; see p. 45 and note 229.

63. *Kjøbenhavnsposten*, 78, February 22, 1836.

64. *Kjøbenhavns flyvende Post*; see note 59 above.

65. *"Critiske Bemærkinger til 'Fædrelandet' Nr. 75"* (under the pseudonym 1116), *Kjøbenhavns flyvende Post, Interimsblad*, 80, February 28, 1836.

66. *Statsvennen*, 3, March 5, 1836, pp. 9-10. The paper was edited and published by Johannes Christian Lange (1785-1850) during the years 1835-37. He also edited *Sandhedsfaklen* for a time.

67. *Kjøbenhavns flyvende Post, Interimsblad*, 76, February 18, 1836. See pp. 6-11.

68. See pp. 6, 10.

69. See p. 11.

70. See p. 6.

71. See p. 7.

72. See p. 10.

73. See p. 6.

74. See p. 10.

75. See Historical Introduction, note 31.

76. A. P. Liunge. See note 77 below.

77. Orla Lehmann (*Le-mand* [man with the scythe]) controlled *Kjøbenhavnsposten* during this period with Jens Finsteen Giødwad. Andreas Peter Liunge remained editor formally until 1837.

78. See Supplement, p. 189 and note 241; cf. p. 38.

79. An order from Frederik VI tightening censorship was published on April 25, 1833. See *Kjøbenhavnsposten*, 83, April 27, 1833.

80. See note 79 above.

81. Orla Lehmann's article "Press Freedom Affair II" in *Kjøbenhavnsposten*, 16, January 16, 1836.

82. An unsigned article, "Against the New Press Law," appeared in *Kjøbenhavnsposten*, 49, February 18, 1836.

83. Lehmann is regarded as the author of the article referred to in note 82 above. Here the pun on his name is based on another meaning of the word *le* [to laugh].

84. Kierkegaard's own copy of *Kjøbenhavnsposten*, 96, March 31, 1836 (*Pap.* I B 4), marked with his underlinings etc., is in the Royal Library, Copenhagen. Kierkegaard wrote "David National Debt" at the foot of p. 383, col.

1 and (abbreviated) "scholastic donkey" (see p. 33) in the margin of p. 385, col. 2. On other markings made by Kierkegaard, see Petersen, *Debut*, pp. 88-93, 166.

85. J. L. Heiberg.

86. See Supplement, p. 142.

87. See p. 13.

88. Lehmann, if he is author of the five-part article on the freedom of the press, as seems certain, maintains anonymity regarding them. For the "reply" elsewhere, see Hage's article in *Fædrelandet*, 77; Supplement, pp. 142-48.

89. I.e., "the whole body or nature of the evidence."

90. See Supplement, p. 134 and note 14 above.

91. *Stændertidende*, January 13, 1836. See Supplement, p. 134 and note 16 above.

92. Cf. *Kjøbenhavnsposten*, 38, February 7, 1836, p. 151, col. 1, p. 152, col. 1.

93. Designation for the political and literary tendencies in France during the reign (1830-48) of Louis Philippe. See p. 64 and note 36.

94. The literary feud between Jens Baggesen (1764-1826) and Adam Oehlenschläger (1779-1850) in the period around 1815. See *Dansk Litteratur Historie*, I-VI, ed. P. H. Traustedt (Copenhagen: Politikens Forlag, 1976-77), II, pp. 85-96.

95. Anders Sandøe Ørsted (1778-1860), Danish jurist and statesman, brother of the physicist Hans Christian Ørsted.

96. The theological dispute between Nicolai Frederik Severin Grundtvig (1783-1872) and Henrik Nicolai Clausen (1793-1877) centered on Grundtvig's *Kirkens Gienmæle* (September 3, 1825), a critique of Clausen's *Catholicismens og Protestantismens Kirkeforfatning, Lære og Ritus* (August 21, 1825), and eventuated in a civil suit won by Clausen.

97. Lehmann's five-part article. See notes 14 and 88 above.

98. See pp. 10, 144.

99. No. 1, May 4, 1836. The identity of the pseudonymous author of *Humoristiske Intelligentsblade*, 1-3, has not been discovered, but it would appear that all three issues are by the same person (as Kierkegaard thought) (see Supplement, p. 211), possibly Peder Ludvig Møller. See Petersen, *Debut*, pp. 149-51, 159, note 4; Henning Fenger, *Kierkegaard-Myter og Kierkegaard-Kilder* (Odense: Odense Universitetsforlag, 1976), p. 178 (chapter omitted in *Kierkegaard, The Myths and Their Origins*, tr. George C. Schoolfield [New Haven: Yale University Press, 1980]). For the Danish texts, see Petersen, *Debut*, pp. 113-43. See also note 281 below.

100. A play on the connection between water and humor; *En vandet Vittighed*—an insipid (wet) joke. Cf. Adam Gottlob Oehlenschläger, *Digte* (Copenhagen: 1803), p. 251 (ed. tr.):

> "What is humor? Nothing other than liquid!
> Namely, what is insipid [*vandet*]."

101. Plant germ used in brewing.

102. Horace, *Ars poetica*, 343; *Opera*, p. 695; Loeb, pp. 478-79: "*omne tulit punctum qui miscuit utile dulce* (He has won every vote who has blended profit with pleasure)." Wessel uses this in his *"Horats og Hans Datter (Impromptu),"* J. H. Wessel, *Samlede Digte af Johan Herman Wessel*, I-II, ed. Adolph Engelbert Boye (Copenhagen: 1832), II, pp. 23-24 (ed. tr.):

> To profit and enjoy,
> Have constantly in mind,
> This was Horace's word,
> While he was on earth.
> Whatever else he means,
> From others can you learn,
> I will not teach you that;
> For my business it is not.
> I will shortly only tell
> Of *Horace's* daughter *Mette*,
> Although she was not wed,
> She found her stays too tight.

103. See J. H. Wessel, *Kierlighed uden Strømper, Johan Herman Wessels samtlige Skrivter*, I-II (Copenhagen: 1787), I, pp. 3-108.

104. Wessel, *"Hundemordet," Skrivter*, I, p. 135 (ed. tr.): "At the end of my work distributing moral saws."

105. Danish: *Fortovsret*, a written or unwritten rule for those wishing to pass on the sidewalk or pavement, stating that where the general rule for passing each other on the right would force the other party out on the street, the one party must hold himself close up against the houses so that the other can pass.

106. See note 100 above.

107. Jens Zetlitz (1761-1821), Norwegian pastor and poet. Lines resembling this are to be found in several places in his poetry, particularly in the poem *"Noahs Minde,"* stanza 11 (ed. tr.): "Yet it is still ennobled water, / And quenches, cheers, and refreshes." Jens Zetlitz, *Samlede Digte*, I-II (Christiania: 1825), II, p. 248.

108. Poetical pastoral name at the time. The Greek god Dionysus is described as having cloven hoofs.

109. Danish: *ætherisk*, "ethereal" in the sense of "airy."

110. See Supplement, p. 149 and note 66.

111. Aglaia (Splendor), Euphrosyne (Mirth), and Thalia (Good Cheer).

112. See p. 8.

113. See pp. 12, 20.

114. The source has not been located.

115. See p. 4.

116. See p. 12.

117. See Supplement, pp. 158-59.

118. The state of nature and the consequence of *jus naturale* according to Thomas Hobbes (1588-1679). *De Cive*, I, 12; *De Cive*, ed. Howard Warrender (Oxford: Oxford University Press, 1983), p. 49.

119. See p. 5.

120. To wear one's cloak on both shoulders, i.e., to run with the hare and hunt with the hounds.

121. Motto of the kings of Spain.

122. See p. 12.

123. See John 20:17.

124. Polemical writers.

125. K(j)øge is a coastal town about twenty miles south of Copenhagen.

126. *Dagen,* a Conservative paper, continually taking issue with *Fædrelandet* and *Kjøbenhavnsposten.* See p. 13 and note 77.

127. The organ of Nicolai Frederik Severin Grundtvig (1783-1872) and his disciple Jacob Christian Lindberg (1797-1857) in the Church dispute of the time.

128. Edited by Jens Peter Tønder (1773-1836) and published 1833-36.

129. *Kjøbenhavns Kgl. Adressecomptoirs alene priviligerede Efterretninger,* the oldest Danish advertising paper, dating back to the eighteenth century.

130. Day flies, i.e., the poorer quality papers of the time, rocket literature.

131. J. L. Heiberg's paper.

132. Probably a reference to the articles in *Flyveposten*, 75, 78, and 79. See Supplement, p. 145 and note 58.

133. The verse refers to J. L. Heiberg's polemic against Christian Wilster in 1830 and is a play on the end of Heiberg's poem *"Epistel til Lanterna-magica-Doublanten i Sorø."* See *Kjøbenhavns Flyvende Post*, 8, 1830, p. 40. See also Christian Wilster, *"Doublet-Billeder til den nye Lanterna-magica,"* *Kjobenhavnsposten*, 9, 1830, p. 33.

134. Kierkegaard. See p. 12.

135. See p. 6.

136. See p. 11.

137. See p. 8.

138. See p. 12.

139. See Matthew 11:5; Luke 7:22.

140. See p. 12.

141. Ibid.

142. See p. 13.

143. Terence, *The Self-Tormentor*, I, 25; *Terentses Skuespil*, I-II, tr. Frederik Høegh Guldberg (Copenhagen: 1805; *ASKB* 1293-94), I, p. 276; *Terence*, I-II, tr. John Sargeaunt (Loeb, Cambridge: Harvard University Press, 1983-86), I, pp. 124-25: *"homo sum: humani nil a me alienum puto* [I am a man, I hold that what affects another man affects me]."

144. Ways of interfering.

145. See Supplement, p. 142.

146. See p. 13.

147. See Historical Introduction, notes 48, 49, and 51.

148. Danish: *Broderpart* [literally, brother's share]. See p. 13.

149. See p. 13.

150. Holberg, *Jacob von Tyboe*, V, 8, *Den Danske Skue-Plads*, I-VII (Copenhagen: 1788; *ASKB* 1566-67), III, no pagination.

151. See Supplement, p. 142.

152. See Supplement, p. 213 (*Pap.* I B 6, p. 181).

153. No. 2, May 4, 1836.

154. See Supplement, pp. 142, 144; cf. p. 14.

155. A broken-off threat: "Whom I ——." See Virgil, *Aeneid*, I, 135; *Virgils Aeneide*, tr. Johan Henrik Schønheyder (Copenhagen: 1812), p. 11; *Virgil*, I-II, tr. H. Rushton Fairclough (Loeb, Cambridge: Harvard University Press, 1978), I, pp. 250-51.

156. This expression was often used about the government and its representatives. The statesman Poul Christian Stemann (1764-1855) and the king heard it as *Vivat* [Long live] when it was shouted at large gatherings.

157. See p. 15.

158. Ibid.

159. Ibid.

160. Ibid.

161. See p. 16.

162. See Matthew 6:3-4; Romans 12:8.

163. See p. 16; cf. Supplement, p. 143.

164. See p. 18.

165. Peter in Thomas Overskou and Anton Ludvig Arnesen's *Capriciosa*, first performed at the Royal Theater on June 11, 1836.

166. See p. 15.

167. See p. 18.

168. See p. 19.

169. See, for example, p. 19.

170. Holberg, *Den politiske Kandestøber*, IV, 5-6, *Danske Skue-Plads*, I, no pagination; *The Political Tinker*, *Comedies by Holberg*, tr. Oscar James Campbell Jr., and Frederic Schenck (New York: American-Scandinavian Foundation, 1914), pp. 90-92.

171. Poul Martin Møller, *"Jæmtelands Befolkning"*:

> The heavy Trønder heroes
> At the Lord's speech laughed;
> For when one word he spoke,
> Then he yapped two.

172. See pp. 19-20.

173. See pp. 19-20.

174. See p. 21.

175. Holberg, *Jule-Stue*, 12, *Danske Skue-Plads*, II, no pagination; *The Christmas Party*, *Seven One-Act Plays by Holberg*, tr. Henry Alexander (Prince-

ton: Princeton University Press for the American-Scandinavian Foundation, 1950), pp. 81-102.

176. *Jule-Stue*, 10, *Danske Skue-Plads*, II; *The Christmas Party*, 11, *Seven One-Act Plays*, p. 93.

177. *Jule-Stue*, 11, *Danske Skue-Plads*, II; *The Christmas Party*, 12, *Seven One-Act Plays*, pp. 96-97.

178. *Jule-Stue*, 12, *Danske Skue-Plads*, II; *The Christmas Party*, 12, *Seven One-Act Plays*, pp. 98.

179. See note 178 above.

180. See p. 21.

181. From Boileau, *Satires*: "*J'appelle un chat un chat, et Rolet un fripon* [I call a cat a cat, and Rolet (an attorney) a scoundrel]," i.e., I call a spade a spade.

182. See p. 10.

183. See p. 22.

184. Ibid.

185. Ibid.

186. King of Babylon (604-562 B.C.).

187. Possibly *Humoristiske Intelligentsblade*, 3.

188. Field Marshal Gebhard Leberecht v. Blücher (1742-1819), who commanded the Prussian forces at Waterloo. His energy and rapidity of movement won him the name "Marshal Forward."

189. Cf. especially Supplement, p. 163.

190. The next section, signed 233/a², an article showing that the terms "Liberal" and "Conservative" are incorrectly applied to various papers, is omitted.

191. No. 3, May 18, 1836.

192. An allusion to the political group in Holberg's *Den politiske Kandestøber*, II, *Danske Skue-Plads*, I, no pagination; *The Political Tinker, Comedies*, pp. 63-73.

193. The title of a vaudeville by J. L. Heiberg. *Kjøge Huuskors* was performed for the first time on November 28, 1831, with Heiberg's wife in the role of Lise. There were nineteen performances before this issue of the *Humoristiske Intelligentsblade* appeared. On *Guldkorset*, see note 199 below.

194. 1234 was almost certainly the pseudonym of Peder Vilhelm Jacobsen (1799-1848). Frithiof Brandt, in *Den unge Søren Kierkegaard* (Copenhagen: 1929), p. 51, argues that Jacobsen's unusual sober style and his view of the Liberal movement is apparent in the 1234 articles.

195. Fenger (*Kierkegaard-Myter*, p. 178) thinks that x was probably Mendel Levin Nathanson (1780-1868). Petersen (*Debut*, p. 172, note 4) argues that x. was Christian Bredsdorff (1765-1853).

196. Kierkegaard. See p. 11.

197. Unidentified author of an article "*Chinesisk Kunstflid i 'Fædrelandet,'*" *Kjøbenhavns flyvende Post, Interimsblad*, 86, April 7, 1836.

198. Peder Hjort (1793-1871) became a lecturer at Sorø Academy in 1822 and is thus "from the provinces." See articles in *Kjøbenhavns flyvende Post*,

Interimsblad, 57-62, October 29-November 13, 1835; 86, April 7, 1836; 88-90, April 13-18, 1836; 92-98, April 23-May 21, 1836; 100, June 7, 1836.

199. J. L. Heiberg's translation and performance of Melesville and Brazier's two-act comedy *Cathérine ou la croix d'or* was a highly topical matter. The play, under the title *Guldkorset* (*Repertoire*, 95, 1836) with Mrs. Heiberg playing the part of Cathérine, had been performed eight times that season since April 25. The performance of the play had given rise to a polemic between Heiberg and playwright Thomas Overskou (1798-1873), but after Overskou's success with *Østergade og Vestergade* (*Repertoire*, 11, 1828), performed seventeen times from December 31, 1828, to the end of the 1835-36 season, Heiberg developed a positive opinion of Overskou, who for his part remained to the end of his life a staunch admirer of Heiberg, despite the *Guldkorset* affair.

200. See note 192 above.

201. Lines identical with those of Herman in Holberg, *Den politiske Kandestøber*, II, 1, *Danske Skue-Plads*, I, no pagination; *Comedies*, p. 63. Cf., for example, Supplement, p. 134.

202. A reference, including the exact figures, to the first part of Johannes Hage's article in *Fædrelandet*, 77, January 22, 1836, col. 635 and 639.

203. Gert Bundtmager's lines in Holberg, *Den politiske Kandestøber*, II, 1, *Danske Skue-Plads*, I, no pagination; *Comedies*, p. 63.

204. J. L. Heiberg, *Philosophiens Philosophie eller den speculative Logik* (pr. as ms., 1831-32), *Prosaiske Skrifter*, I-XI (Copenhagen: 1861-62), I, pp. 111-380; the reference is to pp. 188-284.

205. Heiberg's apotheosis of Hegel and Goethe as the two great spirits of the age is to be found in *Om Philosophiens Betydning for den nuværende Tid* (Copenhagen: 1833; *ASKB* 568), esp. pp. 36-48.

206. See Heiberg, *Philosophiens Philosophie*, *Prosaiske Skrifter*, I, pp. 276-84.

207. See p. 12.

208. See Heiberg, *Philosophiens Philosophie*, *Prosaiske Skrifter*, I, pp. 122-26.

209. Ibid., pp. 121-22.

210. Ibid., p. 118 and note 2.

211. Ibid.

212. Cf., for example, ibid., pp. 116-17.

213. Ibid., p. 115 and note 1.

214. *Fædrelandet*, 57, 1836; cf. pp. 6, 7.

215. Kierkegaard, depicted in a position subordinate to Heiberg.

216. Petersen, *Debut*, p. 148, notes Kierkegaard's musical interest in this period and that he had a weak voice, but perhaps reference should rather be made to the fact that Kierkegaard began his three political articles with fragments of songs and thus came into the debate "singing."

217. See p. 12.

218. A slip made by the author, since "S. K." occurs only once in the article.

219. Cf. p. 24: "I have here medicine that is excellent."

220. See pp. 19, 21, 31, 19, 19, 12, 14, 19.

221. See pp. 26, 31; Supplement, p. 158.
222. See p. 26.
223. See p. 21.
224. See p. 16.
225. Cf., for example, *Letters*, Letter 82, p. 154, *KW* XXV.
226. *Fædrelandet*, 77, 1836, col. 640-41.
227. The quotation has not been located, but it is clearly from Heiberg.
228. A reference to Heiberg's musical comedies.
229. Danish: *Character*, rank, grade/mark, and character.
230. A direct quotation from the article mentioned in note 197 above.
231. Johann Christian Friedrich v. Schiller, *"Die Piccolomini,"* I, 2, *Wallenstein*, I, *Schillers sämmtliche Werke*, I-XII (Stuttgart, Tübingen: 1838; *ASKB* 1804-15), IV, p. 74 (ed. tr.).
232. A continuation of the quotation identified in notes 230 and 197 above.
233. Cf. Virgil, *Aeneid*, I, 204; Schønheyder, p. 15; Loeb, I, pp. 254-55:

> *per tot discrimina rerum*
> *tendimus in Latium*
> [through so many perilous chances,
> we fare towards Latium].

234. An abbreviated translation, *Vandmanden*, was published in *Kjøbenhavns flyvende Post*, *Interimsblad*, 74-78, February 13-22, 1836, and 81, March 9, 1836.
235. See note 199 above.
236. Schiller, *"Das Lied von der Glocke,"* *Werke*, I, p. 374:

> *Jedoch* [But] *der schrecklichste der Schrecken*
> *Das ist der Mensch in seinem Wahn* [delusion].

237. Contemporary politicians. Tage Algreen-Ussing (1797-1872) in the 1830s became prominent by an at times powerful opposition to the government, even though he had been Justice and Home Office Secretary since 1831. He functioned as deputy when the Provincial Consultative Assembly for the Island Dioceses met in Roskilde on October 1, 1835, and his special area of interest was economic affairs. With the passage of time, he tended toward a Conservative position. Peter Christian Stenersen Gad (1797-1851) became the permanent curate at Trinitatis Church in 1831. He was of Liberal outlook and was for three years president of the Society for the Right Use of Freedom of the Press. Johannes Hage (1800-1837), whose interests ranged from agricultural policy to concern with schools in Roskilde, where he was himself a teacher, was a leading Liberal and was regarded as the most important writer for the cause. See Historical Introduction, notes 4, 51.
238. Peder Hjort, *"Af et nyt Brev (som virkelig er kommet) fra Provindserne,"* *Kjøbenhavns flyvende Post*, *Interimsblad*, 86, April 7, 1836.
239. A reference to an article by J. L. Heiberg in *Kjøbenhavns flyvende Post*,

Interimsblad, 91, April 20, 1836, titled: "*Sandfærdig Beretning om den Over-skou'ske Polemiks dødelige Afgang.*"

240. *Fædrelandet*, 71, January 22, 1836.

241. Matthias Winther (1795-1834) started *Raketten* in 1831 as a means of income and as a way of giving vent to his grievances. Left in poor circumstances when his father died, he made a career of writing, and he also did surgical work for the military. Chiefly because of his deficient application in medical study and his ability to make enemies, he gradually lost the good will of those who had supported his efforts and was discharged from his army medical post. The polemical articles in *Raketten* incurred court cases and fines, and finally in 1832 he was sentenced to a short term of imprisonment, from which he never recovered. After his death in 1834, *Raketten*, which was carried on by a friend, perished after less than two years under the name of *Kometen*.

242. At the beginning of the 1830s, several papers were started in Copenhagen with names (tr.) such as *The Rocket, The Rocket with Stars, The Torch of Truth, The Flash of Lightning, Purgatory*, etc. These sensation papers were often known as "rocket literature" after their notorious prototype, *The Rocket*. See Jacob Davidsen, *Fra det gamle Kongens Kjøbenhavn*, I-II (Copenhagen: 1880-81), I, pp. 204-32.

243. A court case was a risky affair, because legislation often could in practice be interpreted according to the pleasure of the ruling power.

244. See Historical Introduction, p. xi.

245. On May 15, 1834, the Provincial Consultative Assemblies were finally constituted. The ordinance for this had been issued on May 28, 1831.

246. A periodical running from 1829 to 1838 and of a very high quality, founded and edited by several of the leading men of the time, including Johan Ludvig Heiberg, Henrik Nicolai Clausen, Hans Christian Ørsted, Johan Nicolai Madvig, and Frederik Christian Petersen.

247. Probably an article by H. N. Clausen in *Maanedsskrift for Litteratur*, VI, 1831, pp. 357-90, containing a violent attack on the authorized form of education favored by the king, the Bell-Lancaster monitor system, imported from Britain.

248. Infringement of the rules laid down by the Ordinance of 1799 and by later amendments could mean sentence to lifelong censorship, as happened, for example, to Grundtvig.

249. See Historical Introduction, note 49.

250. Probably Orla Lehmann and Jens F. Giødwad.

251. See Historical Introduction, note 51.

252. Christian Georg David was prosecuted for statements in articles in *Fædrelandet*, 7, November 9; 10, November 30; and 11, December 7, 1834. He was acquitted on May 18, 1835.

253. *Fædrelandet*, 7, November 9, 1834, contained the article "On the Provincial Consultative Assemblies' Right of Petition," and 11, December 7, 1834, appeared with the article "What Use Is It?"

254. See note 247 above.

255. On February 21, 1835, a petition (with over 570 signatures) against tightening the press laws was handed to the king. The petition was signed by the most prominent figures of the time, for example, H. N. Clausen and F. C. Sibbern, but was rejected. See Historical Introduction, p. xii and note 14.

256. See Historical Introduction, note 40.

257. For the Danish text, see Petersen, *Debut*, pp. 53-54.

258. See p. 53 and title page note.

259. For the Danish text, see Petersen, *Debut*, pp. 29-37.

260. See Ostermann's note, Supplement, p. 199.

261. After "every" there is an unreadable word, perhaps something crossed out.

262. See p. 38.

263. Probably K.L.E. Schønberg, bachelor of law (1797-1857), who, according to the report book of the Student Association for October 31, 1835, read aloud "*Et Bidrag til den danske Trykkefriheds Historie.*"

264. Legation privy counselor P. T. Zartmann (1808-1878).

265. Kierkegaard's brother Peter Christian Kierkegaard (1805-1888), bishop of Aalborg, 1856-75, at whose request Hans Peter Barfod began the publication of Kierkegaard's journals and papers.

266. *Repertoire*, 124 (1840); first performed at the Royal Theater on May 13, 1840. See Supplement, p. 218 and note 316.

267. See p. 53. Cf. Niels Thoroup Bruun, *Skuespilleren imod sin Villie eller Comedien paa Landet* (Copenhagen: 1809); *Sjælvandringen eller Skuespilleren imod sin Villie paa en anden Maneer* (Copenhagen: 1817).

268. See pp. 63, 74-75.

269. See pp. 65-66.

270. See p. 74.

271. Cf. pp. 74-75.

272. Chief character in Holberg's comedy of that name, *Danske Skue-Plads*, I.

273. A recurring character in Holberg's comedies.

274. See p. 61.

275. See p. 62.

276. See p. 64.

277. Genesis 1:2: "without form and void."

278. See p. 65.

279. *Pap.* I B 5 is a fragment concerning Kierkegaard's polemic against *Kjøbenhavnsposten* and *Fædrelandet* in *Kjøbenhavns flyvende Post*, February-April, 1836. See *Af Søren Kierkegaards Efterladte Papirer, 1833-55*, I-VIII, ed. Hans Peter Barfod and Hermann Gottsched (Copenhagen: 1869-81), I, pp. 100-01.

280. I.e., after Orla Lehmann's reply to Kierkegaard's article (see Supple-

ment, pp. 152-58), which reply provoked Kierkegaard's article "To Mr. Orla Lehmann." See pp. 24-34.

281. *Humoristiske Intelligentsblade,* ed. Peder Nicolai Jørgensen (1805-1850), all three issues undated. The pseudonyms in these papers have not been identified. No. 1 is unsigned, 2 is signed X. and 233/a², and 3 is unsigned. Everything points, however, to one author, very possibly Peder Ludvig Møller. See Petersen, *Debut,* pp. 149-51. The three issues appear on a bill dated May 4, 1836, from Reitzel to Kierkegaard. From *Kjøbenhavnsposten,* 130, May 5, 1836, and 146, May 21, 1836, we can date 1 and 2 of *Humoristiske Intelligentsblade* as May 4, 1836, and 3 as May 18, 1836. See Supplement, pp. 160-88.

282. See Wessel, *Kierlighed uden Strømper,* IV, 5; *Skrivter,* I, p. 64. Apart from two unintentional and unimportant deviations from the text, Kierkegaard alters the last line from "thief" to "sophist." See p. 22: "accuses him of being a willful sophist, etc."

283. See note 281 above; pp. 10-11.

284. See Supplement, pp. 160-62.

285. The principle that water seeks its own level.

286. Cf. p. 8.

287. See p. 11; *JP* V 5174 (*Pap.* I A 266); *Pap.* I C 107, p. 279.

288. Johann Wolfgang v. Goethe, *Faust,* I, 2293-94, *Goethe's Werke. Vollständige Ausgabe letzter Hand,* I-LX (Stuttgart, Tübingen: 1828-42; *ASKB* 1641-68 [I-LV]), XII, p. 115; *Faust. Eine Tragödie* (Stuttgart, Tübingen: 1834; *ASKB* 1669), p. 115; *Faust,* tr. Bayard Taylor (New York: Random House, 1950), p. 81.

289. Cf. *JP* II 1287 (*Pap.* I A 83).

290. See p. 33.

291. See Genesis 41:1-4.

292. See Supplement, pp. 168, 173-74, and notes 150, 170, 175-179.

293. Grundtvig, *Nordens Mythologi eller Sindbilled-Sprog historisk-poetisk udviklet og oplyst* (Copenhagen: 1832; *ASKB* 1949).

294. A word Grundtvig used instead of *Grottuns-Gaard* to translate the original Icelandic place name.

295. See Supplement, pp. 211-14 (*Pap.* I B 6).

296. Knud Lyne Rahbek, best known for his passionate interest in the theater and for his home, Bakkehuset; see Historical Introduction, note 31.

297. Poul Martin Møller. See Historical Introduction, note 26.

298. See Historical Introduction, note 35.

299. Emil Boesen (1812-1879), pastor and Kierkegaard's lifelong friend and confidant. See *Letters,* Letter 60, *KW* XXV.

300. Jens Finsteen Giødwad (*juridisk Licentiat,* the equivalent of B.LL.) was editor of *Kjøbenhavnsposten* from April 1, 1837. Three charges of infringement of the press laws were pending against Giødwad and a fourth was made on April 23, 1838. He was acquitted of the several charges on April 24, April 28, May 8, and November 6, 1838, but he had to pay the court costs involved in two of them. See also Historical Introduction, note 48.

301. Caspar Claudius Rosenhoff (1804-1869), editor of several papers, mentioned here as editor of *Den Frisindede* (1835-46), a weekly of mixed content, and of *Concordia* (1835-39), a weekly containing items of general interest. Three basins indicated that the barber held the position of "county barber," of whom there were very few in each town.

302. See *Irische Elfenmärchen* (tr. of Thomas Crofton Croker, *Fairy Legends and Traditions of the South of Ireland*, I-III [London: 1825]), tr. Jakob Ludwig Karl and Wilhelm Karl Grimm (Leipzig: 1826; *ASKB* 1423), p. xxxvii; *Irony*, p. 151, *KW* II (*SV* XIII 236).

303. See Jakob Ludwig Karl and Wilhelm Karl Grimm, "*Die kluge Else* [Clever Elsie]," *Kinder- und Haus-Märchen*, I-III (Berlin: 1819-22; *ASKB* 1425-27), I, 34, pp. 173-76; *The Complete Grimm's Fairy Tales*, tr. Margaret Hunt and James Stern (New York: Pantheon, 1944), pp. 171-72. The story centers around the consequences of a series of imagined conditions or "if" clauses. Except for a reference in *Anxiety*, p. 50, *KW* VIII (*SV* IV 320), no use of the story is found in the works or the papers. The story is summarized in *KW* VIII, p. 236, note 60.

304. Ludvig Holberg, *Niels Klims Reise under Jorden* (Copenhagen, Aalborg: 1745); Klim is the main character in Jens Baggesen, *Niels Klims Underjordiske Reise* (based on the Latin work by Ludvig Holberg), *Danske Værker*, I-XII (Copenhagen: 1827-32; *ASKB* 1509-20), XII, pp. 167-524; Holberg, *Journey of Niels Klim to the World Underground*, tr. anon., ed. James I. McNelis, Jr. (Lincoln: University of Nebraska Press, 1960). In Niels Klim's fall to the center of the earth, the caraway kringle he threw away in sudden revulsion at earth food went into orbit around him (*Niels Klims Reise*, p. 8; *Værker*, XII, p. 180; *Niels Klim*, p. 11).

305. The stated aim of *Kjøbenhavnsposten* was to meet the demands of the times and to concentrate on current local news of Copenhagen.

306. See the article *"Om Almeenaand," Kjøbenhavnsposten*, 239-40, August 28, September 1, 1838.

307. Presumably most of the entries *Pap*. II A 768-85 were jottings in connection with the early years; the Andersen entries must be seen in relation to *From the Papers* (September 7, 1838). See pp. 53-102.

308. This is Kierkegaard's first use of the expression "armed neutrality." See *Armed Neutrality*, in *Point of View*, *KW* XXII (*Pap*. X⁵ B 107).

309. See J. L. Heiberg, *Kong Salomon og Jørgen Hattemager*, 3, *Skuespil*, I-VII (Copenhagen: 1833-41; *ASKB* 1553-59), II, p. 317 (ed. tr.):

> No, Knight, so many
> From ladders fell down,
> But the church door's way
> Is sure and broad.
> Eia!

It is difficult to be sure to what extent Kierkegaard deliberately alters his version and to what extent he remembers the verse incorrectly. He emphasized the word "churchyard"; therefore it would seem that this word is a deliberate alteration and probably a pun on his own name: *Ki[e]rkegaard* ("graveyard," "churchyard," more accurately "church farm").

310. See Exodus 3:5.

311. Under pain of exclusion and loss of the right to speak, a formula used in a public summons.

312. Oehlenschläger, *Digte*, p. 29.

313. See *JP* V 5405 (*Pap*. II A 533).

314. Wessel, *"Om en Jødepige,"* *Skrivter*, II, p. 130.

315. Claudius, *Werke*, II, pp. 112-38.

316. This journal entry is an unpublished reply to Hans Christian Andersen's parody of Kierkegaard in *En Comedie i det Grønne*. See Supplement, pp. 202-04.

317. A famous peasant clown in northern Germany in the fourteenth or fifteenth century. Kierkegaard mentions him several times, for example, in *JP* V 5082, 5110 (*Pap*. I A 51, C 61). See also *En gandske ny og lystig Historie om Ulspils Overmand Eller Robertus vom Agerkaal* (Copenhagen: 1724; *ASKB* 1467); *Underlig og selsom Historie, Om Tiile Ugelspegel* (Copenhagen: 1701; *ASKB* 1469).

318. In Denmark between 1814 and 1874, a *skilling* (shilling) was worth 1/96 of a rix-dollar and 1/16 of a mark.

319. See note 307 above.

320. On May 13. It was performed again on November 8, 1840.

321. Hans Christian Andersen, *En Comedie i det Grønne, Vaudeville i een Akt efter det gamle Lystspil: "Skuespilleren imod sin Villie,"* advertised under *Nye Sager* in *Berlingske Tidende*, 249, October 26, 1840; *Repertoire*, 124 (Copenhagen: 1840; *ASKB U* 14). See note 316 above.

322. In *Berlingske Tidende*, 256, November 3, 1840, "the poet Andersen" appears in the list of passengers who on October 31 sailed on the steamship Christian VIII to Kiel.

323. See Holberg, *Mester Gert Westphaler eller den meget talende Barbeer*, VII, *Danske Skue-Plads*, I, no pagination; *Master Gert Westphaler or The Talkative Barber*, VII, *Seven One-Act Plays by Holberg*, tr. Henry Alexander (Princeton: Princeton University Press for the American-Scandinavian Foundation, 1950), p. 28. R is an abbreviation of Roven (Rouen), naughty assimilation to *Røven* [arse].

324. See p. 67.

325. See Historical Introduction, p. xxxi and note 100.

326. By Leonhard Groth (pseud. of Grimur Thomsen). See *Fædrelandet*, 1120, January 16, 1843, col. 8995. Holst had written *Et Bidrag til den nyere danske Litteratur-historie* (Copenhagen: 1840), the publication of which was advertised in *Berlingske Tidende*, 241, October 16, 1840. In the same issue of the paper, "the teacher Holst" appears in the list of passengers who on October 15 sailed on the steamship Frederik VI to Kiel.

327. See Holberg, *Ulysses von Ithaca*, I, 7, *Danske Skue-Plads*, III, no pagination.

328. See Supplement, p. 202.

329. See H. C. Andersen, *Billedbog uden Billeder* (Copenhagen: 1840), pp. 44, 47. It was reviewed in *Fædrelandet*, 78, February 23, 1840.

330. See pp. 65–66. Kierkegaard is incorrect in regarding Dalby's speech as a "verbatim" reprint. See note 331 below.

331. *Comedie i det Grønne.* See Supplement, p. 203.

332. See note 322 above.

BIBLIOGRAPHICAL NOTE

For general bibliographies of Kierkegaard studies, see:

Jens Himmelstrup, *Søren Kierkegaard International Bibliografi*. Copenhagen: Nyt Nordisk Forlag Arnold Busck, 1962.

Aage Jørgensen, *Søren Kierkegaard-litteratur 1961-1970*. Aarhus: Akademisk Boghandel, 1971. *Søren Kierkegaard-litteratur 1971-1980*. Aarhus: privately published, 1983.

François H. Lapointe, *Søren Kierkegaard and His Critics: An International Bibliography of Criticism*. Westport, Connecticut: Greenwood Press, 1980.

International Kierkegaard Newsletter, ed. Julia Watkin. Copenhagen, 1979- .

Kierkegaard: A Collection of Critical Essays, ed. Josiah Thompson. New York: Doubleday (Anchor Books), 1972.

Søren Kierkegaard's Journals and Papers, I, ed. and tr. Howard V. Hong and Edna H. Hong, assisted by Gregor Malantschuk. Bloomington: Indiana University Press, 1967.

For topical bibliographies of Kierkegaard studies, see *Søren Kierkegaard's Journals and Papers*, I-IV, 1967-75.

INDEX